The U.S. Navy
in the 1990s

James L. George

THE
U.S. NAVY
IN THE 1990s

Alternatives for Action

Naval Institute Press   Annapolis, Maryland

Library of Congress Cataloging-in-Publication Data

George, James L.
    The U.S. Navy in the 1990s : alternatives for action / James L.
George.
        p.   cm.
    Includes bibliographical references and index.
    ISBN 1-55750-325-7. — ISBN 1-55750-326-5 (pbk.)
    1. United States.   Navy. 2. Sea-power—United States—
History—20th century.   I. Title.   II. Title: US Navy in the 1990s.
VA58.4.G46   1992
359'.00973'09049—dc20

92-9917
CIP

Printed in the United States of America on acid-free paper ∞

9   8   7   6   5   4   3   2

First printing

To my favorite daughters,
Laura M. George
and
Leslie M. George

You've got to air creative ideas no matter how controversial. You've got to innovate. You've got to see old and new problems with a fresh view, and a steady eye on the process of learning the lessons of the past, be it recent or further back, for the fleet that will sail into the future.

—*Secretary of the Navy H. Lawrence Garrett III*
Sea Power Forum, 1990

Contents

List of Tables and Figures   xi
List of Abbreviations   xiii
Preface   xix

1 Introduction: Concentrating on the Knowns   1
2 Background: Will the Past Be Prologue?   7

Part I: The Missions
3 The Changing Missions of the 1990s   27
4 Nuclear Deterrence: All at Sea?   32
5 NATO: The Emergence of SACLANT   48
6 Third World Operations: The Past Is Prologue   62
7 Maritime or National Missions?   78

Part II: The Forces
8 Concepts for the New Interwar Period: The Need for
Alternatives   89
9 Naval Air Forces: "Where Are the Planes?"   103
10 Submarine Forces: Transition Time?   127
11 Surface Combatants: Quantity Versus Quality   142
12 Balance of the Fleet: Maintaining the "Blue"   159

Part III: Comments and Conclusions

13 Lessons of Desert Shield/Desert Storm:
   Forerunner or Fluke?   183
14 Naval Arms Control: An Unknown Factor   194
15 Other "New World Paradigms": Do They Really Matter?   203
16 Conclusions: The Perils of "Less of the Same"   215

   Notes   229
   Select Bibliography   239
   Index   241

List of Tables and Figures

TABLES

2-1.	Major U.S. Marine Corps Landings Since World War II	12
2-2.	Size of the U.S. Active Fleet	16
2-3.	Base Force Structure	19
4-1.	SALT I Limits	34
4-2.	SALT II Limits	34
4-3.	START I Limits	35
4-4.	Current U.S. Strategic Inventory	36
4-5.	Possible START II Force Mix and Limits	40
6-1.	Missile Proliferation	64
6-2.	Chemical Weapons Proliferation	66
6-3.	Nuclear Proliferation in the 1990s	66
8-1.	Building and Transitional Concepts	91
8-2.	Research and Development Concepts	95
8-3.	Reserve Concepts	97
8-4.	Deployment Concepts	99
9-1.	Aircraft Carrier Modified Mix Alternatives	110
9-2.	Airplane Modified Mix Alternatives	120
10-1.	Submarine Modified Mix Alternatives	136
10-2.	Air-independent Propulsion Concepts	137

11-1.   Surface Combatant Modified Mix: 1950–2000   150
11-2.   Surface Combatant Modified Mix Alternatives   151
12-1.   U.S. Navy Auxiliary and Support Ship Types   161
12-2.   U.S. Navy Auxiliary Force   162
12-3.   U.S. Navy Amphibious Force   168
12-4.   Comparison of Marine and Army Units   174
12-5.   Auxiliary, Amphibious, and Mine Craft Modified Mix
        Alternatives   179
13-1.   Theater Coalition Ships   186

FIGURES

 2-1.   DoD Budget Authority   23
 9-1.   Aircraft Carrier Retirement Schedule   105
10-1.   Submarine Retirement Schedule   130
11-1.   Surface Combatant Retirement Schedule   145
12-1.   Amphibious Ships Retirement Schedule   170
16-1.   New U.S. Fleets and STANAVFORs   226

List of Abbreviations

A	Attack (prefix for attack/bomber aircraft)
AA	Antiaircraft
AAAM	Advanced Air-to-air Missile
AAW	Antiair Warfare
AE	Ammunition Ship
AEW	Airborne Early Warning
AIP	Air-independent Propulsion (submarine)
ALCM	Air-launched Cruise Missile
AMRAAM	Advanced Medium-range Air-to-air Missile
AO	Oiler
AOE	Fast Combat Support Ship
AOR	Replenishment Oiler
APD	High-speed Transport (modified DE)
APDG	High-speed Transport, Guided Missile
ARG	Amphibious Ready Group
ASuW	Antisurface Warfare
ASW	Antisubmarine Warfare
ASWFZ	ASW Free Zones
ATA	Advanced Tactical Aircraft
ATF	Advanced Tactical Fighter
ATS	Advanced Tactical Support (airplane)

BB	Battleship
BBBG	Battleship Battle Group
BFC	Battle Force Combatant
BW	Biological Weapons
CAS	Close Air Support
CAT	Conventional Arms Talks
CBM	Confidence Building Measures
CBO	Congressional Budget Office
CD	Committee on Disarmament
CDE	Conference on Disarmament in Europe (talks/accords)
CDG	Carrier Dock Guided Missile
CDM	Carrier Dock Multimission
CDV	Carrier Dock Multimission Aviation
CENTCOM	Central Command
CFE	Conventional Force in Europe (talks/treaty)
CG	Cruiser, Guided Missile
CGN	Cruiser, Guided Missile, Nuclear Powered
CILOP	Conversion in Lieu of Procurement
CINC	Commander-in-Chief
CINCLANT	Commander-in-Chief Atlantic
CINCLANTFLT	Commander-in-Chief Atlantic Fleet
CINCPACFLT	Commander-in-Chief Pacific Fleet
CL	Light Cruiser
CLF	Combat Logistics Force
CLG	Guided Missile Cruiser
CMC	Cruise Missile Carrier
CNO	Chief of Naval Operations
CODOG	Combined Diesel—Gas Turbine
COMUSNAVCENT	Commander U.S. Naval Forces Central Command
COOP	Craft of Opportunity Program (minecraft)
CSBM	Confidence and Security Building Measures
CSGN	Strike Cruise, Nuclear Powered
CTOL	Conventional Takeoff and Landing
CTS	Common Tactical Support (airplane)
CV	Aircraft Carrier, Conventional Powered

CVBG	Carrier Battle Group
CVN	Aircraft Carrier, Nuclear Powered
CW	Chemical Weapons
DCA	Dual-capable Aircraft (conventional and nuclear)
DD	Destroyer, General Purpose (ASW)
DDG	Destroyer, Guided Missile
DE	Destroyer Escort
DVS	Destroyer Variant Study
ECM	Electronic Countermeasures
EW	Electronic Warfare
F	Fighter (prefix for fighter aircraft)
FF	Frigate, General Purpose (ASW)
FFG	Frigate, Guided Missile
FMS	Foreign Military Sale
FOL	Follow-on to Lance
FSS	Fast Sealift Ships
FY	Fiscal Year
GLCM	Ground-launched Cruise Missile
GPS	Global Positioning System
IAEA	International Atomic Energy Agency
ICBM	Intercontinental Ballistic Missile
INF	Intermediate-range Nuclear Force (treaty)
IOC	Initial Operational Capability
IOZP	Indian Ocean Zone of Peace
IRBM	Intermediate Range Ballistic Missile
JSTPS	Joint Strategic Target Planning Staff
LAMPS	Light Airborne Multipurpose System (helicopter)
LAV	Light Armored Vehicles
LCAC	Landing Craft Air-cushion
LHA	Amphibious Assault Ship (*Tarawa* class)
LHD	Amphibious Assault Ship (*Wasp* class)
LPD	Amphibious Transport Dock
LPH	Amphibious Assault Ship (*Iwo Jima* class)
LSD	Landing Ship Dock
LST	Landing Ship Tank

MAGTF	Marine Air-ground Task Force
MBFR	Mutual Balanced Force Reduction (talks)
MCM	Mine Countermeasure Ship
MEB	Marine Expeditionary Brigade
MEF	Marine Expeditionary Force
MEU	Marine Expeditionary Unit
MHC	Coastal Mine Hunter
MIRV	Multiple Independently Targeted Vehicle
MPS	Maritime Prepositioning Ships
MRF	Multirole Fighter
MSC	Military Sealift Command
MSO	Ocean Minesweeper
MSTS	Military Sealift Transportation Service
MTCR	Missile Technology Control Regime
NAC	Naval Arms Control
NATF	Navy Advanced Tactical Fighter
NCA	National Command Authority
NCND	Neither Confirm Nor Deny (policy)
NDFR	National Defense Fleet Reserve
NFR-90	NATO Frigate Replacement for the 1990s
NNA	Neutral Nonaligned (nation)
NOAA	National Oceanic and Atmospheric Administration
NSTT	Navy Strategy Think Tank
NWFZ	Nuclear Weapon Free Zones
OBE	Overtaken by Events
OMB	Office of Management and Budget
OPNAV	Office of the Chief of Naval Operations
OSD	Office of the Secretary of Defense
OTH	Over the Horizon
PAL	Permissive Action Links
PHM	Missile Hydrofoil Patrol Combatants
POMCUS	Prepositioned Overseas Material Configured in Unit Sets
POS	Protection of Shipping
RARG	Reserve Amphibious Ready Group
RBBBG	Reserve Battleship Battle Group

RBG	Reserve Battle Group
RCVBG	Reserve Carrier Battle Group
RO/RO	Roll-on/Roll-off
RRF	Ready Reserve Force
SAC	Strategic Air Command
SACEUR	Supreme Allied Commander Europe
SACLANT	Supreme Allied Commander Atlantic
SAG	Surface Action Group
SALT	Strategic Arms Limitation Talks
SAM	Surface-to-air Missile
SAR	Search and Rescue
SCS	Sea Control Ship
SDI	Strategic Defense Initiative
SLAM	Stand-off Land Attack Missile
SLBM	Submarine-launched Ballistic Missile
SLCM	Sea-launched Cruise Missile
SLEP	Service Life Extension Program
SLOC	Sea Lines of Communication
SNDV	Strategic Nuclear Delivery Vehicle
SNF	Short-range Nuclear Forces
SRAM	Short-range Attack (Nuclear) Missile
SS	Submarine, Conventional Powered
SSBN	Strategic Ballistic Missile Submarine, Nuclear Powered
SSG	Guided Missile Submarine, Conventional Powered
SSGN	Guided Missile Submarine, Nuclear Powered
SSn	Submarine, Combined Nuclear/Conventional Powered
SSN	Submarine, Nuclear Attack
SSOD	Special Session on Disarmament (U.N.)
STANAVFOR	Standing Naval Force
STANAVFORLANT	Standing Naval Force Atlantic
START	Strategic Arms Reduction Talks
STOL	Short Takeoff and Landing
STOVL	Short Takeoff and Vertical Landing
STRATLANT	Strategic Atlantic

STRATPAC	Strategic Pacific
SWATH	Small Waterplane-area Twin Hull (ship)
TASM	Tactical Air-to-surface Missile
TLAM	Tomahawk Land Attack Missile, Conventional
TLAM-N	Tomahawak Land Attack Missile, Nuclear
UNDC	U.N. Disarmament Committee
UNREP	Underway Replenishment
USCG	United States Coast Guard
USMC	United States Marine Corps
USN	United States Navy
V/STOL	Vertical/Short Takeoff and Landing
VERTREP	Vertical Replenishment (helicopter)
VLS	Vertical Launch System (for missiles)
VSS	V/STOL Support Ship

Preface

THE WORLD HAS entered the new post–Cold War era. If history is any guide, it could well be another interwar period requiring constant vigilance. The recent 1991 Iraq crisis illustrates this ongoing need. Lest anyone forget, Alexis de Tocqueville made his famous prediction of an eventual U.S.–Russian competition some eighty years before there was a Soviet Union. As during all such postwar eras, however, the military has fallen on harder times, sustaining major cutbacks and decreased budgets. Although all the services have problems, the Navy appears to be in particular trouble. Indeed, the word "disarray" seems to be the favorite term used by reporters and analysts describing current Navy plans. An active-duty admiral, in a rare outburst of candor, even described his own programs as in a "complex dilemma" and a "modernization crisis."

The reasons for these unflattering descriptions are not hard to fathom. One merely needs to examine the main naval warfare areas. Just a very few years ago, the Navy had five new airplanes on the drawing board; one by one, they have all been canceled. The latest and worst example is the cancellation of the A-12 attack aircraft, meaning the Navy will have to rely on a compromise plane lacking some capabilities of 1950-era planes. In surface ships, the Navy is building $1 billion destroyers for the twenty-first century without any flexible helicopter capabilities. If that were not bad enough, to save money the Navy actually looked at a destroyer design without sonar, which probably has not happened since the 1920s. The submarine community is constructing an unaffordable

$2 billion attack submarine, driving building rates down to only one a year, which could eventually mean a thirty-ship force—pre–World War I numbers.

As bad as these examples may seem, they are simply the visible symptoms of two more serious underlying problems: the lack of a new mission analysis for force planning and a comprehensive building philosophy for the new era. The first priority must be a mission analysis for the new post–Cold War conditions. Mission analysis is important in filling that necessary planning gap between the broad national security statements from the national command authorities and the military requirements of the local area commanders, the CINCs. Even though the capabilities the Navy and Marine Corps bring should predominate in this new era, without a proper mission analysis they could end up the big losers in a post–Cold War command shuffle. Building concepts are important as touchstones and guidelines showing the way to build, phase in, and, if necessary, quickly reconstitute programs. The Navy has abandoned its more traditional building concepts such as constructing a multiple mix of weaponry, and now finds itself in trouble with only high-level, expensive systems it can no longer afford and may not even need in all situations.

Mission analysis and building concepts are also important for evaluating alternatives—and, contrary to some opinions, there are currently available alternatives. For example, naval air "presence" (not capabilities) could be doubled overnight simply by adding ski jumps to amphibious assault ships. Thus, the first priority for naval air might be capable short takeoff and vertical landing (STOVL) rather than expensive stealth aircraft. Since several allied navies operate ski-jump carriers, this could be a multinational project, thus decreasing costs. The surface warfare community could consider building corvettes for certain mission requirements, such as Persian Gulf patrols. The United States is, in fact, building an extremely capable corvette chockablock with weaponry across the complete spectrum of warfare (including both a helicopter and sonar) requiring a crew of only fifty-eight, but these are for export. The submarine community could take a look at the new "air independent propulsion" (AIP) proposals that now answer the main Navy objection to building nonnuclear subs. Building corvettes and AIP subs has additional advantages—from keeping the force numbers up to allowing for some lieutenant commander commands (bringing fun back into the Navy while increasing responsibility) and, best of all, saving money for the real need: truly futuristic "dreadnoughts" for the twenty-first–century environment.

Perhaps the major problems with the current, unimaginative "less of the same" building program is that it will squeeze out those weapon systems truly needed for the upcoming century. This is already happening in the surface warfare community. The DDG-51 Block III destroyer with full helicopter capabilities and a large magazine space is now being post-poned for lack of funds. A better building philosophy, especially during this first decade of transition in the new interwar period, might be to live off the buildup of the Reagan years for a time and construct some less costly systems to maintain the numbers and the industrial base, while building a series of experimental dreadnoughts in all areas, that is, new weaponry that makes all else obsolete, selecting the best for possible mass production in the twenty-first century.

The purpose of this book is to explore all these notions and more. First will be an analysis of the changing missions, showing how the Navy should become the dominant service in all three major traditional areas of concern: nuclear deterrence, the still important possible U.S.–Russian commonwealth scenario, and Third World crisis response operations. Second will be development of some building, transition, and reconstitution concepts for the new era; third will be an exploration of some reasonable and affordable alternatives. Finally, the book will briefly examine some of the unknown variables of the post–Cold War period, such as possible naval arms control agreements, the future of the new Russian-dominated Commonwealth of Independent States (CIS)* and other so-called new world paradigm possibilities. One thing seems certain—regardless of how the new interwar period ends, the United States will still need a large, strong, and flexible navy.

* * *

There are several people I would like to thank for assisting in this book. At the top of the list are Jim Sutton, marketing director, and Mark Gatlin, acquisitions editor, of the Naval Institute Press, who came up with the idea for a book on the Navy's future and had the wisdom, or perhaps the misfortune, to approach me on the project. I would also like to thank others at the Institute for their support, including Tom Epley, press director, and Jim Barber, executive director. Also, special appreciation to Randy Baldini, who had the tedious chore of editing the book.

There are several other people I would like to thank, either for supplying me with information or for taking the time to read and comment on my work. These are Jeff Barlow, Al Bowen, John Byron, Larry Cavaiola, Bert Cooper, Bob Hale, Bob Hofford, Tom Houston, Spence

---

*The official name of the USSR's successor state is the Commonwealth of Independent States (CIS). However, since Russia is by far the dominant republic this book will use the term "Russian commonwealth."

Johnson, Mark Lowenthal, Alice Maroni, Paul Moses, Jerry O'Rourke, Ron O'Rourke, Robin Pirie, Bill Ruhe, Peter Tarpgaard, and Milan Vego.

I also appreciate the wisdom and camaraderie of my former shipmates from the Strategic Policy Analysis Group (SPAG), many of whom commented on the book. I miss our brown-bag lunches, and now you know I was taking notes but not names. Supporting corvettes, nonnuclear submarines, and STOVL planes might not enhance one's career.

Finally, I would like to thank my beloved typist and editorial assistant, Jeanne Carolan, whom I will marry after she checks her corrections.

* * *

A note on timing. When this book was started, although the Berlin Wall had fallen and further changes were obvious, the Warsaw Pact and the Soviet Union were still dominant players on the international scene; President Gorbachev had just been named "man of the decade" by *Time* magazine; Saddam Hussein was considered just a minor, faraway irritant; and although the U.S. Navy's 600-ship goal was forgotten, there were still hopes for a relatively large fleet. Since then, the Warsaw Pact has dissolved (although Russian troops are still in some Eastern European countries), the Soviet Union minus a few old republics has now become the CIS, while President Gorbachev was forced to resign in disgrace. Many analysts are predicting that the CIS will eventually dissolve, with new Russian President Boris Yeltsin not far behind Gorbachev. Regardless of the final outcome, there will still be a strong Russia—meaning that most of the conditions described throughout this book will still pertain for many years. And just when many started spending the end of the Cold War peace dividend, Iraq invaded Kuwait, necessitating the largest movement of troops since World War II. Saddam is now, once again, a minor irritant.

In the United States, although a so-called base force of approximately 450 ships was announced in 1990, shipbuilding rates have fallen to numbers capable of sustaining only 300. Although this book incorporates the latest FY93 budget submission of February 1992, there are ongoing debates on the further direction of the military. A final defense budget remains elusive.

In short, events are moving very quickly in this new post–Cold War era, and today's truth and wisdom soon become tomorrow's latest casualty. The purpose of this book, therefore, is not to try to chronicle and capture the lessons from the latest event, crisis, or budget change. In this rapidly changing world, that is impossible. Every day's newspaper seems to bring something new, and some of the "latest" items mentioned herein will undoubtedly become "overtaken by events" (OBE) by the time of publication. Whether Boris Yeltsin or Saddam Hussein survives, a nuclear-armed Russia will always be of some concern and the Middle East always a potential tinderbox.

Rather, the purpose of the book is to capture certain trends, and more important to present some basic concepts, principles, and especially alternatives that will continue to pertain regardless of the latest international crisis or defense budget change. In fact, the more current events do change, the greater will be the need for many of the alternatives and options presented in this book.

The U.S. Navy
in the 1990s

1 / Introduction

Concentrating on the Knowns

THE WORLD IS entering what might be considered a new "interwar" period—measured from the end of the Cold War to who really knows what? Like all such periods, it is a time of hope but also uncertainty. Just when many were starting to spend the end of the Cold War "peace dividend," Iraq invaded Kuwait, necessitating the largest movement of American forces since the Vietnam War and the greatest collection of allied navies since World War II. This first post–Cold War crisis illustrated the dangers and delusions of all such interwar periods. Among the many lessons to be learned from the Iraq crisis, undoubtedly the most important is that it will certainly not be the last.

There have been three previous inter- or postwar periods in modern times: from the end of World War II to the Korean War; the end of the Vietnam War to the Reagan buildup, which finally brought U.S. and Soviet forces into balance; and of course, by far the most famous, the twenty-odd years between the two world wars. All have had an impact, usually perceived as detrimental, on the military and especially on the Navy. During the first interwar period, although official policy was to build a navy "second to none," construction virtually stopped, with the major Washington and London naval arms control agreements contributing to the disillusionment and appeasement of that period. From World War II to the Korean War, the Navy and Marine Corps were in the bureaucratic fight of their lives as the fleet quickly deteriorated from its wartime strength and readiness. Following the Vietnam War, the Navy shrank by 50 percent as part of the "no more Vietnams" syndrome and was heading, by some estimates, to about 30 percent of its former strength before the trend was reversed by the Reagan administration.

While these postwar periods are usually perceived unfavorably for some of the reasons cited above, they can be times of progress and imagination. For example, between the world wars the Marines studied and developed amphibious techniques despite the conventional wisdom about the fiasco at Gallipoli, which supposedly proved that such warfare was no longer feasible in the modern era. Despite the preponderance of "battleship admirals" in the Navy, there were also advances in naval air power that proved important in World War II, especially in the Pacific. Also, the Navy did not make the Japanese mistake of building only one or two types of aircraft, which, although initially quite good, became obsolete later in the war. Instead, the United States had many models under development that eventually proved superior to those early enemy planes, illustrating once again the constant need for research and development even in peacetime.

During the post–World War II period, despite the intense political and bureaucratic fights over defense reorganization and responsibilities, important principles were established in the Key West and Newport agreements on service roles and missions, agreements that essentially saved both the Navy and the Marines. The Marines even had certain strengths and duties written into law. During the post-Vietnam period, important doctrine was established such as the Guam or Nixon Doctrine, which declared that the United States would simply help indigenous forces in the future and not shoulder the complete burden. Equally important, this post-Vietnam period saw a renaissance in naval conceptual thinking marked by innovations such as the high-low mix, the use of V/STOL, the emergence of nuclear power for surface combatants, and even the elements of the current Maritime Strategy itself.

None of these progressive programs was without cost; and in many cases, they were advanced by imaginative mavericks who challenged traditional naval parochialism. During the first interwar period, amphibious warfare was pushed by the likes of the eccentric Lt. Col. Earl H. "Pete" Ellis with naval air developments originating from men such as Adm. William A. Moffet, chief of the Bureau of Aeronautics, who flew his flag on a plane. During the post–World War II period, the "Admirals' revolt" was at least indirectly responsible for saving the Navy. Without Adm. Hyman Rickover's dogged persistence, nuclear-powered ships probably would have been developed much later. In the post–Vietnam War period, the maverick ideas came from the very top. The first post-Vietnam Chief of Naval Operations, Adm. Elmo Zumwalt, led the way. Although famous for his "Z" grams, more important were his rebuilding concepts, directed toward the goal of a 600-ship navy. The next CNO, Adm. James Holloway, an aviator, challenged his own air community by planning for a transition to V/STOL: from large-deck nuclear carriers, CVN, to slightly smaller fossil-fuel carriers, CVV, and finally to V/STOL-only capable ships, VSS. In the late 1970s, when the fleet had shrunk to its lowest (and what some might have considered only defensive) levels, Adm. Thomas P. Hayward developed the concept of forward deployments, which eventually led to the Maritime Strategy fully pushed by another maverick, Secretary of the Navy John Lehman.

The question is, what will this new interwar period bring forth—only problems, or progress as well? Equally important, will it bring forth the mavericks, with their alternatives to show the way? That is the primary purpose of this study: to present some alternatives. First, this book will look at the rapidly changing world environment, which requires new missions and responsibilities in the three traditional areas of concern: nuclear deterrence, the European theater, and Third World operations. Then it will look at current forces and, more important, some alternatives for the future to meet new mission challenges in an era of decreasing defense budgets.

There seems to be a lack of alternative strategies today. As already noted, during the last postwar period following the Vietnam War there were many different proposals put forward: the high-low mix, nuclear propulsion for all large surface combatants, transition to V/STOL, even radical plans such as the somewhat infamous White Paper by Senators Taft and Hart, and Bill Lind. Another senator, Bill Brock, called for new building and R and D concepts such as "capability without production," better phasing in and phasing out of systems, and a clearer definition of service roles and missions. At least to date, the alternatives suggested for the new postwar period boil down to moving a few ships to the reserves and building "less of the same." Moving some ships to the reserves probably makes sense, although the Navy should not make what might be called the "Army mistake," that is, moving so much to reserves that it cannot deploy without major call-ups. Because of the Reagan buildup and early retirements, "less of the same" building programs might work for a while, but eventually they will result in a smaller fleet and block obsolescence; worse, such programs will probably squeeze out those futuristic new ships truly needed for the sophisticated twenty-first-century environment. There are already signs of this trend.

While every interwar period is full of uncertainty, the book will try to concentrate on the "knowns" rather than building abstract new world models or paradigms, a favorite think-tank guessing game these days. There are some unknowns that will be discussed, such as suggested naval arms control accords, the future of the Russian commonwealth and the possible movement toward a multipolar or even a U.S.–Russian condominium world. But the knowns are considerably more important and themselves constitute quite a long list. For example, we know that the arms control rules of the game will change drastically in the next few years and, for the first time, bring real reductions. The 1987 Intermediate Nuclear Force (INF) Treaty eliminated two complete classes of theater nuclear weapons, the long- and medium-range systems. Both sides had also agreed to eventually negotiate cuts in theater short-range nuclear forces (SNF), although Presidents Bush and Gorbachev's unilateral decisions to eliminate these systems might now make that unnecessary. This means that naval systems such as sea-based dual-capable aircraft (DCA) and especially the much maligned Tomahawk nuclear sea-launched cruise missile (SLCM), the TLAM-N (to be placed in garrison) could well constitute the only theater nuclear deterrent in a very few years.

There should be similar changes in strategic weaponry. Unlike the two earlier SALT I and II accords, which simply froze existing strategic nuclear forces, START I will reduce weaponry and could cause major dislocations in the old U.S. nuclear triad of long-range bombers, land-based ICBMs, and strategic submarines (SSBNs). This might be replaced by a dyad consisting of Navy systems and Air Force bombers, with ICBMs slowly withering away. Both Presidents Bush and Yeltsin have proposed further cuts, and a START II or even III might be possible by the turn of the century.

There will also be at least one, and possibly as many as three, conventional arms control agreements in Europe over the next decade. As European-based U.S. Army and Air Force contingents are drawn down, the importance of Navy forces should rise—an almost inverse relationship. In fact, it would not be too surprising to see the senior NATO naval commander, Supreme Allied Commander Atlantic (SACLANT), emerge as the senior NATO military official in the next few years.

The Iraqi invasion of Kuwait illustrates the dangers in the so-called Third World. One must use the caveat "so-called" because the recent proliferation of sophisticated weaponry including ballistic missiles, chemical weapons, and possibly even nuclear munitions hardly seems to be characteristic of developing countries. Antiship missiles, mines, and even submarines are also entering Third World inventories. These are not the type of weapons for use in what is popularly called "low-intensity" warfare. The day when a mad Mike Hoare and a handful of mercenaries with Uzis could threaten a Third World government, with its army carrying only World War I–vintage Enfields, has passed. Since Third World crisis response operations have traditionally fallen to the Navy and Marine Corps, they may be the most affected by these new conditions.

Finally, there is another major "known" that must be considered—declining, perhaps drastically declining, defense budgets. The recent Iraq crisis has not caused any delays in cutting the defense budget, and further reductions are inevitable. Ranges vary from optimistic administration projections of about 3 percent per year in real declines (about 6–7 percent with inflation) to some predicting 50 percent cuts by the end of the decade. The administration has already announced a 25 percent cut in forces, indicating a fleet of approximately 450 ships; some commentators predict an eventual 300-ship Navy. A final defense budget figure often heard these days is about $200 billion by the turn of the century (in FY90 dollars)—about a one-third reduction in nominal terms. These cuts will come at a time when naval responsibilities should be increasing across the board, in nuclear deterrence, NATO, and Third World operations. While some consensus seems to be emerging that the Navy should get the largest slice of the budget pie, that will still be a decreasing pie—perhaps only a cupcake if some have their way.

There are, of course, many unknowns that should be considered. Naval arms control remains an unknown; but agreements will probably center on confidence building measure (CBM) accords, such as advance notice requirements, and not on force levels, although they cannot be completely ruled out. Another major unknown is the future of the new Russian-dominated Commonwealth of Independent States (CIS) and its navy (or perhaps even navies). Despite the breakup of the Soviet Union, the Russian commonwealth will remain a major power, in part due to its nuclear arsenal but also because of its extremely large army, air force, and navy. Although their naval operations have declined recently and the Russians are finally retiring some older ships, many simply rusting "hangar queens," until quite recently they were still building at old, Cold War rates. The Soviet Navy recently launched ten submarines, the largest number in years. It should also be kept in mind that if the Russian commonwealth wants to influence world events directly, it will probably have to use its navy. Moving army troops and equipment back into Eastern Europe might be impossible, but sailing the fleet is not.

There are many who foresee completely new international paradigms, from a U.S.–Russian alliance (or at least condominium) to a multipolar world with a return to traditional nineteenth-century balance-of-power politics. Those most mentioned for promotions to superpower status are Japan and a reunited Germany. Economically, of course, multipolarity exists today, but military multipolarity is quite a different matter. Naval historians like to point out that Germany started World War II with only sixty-two submarines. Today, Germany has twenty-four. More likely to emerge will be regional powers such as India, China, Iraq, and perhaps

Brazil; a militant, black South Africa (possibly with nuclear weapons) cannot be ruled out. At least for the foreseeable future, only the United States and the Russian commonwealth will remain in the superpower category, but this does not necessarily make the world safer. As we have recently seen, a dominant Iraq in the Persian Gulf and the Middle East can be extremely destabilizing. Regardless of the shape of the new political world, however, flexible navies will always be important.

While some conclusions and personal recommendations will be presented, the aim of this book will be to look first at the new problems and changing missions of the 1990s, and then at some alternative concepts and strategies. As will be shown in Part II, there are other alternatives besides simply moving a few ships into the reserves and building less of the same. For example, there are not just one or two but over twenty different building and R and D concepts, at least eight different reserve alternatives, and even some seven different basic deployment patterns available. In the rapidly changing world of this new interwar period, there is probably no one right answer, and what might sound just perfect today may not tomorrow. As Secretary of the Navy H. Lawrence Garrett said at the Center for Naval Analyses 1990 Sea Power Forum:

> The "nice to have" items in our shopping cart are going to get tossed out by the people who pay the bills. And if we're not careful, those items that are absolutely "need-to-have" are going to get tossed out with it—certainly, if they're not part of a lean, dramatic and utterly convincing concept of seapower, convincing not just to strategists, but also decision-makers. So I ask you and I encourage you, as you think about the Navy's future, and I mean the future, you've got to ask those critical questions.
>
> *You've got to air creative ideas no matter how controversial. You've got to innovate.* You've got to see old and new problems with a fresh view, and a steady eye on the process of learning the lessons of the past, be it recent or further back, for the fleet that will sail into the future.
>
> And I don't think there's any question—certainly, there is no question in my mind but that we are at a historic threshold. We may be at a point in history that happens once every century. In a sense, we are fortunate. In another sense, we're not so fortunate. But it is a tremendous challenge. (emphasis added)

What is needed, therefore, is a complete and flexible spectrum of choices. If the first post–Cold War crisis in the Persian Gulf has taught the world any lessons, it is that uncertainty will continue to be the watchword. Uncertainty demands flexibility and many different alternatives and approaches.

2 / Background

Will the Past Be Prologue?

ALTHOUGH EACH inter- or postwar period had its own peculiarities, history still provides the only available guidelines. Thus, in order to set the stage, this chapter will review briefly the uses and missions of navies throughout history, concentrating on the post–World War II period. A look at the size of the fleet and certain budget trends since World War II will follow.

There is an obvious tendency, when writing any book, to overemphasize the subject. That fate befell early advocates of the Maritime Strategy, enunciated in the early 1980s, who were then accused of being "neo-Mahanians"[1]—whatever that might have really meant. It was obviously a pejorative term intended to imply that the advocates of the Maritime Strategy felt the Navy itself could win any war in Europe. This was never their intent.

Critics of maritime strategies should be reminded that Mahan's great work was *The Influence of Seapower on History,* and that he pointed out many other factors such as geography, the number and character of peoples, and the like. Colin Grey and Roger Barnett note the many differences between land and sea power, concluding that "states seek to control the open seas in order to affect or influence what is happening on the land."[2] While seapower has had great "influence," there have been very few naval wars, or cases where a great naval battle alone was enough to decide a conflict. There are some. The Peloponnesian Wars between Athens and Sparta hold fascination not only because of the writings of Thucydides, often called the first historian, but because of the classic struggle between Athens, a democracy and sea power, and Sparta, an autocracy and land power—a conflict with striking similarities to that between the United States and the Soviet Union. It was only when Sparta went to sea that it was able to defeat Athens. The struggle between traditional maritime power Carthage and land power Rome ended similarly. Carthage was defeated partly because it finally lost control of the seas to Rome. While seapower was important, Carthage was defeated on land.

There have also been great sea battles that decided the outcome of wars. The Battle of Salamis in 480 B.C. stopped Persian King Xerxes' invasion of Greece. The Battle of Lepanto in 1571 between the Ottoman Empire navy and a coalition of European fleets halted the Turkish advance into Europe and ended its domination of the Mediterranean. Japanese fleets, along with favorable "divine winds," kept that island nation safe from invasion for years. And, in perhaps one of the most famous naval battles of all time, the defeat of the Spanish Armada not only saved England but marked the decline of Spain and the ascendancy of Great Britain—all on the strength of the Royal Navy. The history of Great Britain as a major power for some four hundred years, and especially during the Pax Britannia years of the nineteenth century, is truly remarkable when one considers the nation's resources. But England was not the only relatively small country to exert power through maritime strength. Portugal, the Netherlands, and even city-states such as Venice were, for a time, considered great powers because of their seapower.

Despite these great battles and uses of maritime strength by smaller nations, the influence of seapower should not be taken out of context. Athens and Sparta finally settled their differences on land, as did Rome and Carthage, and Christians and Moslems. The smaller sea powers such as Venice, Portugal, and the Netherlands were subdued on land, and even the world's greatest sea power, Great Britain, landed troops to finally defeat Napoleon, despite the great sea victories over the French navy by Lord Nelson and his band of brothers.

During the more modern "era of steam," seapower has had mixed results. The United States won an overseas empire through two major sea battles during the Spanish-American War. What some historians consider the first modern sea battle, the Battle of Tsushima, in which the Japanese fleet destroyed the Russian fleet after its sojourn from European Russia to Asia, was decisive in ending their war. On the other hand, the great Jutland sea battle had virtually no effect on World War I. In World War II, the Battle of the Atlantic was crucial to the win in Europe, but, as in World War I, there was no decisive sea battle to end that campaign.

Such was not the case in the Pacific theater. In fact, it can reasonably be argued that the World War II campaign in the Pacific constitutes one of the very few truly maritime wars in all of history. That is, the complete outcome of the struggle centered on seapower, including great sea battles, convoys, blockades, and amphibious landings, or what would today be called power projection ashore. With the possible exception of the Peloponnesian Wars, there are few examples in history in which seapower played such a dominant role. Even during the great days of Royal Navy predominance and influence, Great Britain almost always had to land troops to decide its conflicts.

POSTWAR USES AND MISSIONS

Despite this long history of naval uses and influence including the recent U.S. Navy record in the Pacific, many thought the atomic bomb that ended the war with Japan also ended the era of seapower. Pundits of the day began writing epitaphs for both the Army and the Navy, particularly the latter. Wars in the nuclear age would be fought by air forces, won or lost through strategic bombing. The active Navy fleet shrank from its wartime high of 5,700 ships to about 600, only one-third of which were considered combat-ready. This first postwar 600-ship Navy was virtually the same size as before the war, when the USN could still rely on the other world sea power and ally, Great Britain. At the end of World War II, the USN stood virtually alone.

The size of the fleet was not the only problem for the Navy and Marine Corps as they entered this new interwar period. They were about to begin the bureaucratic fight of their lives, one that still deeply affects their attitudes. More ominous than the new Air Force fighting for recognition and roles was the establishment of the Department of Defense (DoD), which all services, but particularly the Navy, thought would restrict their responsibilities. The admirals felt they would constantly lose "two to one," with the Air Force and its old parent service, the Army, ganging up on them. They had reason to be concerned. There were proposals to eliminate the Marine Corps by folding it into the Army, and the Air Force tried to take over certain naval air missions while denying the Navy any role in strategic bombing even though land-based bombers had limited range in those days.[3]

After several years of bureaucratic infighting, the debate over service roles and missions was finally settled at two informal meetings between the services and the Secretary of Defense at Key West and then at Newport. The Navy retained virtually all of its traditional responsibilities, and despite opposition by President Truman, the Marines even had their strength of three divisions written into law. That did not, however, end the squabbles. The biggest fight was yet to come: the great Navy–Air Force fight of 1949 and subsequent "Admirals' revolt."

The Navy–Air Force fight, like most bureaucratic conflicts, was ostensibly over funds, although other issues were involved. For years, the Navy had wanted a new "supercarrier" to carry modern planes. While the *Essex*-class carriers built late in World War II dwarfed their prewar predecessors, they were still considered small for new jet planes, especially attack or bomber aircraft. After years of planning, the Navy finally won approval for a new carrier, the *United States*. However, only a few days after the keel was laid, Secretary of Defense Louis Johnson canceled the ship. There were several reasons. A major culprit was the overall reductions in defense spending demanded by President Truman, but what really precipitated the fight was the Air Force's request for the B-36 long-range bomber and Secretary Johnson's views. According to press accounts, the Navy's carrier was canceled to make way for the Air Force's new bomber; and Secretary Johnson did want to prevent the Navy from participating in long-range or strategic bombing. This precipitated the so-called "Admirals' revolt."

The Korean War erupted shortly thereafter, ending that interwar period and that dispute, but the Navy–Air Force fight has had an indelible impact, disproportionate to the original incident. As the Korean War once again proved, aircraft carriers are crucial, and the Navy has built many since the cancellation of the *United States*. But the effects of the fight remain. Some historians view the fight as much ado about nothing, with as much myth as fact (e.g., no admiral actually was forced to resign, and only the CNO was removed from his position),[4] but the battle is still being fought to this day on the pages of Navy and Air Force professional magazines.[5] This incident, coupled with the general military "circling of the wagons" during the McNamara era, when civilian so-called whiz kids ignored military advice, meant one service would no longer challenge another's roles. While uncritical acceptance of other services' missions might have been appropriate during the Cold War, it may not be suitable for this new interwar period.

*　　*　　*

On the morning of 25 June 1950 the post–World War II interwar period ended when North Korea invaded South Korea across their artificially drawn border. (Often overlooked is the fact that North Korea also executed two end-run amphibious operations, landing 10,000 troops at Kangnung and Samchock on the east coast.) Seapower was crucial in this first major postwar confrontation. Within days, both American and Royal

Navy carrier-based aircraft were responding in support of South Korean and some hastily dispatched American troops. Thus, from the very beginning of the conflict and with the help of carrier-based forces, the allies never lost air superiority. Despite this control of the skies, however, the allies were quickly pushed into the Pusan peninsula, where seapower played another, and more traditional, role—sealift. Although flying planes into the peninsula was not impossible, it was extremely dangerous; and planes could provide only limited supplies. Seapower was not only safer, it could supply immeasurably more tonnage. This made possible the buildup and eventual breakout.

Of course, the most spectacular use of seapower was the daring amphibious assault at Inchon, which trapped the North Korean troops and led to their complete rout in a matter of weeks. Without the Chinese intervention, the Korean conflict might have been another Spanish-American War, measured in days instead of years. The Chinese intervention led to the fourth dramatic use of seapower. The Marines trapped in the Chosin Reservoir staged what many consider a classic withdrawal to the sea, where American seapower was able to extract them as well as many civilians.

But seapower should not be overemphasized. The Korean War was a land war. However, seapower played an important role. From the early establishment of air superiority maintained by carriers and the supply of the beleaguered forces at Pusan, to the Inchon landing and the extraction of Marines trapped in the Chosin Reservoir, the influence of seapower was indeed significant—and in at least those four cases, crucial.[6]

While there was nothing comparable to Inchon during America's next major conflict, in Vietnam, the Navy still played an important role. As in Korea, carriers helped maintain absolute air superiority and conducted approximately half of all bombings and air sorties. The two to four carriers constantly deployed off the Vietnamese coast on "Yankee Station" became a crucial part of the air war in Vietnam. Surface combatants, which then included gun cruisers and even, for a time, a battleship, provided critical gunfire support. The Navy also played an important role as a riverine, "brown water" force helping to stop infiltration and supplies from the north. But, Vietnam, like Korea, was essentially a land war. The Marines conducted a few amphibious landings in Vietnam but mostly operated as land forces.

The Navy did play a role in the mining of Haiphong harbor, which many felt was the final straw that brought the North Vietnamese around to serious negotiations. President Nixon has said that his only major mistake was not mining earlier. And, considering the outcome, one of the most important naval benefits from Vietnam was that all Navy bases, that is, surface ships, carriers, and planes, came home, whereas all the Army and Air Force bases and considerable equipment were lost.[7]

Korea and Vietnam were by far the largest American involvements in the postwar period, but there were also several other minor interventions, most involving just the Navy–Marine Corps team. Table 2-1 lists the various landings since World War II, which, in addition to Inchon, include Lebanon in 1958, the Dominican Republic, the *Mayaguez* incident, Grenada, and Lebanon again in the 1980s. With the exception of Inchon, all were relatively small in size, although each was important in its own way and, with the exception of the 1980s Lebanon mission, very successful. The table also helps to illustrate the true influence of the Navy in the postwar period: its roles and missions in the Third World.

The Korean and Vietnam wars are, fortunately, the exceptions. More frequent have been the dozens of Third World incidents and crises, and in most cases the U.S. response has been carried out by naval forces. As the famous 1975 Brookings study stated:

> Throughout the postwar period the United States has turned most often to its Navy when it desired to employ components of the armed forces in support of political objectives. Naval units partici-

Table 2-1. Major U.S. Marine Corps Landings Since World War II

Operation	Year	Number of troops in initial landing
Inchon	1950	19,500[a]
Lebanon	1958	1,700[b]
Dominican Republic	1965	500[c]
Mayaguez Incident	1975	300[d]
Grenada	1983	500[e]
Lebanon	1982–84	1,200[f]

Source: Congressional Budget Office.

[a]Approximately 2,760 U.S. Army troops and 2,790 Republic of Korea Marines also participated in the assault.

[b]Total U.S. forces in Lebanon in 1958 peaked at about 14,000—6,000 Marines and 8,000 Army troops—before they were withdrawn.

[c]A force of about 500 Marines landed on 28 April 1965. Two days later, the force had grown to 1,700 Marines and 2,500 U.S. Army troops. Total U.S. forces peaked at about 23,000, about 6,000 of which were Marines.

[d]Landing force on Koh Tang Island and troops used to seize the SS *Mayaguez.*

[e]About 2,200 Army troops also participated in the initial landing. Forces on Grenada totaled about 6,000—500 Marines, 5,500 Army and support forces—several days after the operation began.

[f]Different Marine Expeditionary Units rotated in and out of Lebanon for peacekeeping duties. Approximately 800 Marines went ashore to serve as part of a multinational peacekeeping force in 1982, and subsequently withdrew. A force of about 1,200 Marines returned to Beirut nineteen days later.

pated in 177 of the 215 incidents, or more than four out of every five. . . .

In short, the Navy clearly has been the foremost instrument for the United States' political uses of the armed forces: at all times, in all places, and regardless of the specifics of the situation.[8]

Despite the Brookings study, which is cited in virtually every CNO's annual posture statement in one form or another, the Navy has generally planned forces and missions around two scenarios: strategic nuclear deterrence and a conventional war against the Soviet Navy.

The Navy has always had an important, if often unrecognized, role in nuclear deterrence. In the early days, and despite the Navy–Air Force fight, the Navy was given the nuclear mission for naval targets and some land-based targets reachable by carrier-based heavy bombers such as the A-3 Skywarrior. The emergence of ballistic missiles saw the Navy's role increase, but again not without a fight. Although overshadowed by the more famous 1949 Navy–Air Force fight, there was a somewhat similar squabble in the late 1950s over service strategic roles.[9] Admiral Burke put forth the notion of finite deterrence: that only a limited number of invulnerable sea-based missiles were needed. The Air Force, still under the influence of massive retaliation, wanted a first-strike capability requiring a very large inventory. While President Eisenhower officially rejected both policies, these basic notions still influence strategic thinking. The Navy's SSBNs and SLBMs are usually considered the invulnerable, second-strike, mutual assured destruction (MAD) force, while the Air Force's historically more accurate silo-based ICBMs are the quick response, "hard-target kill" systems. Perhaps more important, since the earliest days the Navy's SLBMs have carried the overwhelming majority of warheads. Today, of the 6,300 odd ballistic warheads, about 4,000 are on the Navy's SLBMs.

The Navy's role in theater nuclear deterrence has generally been more limited. From the earliest days of the Cold War, carriers had both nuclear and conventional DCAs, but Air Force medium-range bombers and land-based theater nuclear systems were considered more important for NATO deterrence. During the late 1950s and early 1960s, there were many different schemes for making NATO a fourth nuclear power, some involving sea-based systems.[10] One proposal called for a nuclear multilateral force (MLF). In fact, for several years an American destroyer operated with a multinational crew to demonstrate the concept, although it never carried nuclear weapons. Finally, as a compromise, some 400 SLBM warheads were allocated for theater use to SACEUR, but only as a last resort.

In the mid-1970s, in order to balance the Soviet buildup of theater nuclear forces and the recently deployed SS-20s, NATO looked at various countermeasures, including a new medium-range bomber, sea-launched cruise missiles, and new land-based systems.[11] Naval systems were dismissed as not "visible" enough for deterrence, and the decision was made to build and deploy ground-launched cruise missiles (GLCMs) and a new Pershing II mode (P-II). These deployments were coupled with calls for reductions—the "two track" decision to negotiate while also planning deployments. Shortly after the GLCMs and P-IIs were deployed, the United States and Soviet Union signed the INF agreement. Both sides have since agreed to start negotiations on the remaining short-range nuclear systems, although that might have become "overtaken by events" since Presidents Bush and Gorbachev's decision to remove these forces.

* * *

There have been, fortunately, no serious confrontations between the U.S. and Soviet fleets. During the Cuban missile crisis, the U.S. Navy stopped some Soviet merchant ships and forced a few submarines to the surface, and over the years there have been several bumping incidents between warships of the two countries (which led to the Incidents at Sea Agreement). Perhaps the most potentially dangerous time came during the 1973 Arab-Israeli war, when both sides had large fleets in the Mediterranean and there were some fears that they might be drawn into that conflict by their respective client states. The USN was in a downward trend from the post–Vietnam War period, while the Soviet Navy was starting to modernize. In this crisis, the Soviet Mediterranean fleet actually outnumbered the American Sixth Fleet, and Admiral Zumwalt in his memoirs stated that the outcome of any conflict could have been in serious doubt.[12]

Despite the rarity of these confrontations, the U.S. Navy has generally planned its forces to deter and, if necessary, to fight the Soviet Navy. The Soviets' greatest strength was their submarine force, which numbered approximately 300 throughout the Cold War. In the late 1950s, they started to build modern surface combatants with what one analyst called a "fierce look," bristling with missiles, but they turned out to be short-range, single-shot ships. However, in the late 1970s and 1980s, they finally began building new surface combatants that, although perhaps not quite up to American standards, were still considered very capable ships. Their latest battle cruiser even has a phased-array radar system, perhaps comparable to the American Aegis.[13] The most disturbing new development is the emergence of a new generation of quiet submarines. No longer could Soviet subs be heard "an ocean away." It is somewhat ironic, although perhaps fortunate, that at about the same time the Soviet/Russian Navy might finally be matching USN ships in quality, both sides are entering the new interwar period.

Although conflicts with the Russian Navy seem increasingly remote, they cannot be ruled out. More likely are conflicts in the Third World. Overshadowed by the Iraqi invasion of Kuwait was another successful use of seapower during the Liberian civil war. An Amphibious Ready Group (ARG) with V/STOL Harriers steamed off the Liberian coast for weeks, protecting American lives. A small ARG was also used to rescue both American and foreign diplomats from Somalia. During the Iraq crisis, Navy and Marine Corps forces were among the first on station, and, as with all overseas operations, approximately 95 percent of the supplies came by sea. Despite the seriousness of the Iraq crisis, it will probably not be the major event to end this current interwar period, but rather simply another reminder of the dangers of such times.

Size of the Fleet

Throughout much of the Cold War period, the fleet stood at just under 1,000 ships. As shown in Table 2-2, the Navy had some 5,700 ships at the close of World War II; this quickly dropped to about 600 active ships, rising again during Korea to approximately 1,000. It stayed just under that level with some consistency for the next twenty years. The fleet dipped to around 800 in the early 1960s, then rose to just under 1,000 again during the Vietnam conflict. Maintaining those large numbers created few ship-building problems. During the 1950s and 1960s, while some new ships were built, the Navy generally lived off the fat of the vast World War II buildup. Because of that buildup and the shortness of the World War II–Korea interwar period, the fleet could quickly be ratcheted up from 600 to 1,000—with many of those ships still functional for the Vietnam War. At the end of the Vietnam conflict, the fleet still stood at just under 1,000. But in a very few years, it was at fewer than half that number and declining.

There were three reasons for this rapid decline in the post-Vietnam period. First, the thousands of ships built during World War II were reaching the end of their normal thirty-year life cycle. While those built at the end of the war probably could have been kept active for a few years, the decision was made to retire them in order to free up funds. Second, the need to finance the Vietnam War meant that shipbuilding rates during the late 1960s were relatively low. Finally, the rising cost of construction, due in part to inflation but also to the need for more sophisticated ships, meant fewer could be built. As then Rear Admiral

Table 2-2. Size of the U.S. Active Fleet

Type of ship	1940	1945	1950	1955	1960	1968	1970	1975	1980	1985	1990
Carriers											
Attack	6	25	11	16	14	15	15	15	13	13	14
Support		73	4	8	9	8	4				
Surface combatants											
Cruisers/BB	52	95	14	20	14	14	10	27	27	29	45
Destroyers	239	372	137	249	226	240	176	70	80	68	69
Frigates/DE		365	10	64	41	50	47	64	71	105	100
Submarines											
Strategic					2	41	41	41	41	36	36
Nuclear attack				1	8	33	47	64	78	95	95
Nonnuclear	101	237	72	108	103	72	56	11	5	4	2
Amphibious											
Helo-carriers					4	8	7	7	8	12	13
Other		1,256	91	175	109	151	90	57	55	49	53
Support ships	208	3,295	279	389	282	344	250	140	84	114	148
TOTALS	606	5,718	618	1,030	812	976	743	496	462	529	575

Source: Naval Historical Office, various annual posture statements.

Trost explained, "The increase in decommissionings reflected a judgment that some risk was necessary during the 1970s in order to construct greater numbers of more capable ships for the future."[14]

However, because of continuing budgetary restraints, inflation, and the lingering "no more Vietnams" syndrome, still other concepts had to be adopted in order to keep the numbers up. One of the most controversial was Admiral Zumwalt's high-low mix, which balanced larger, sophisticated, very expensive ships with smaller, less expensive craft. There was really nothing new about this concept, of course. From earliest times, navies have always balanced larger warships with smaller, less expensive ones, for mission reasons as well as budgetary concerns. In the days of galleys, three-banked triremes were balanced with two-tiered vessels. During the age of sail, 100-gun ships of the line were balanced with thirty-gun frigates; and in modern times, battleships with cruisers and even multimission destroyers were balanced with smaller, less expensive destroyer escorts. One reason is financial, but smaller ships are also useful as scouts and outlying warning systems, while allowing more dispersal for "show the flag" missions.

Yet the high-low concept brought forth a maelstrom of criticism. Most was leveled at lows such as the proposed 14,000-ton helicopter and V/STOL "sea control ship" (SCS), which was never built, and particularly the FFG-7 *Oliver Hazard Perry*–class frigate, built in large quantities. (Undoubtedly adding to the FFG-7 problem was the fact that *Perry* started out as a patrol frigate to avoid legislation requiring nuclear power for large warships, and there were even suggestions to use a Coast Guard cutter hull.) This ship became so controversial that the Naval Institute *Proceedings* devoted a large section to the pros and cons of the FFG-7. Yet it has turned out to be a very fine, extremely versatile ship, and, more important, it was built in quantity. Currently, the fifty-one FFG-7s represent about a third of the surface combatant force. Often overlooked is that many high-end ships were actually built during this period, including the last nuclear-powered surface combatants, the four *Virginia*-class CGNs; the large, almost cruiser-sized DD-963-class ASW destroyers (whose hull was then used for a cruiser, the sophisticated Aegis-class CG-47); and the large SSN-688-class attack submarine still under construction.

Another post-Vietnam controversy erupted over the future of aircraft carriers. The many carriers built during World War II had reached the end of their useful lives and were retired. Only the *Midway* CV-41 and the *Coral Sea* CV-43, commissioned shortly after the war, remained. The Navy had eight postwar, large-deck, fossil-fuel carriers (CV) but wanted more nuclear-powered *Nimitz*-class (CVN) ships to maintain a force of at least twelve carrier groups. At the same time, V/STOL planes such as the

Harrier started to enter inventories, and many planners pushed for smaller, V/STOL-only carriers. As a compromise, still others suggested smaller conventionally powered carriers, CVVs, in the 40,000- to 60,000-ton range, in contrast to the 90,000-ton CVNs. It was once claimed that two CVVs could be built for every CVN. The Carter administration decided to build CVVs, planning for an eventual transition to V/STOL, but they were curtailed first by Congress and then by the Reagan administration. Over an initial veto, Congress forced President Carter to accept another *Nimitz*-class carrier, but most felt that that would be the last large-deck flattop ever built.

Thus, going into the 1980s, the future of the Navy looked particularly bleak. On the eve of the Reagan administration, Norman Polmar wrote: "During the 1980s the United States Fleet will probably decline in size, from the current 460-odd active, Navy-manned ships to possibly as few as 350. At the same time, the Navy will have difficulty manning even these ships with the quality of personnel needed to operate them effectively and continuously."[15] In 1980, few would have argued with that assessment. However, true to his campaign promise, President Reagan took early action to increase shipbuilding rates. He added ships in a supplemental request, and the following year he requested not one, but two CVNs. Many thought this was simply the old ploy of asking for two in the hopes of getting one, but the two were approved. This concurrent purchase saved millions of dollars, bringing into question the rationale for the CVV. Requests for other ships were also increased, with the annual shipbuilding rate reaching the twenty per year required to sustain a 600-ship Navy (i.e., assuming the normal thirty-year life, 20 × 30 = 600). The Reagan administration once more resurrected the goal of a fifteen-carrier, 600-ship Navy for 1990, and almost made it. The decision to retire fourteen frigates earlier than needed in 1989 ended that quest. The Navy would have had the fifteen carrier groups had it not been for another decision to retire the aging *Coral Sea* a few years early.

Virtually all the ship types requested by the Reagan administration fall into the high end of the building spectrum. FFG-7 production was stopped at fifty-one, with no further frigate type planned. The large DD-963 ASW destroyers were followed by the ultrasophisticated CG-47 Aegis-class cruisers, which are now being followed by the new DDG-51 Aegis-class destroyers. As noted, the CVV and proposed VSS were canceled, with only CVNs authorized. The new SSN-688s, built in quantity, are now being superseded by the SSN-21. What might be considered medium-level amphibious ships were built—the LSD-41 and LSD-41(CV) (cargo-variant)—but they are now being followed by large amphibious assault *Wasp*-class LHDs, the size of World War II carriers. The only low-

Table 2-3. Base Force Structure

	FY90	FY95
Army divisions	28 (18 active)	18 (12 active)
Aircraft carriers	15 + 1 training	12 + 1 training
Carrier air wings	15 (13 active)	13 (11 active)
Battle force ships	546	451
Tactical fighter wings	36 (24 active)	26 (15 active)
Strategic bombers	268	180

Source: Department of Defense, FY93 briefing charts.

end ships built during the 1980s were much-needed minesweepers. Virtually all the ships built in the last decade would have been considered in the high end of the spectrum, an observation that is certainly not meant as a criticism. As noted, it was in the late 1970s that the Soviet Union started to build their own modern, sophisticated ships.

However, what might have been appropriate for the 1980s may not be for the 1990s. In 1990, the Bush administration announced a 25 percent cut in defense and a new, so-called "Base Force." As shown in Table 2-3, all the services will take major reductions by the time the Base Force is phased in for FY95. The numbers for the Navy have been broken down as follows (all numbers are estimates except those for strategic submarines and aircraft carriers):

Strategic submarines (SSBNs)	18
Aircraft carriers	12
Attack submarines	80
Surface combatants	150
Amphibious ships	50
Combat logistics force	50
Support, reserve, and other	90

However, even these numbers might be hard to maintain. Between decreasing budgets and the increasing costs of ships, the warship building rate is declining to less than ten per year; the FY93 plan calls for only six. Without a more traditional shipbuilding balance, the results could be disastrous, ending in a 300-ship Navy (again assuming the usual thirty-year life). There are also drastically changing mission requirements in the post–Cold War era. For example, recently retired chairman of the Joint Chiefs of Staff, Admiral Crowe, has suggested that smaller ships might actually be more appropriate for new missions such as Persian Gulf–type operations.[16] Because of the buildup from the early Reagan years, as with the buildup in World War II, the Navy can live off the fat of the land for a time, but the day of reckoning will eventually come. The Navy may soon find itself in a situation very similar to the post-Vietnam period, when it was faced with both block obsolescence of the World War II ships and declining budgets—a period that required new shipbuilding and fleet strategies.

THE POSTWAR DEFENSE AND SERVICE BUDGETS[17]

As can be expected, the defense and service budgets reflect the post–World War II interwar period. At the close of World War II in 1945, defense spending or outlays were just over $800 billion. That figure dropped by almost half to approximately $416 billion in 1946, and by another two-thirds to $114 billion in 1947. The postwar nadir came in 1948 with budget outlays of only $78 billion, approximately the prewar level of $73 billion in 1941. They rose to just over $100 billion in 1949 and 1950 before rising to approximately $300 billion during the Korean War years. The Korean War high was $331 billion in 1953. After Korea, defense spending dropped to the $250–260 billion range and stayed there until Vietnam, when it once again increased to over $300 billion during the late 1960s. The highest Vietnam-era budget was 1968 with outlays reaching $324 billion, remarkably close to the Korean high of $331 billion in 1953.

During the post-Vietnam period, defense outlays dipped to their lowest levels since the Korean War. From the over $300 billion of the Vietnam years, defense spending quickly fell to approximately $210 billion. The nadir of this postwar period was 1976, with defense outlays totaling only $203 billion. This was finally reversed by the Reagan administration as spending once again rose to the $250 billion post-Korean range, peaking at about $330 billion before leveling off at approximately $290 billion, where it has been for the last few years.[18]

Service budget-authority trends (as contrasted to the actual defense outlays noted above) are interesting and, in some cases, surprising.[19] For example, during the post–World War II interwar period, the Navy got the largest slice of the budget pie for two years, 1948 and 1949. However, by far the largest recipient of funds during the 1950s and 1960s was the Air Force. In fact, even during the Korean and Vietnam wars, except for one year (1952), the Air Force had the largest budget authority. This was, of course, the era of massive retaliation with long-range bombers and Strategic Air Command (SAC) predominance in the 1950s, followed by the ICBM buildups of the 1960s. Throughout most of the 1950s and 1960s, the Air Force budget was in the $90–100 billion range; the Navy budget was around $65–70 billion through the early 1960s, rising to $85–$90 billion during Vietnam; while the Army budget was $55–60 billion through that same early period, rising to $95–100 billion for the late 1960s Vietnam years.

During the post-Vietnam period of the 1970s, the Navy's budget authority was approximately $70–75 billion, followed by the Air Force with decreasing budgets in the $65–70 billion range and the Army at around $55–58 billion. The Navy once more received the largest share during the Reagan years, going from $75 billion in 1980 to a high of $121 billion in 1985 and then to around $100 billion in 1990. The corresponding 1980, 1985, and 1990 figures for the Air Force are $65 billion, $120 billion, and $83 billion, and for the Army, $58 billion, $91 billion, and $78 billion.

All budgets are being decreased further. Here are the new FY93 requests in billions of 1992 dollars, compared with prior years:

	1990	1991	1992	1993
Army	$77.9	$72.5	$67.0	$63.3
Navy	99.5	94.9	84.8	84.6
Air Force	92.4	83.6	80.2	83.9

Although many are predicting a large "peace dividend" from the end of the Cold War, the defense budget has in fact been in significant decline since its zenith year of $351 billion in 1985. Since then the funding for defense has declined, as shown below:

Fiscal Year	Budget Authority (in billions of 1991 dollars)
1985	$350.7
1986	335.1
1987	322.3
1988	315.5
1989	311.3
1990	302.9
1991	295.1 (requested)
1991	288.3 (authorized)
1992	290.8 (requested)

In short, there has already been a peace dividend of over $60 billion from 1985 to 1991—and actually more, considering the original requests. Real declines in defense spending over the last six years have averaged about 3 percent a year.

The future also looks bleak. After the budget summit agreement of late 1990, Senator Robert Byrd of West Virginia, chairman of the Senate Appropriations Committee, inserted the following defense budget estimates with original baseline requests into the *Congressional Record*; but these have already been overtaken by events, as the 1993 figures show:

	1991	*1992*	*1993*	*1994*	*1995*	*1996*	*1997*
1990 agreement	$288.3	$290.9	$291.9	$292.0	$295.0	n/a	n/a
summer baseline	313.8	326.0	338.5	351.5	364.9	n/a	n/a
difference	25.5	35.1	46.6	59.5	69.9	n/a	n/a
1993 submission	n/a	283.8	280.9	281.7	284.4	$285.7	$290.6

To illustrate all of the recent changes in the defense budget, Secretary of Defense Dick Cheney brought out during his FY93 presentation what he called his "favorite . . . pitchfork chart" (Figure 2-1). It shows all the different estimates and projections made since the Bush administration's initial April 1989 request for real increases of 1.2 percent per year, including the latest plan for a 7 percent real decline. In constant dollars, the budget appears to be heading to the old 1950–1960 levels of approximately $250 billion. At least to date, the figures are far from the two post–World War II interwar budget lows of approximately $110 billion and $210 billion for the pre-Korea and post-Vietnam periods, respectively. However, there are many in Congress who would like to return to those levels. In fact, a number often heard is $200 billion in constant dollars by the end of the decade, which would probably come close to $300 billion in current funding. Although the administration had originally planned only a 2 percent real decline per year, actual reductions during the late 1980s came closer to 3 percent and are now increasing to 4 percent. A senior defense budget official has predicted a defense budget falling from approximately 5 percent to only 3.5 percent of GNP.

In short, it appears that the defense budget will vary from, at best, continued real declines in the 4–5 percent range, allowing for only slight growth in current-year dollars. Minor increases in current-year (inflated) dollars would permit politicians to claim that the defense budget was "increasing," even though in real terms it would be decreasing rapidly. While there is some consensus that the Navy should continue receiving the largest slice of the budget, that slice will still be decreasing to, in real terms, 1970s interwar levels by the end of this decade.

ENTERING THE NEW INTERWAR PERIOD

Throughout the post–World War II, Cold War period, the Navy has had many different uses, roles, and missions. From participation in the major "limited" wars, Korea and Vietnam, and the two-hundred-odd crises and incidents, mostly in the Third World, to its stake in nuclear strategy as

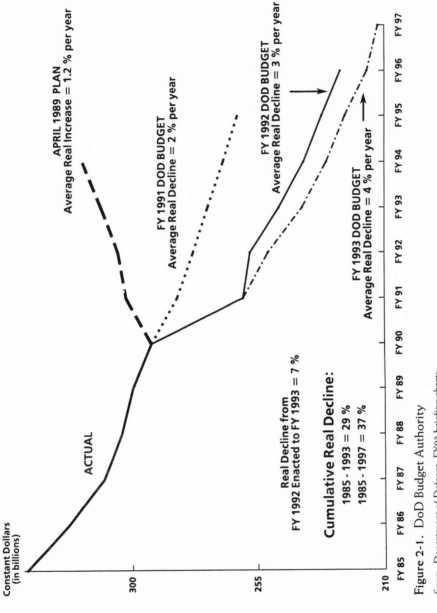

Figure 2-1. DoD Budget Authority

Source: Department of Defense, FY93 briefing charts.

Note: Excluding Desert Shield/Desert Storm costs

part of the triad and in deterring the Soviet naval threat, the U.S. Navy has played an important role. While the old Soviet threat may be abating, at least in the short term, there are still many dangers in the world, as the recent Iraq crisis demonstrates. As serious as the Iraqi crisis was, however, it will probably not be the significant event that ends this new post–Cold War interwar period. Rather, it will simply be a reminder of how dangerous interwar periods are, and why they still require a large fleet.

If history is any guide, the size of the fleet will decline during the 1990s, although there could easily be a five- to ten-year respite. Because of the early Reagan administration's shipbuilding rates of well over twenty ships a year, the fleet should be in relatively good shape for the next few years. In other words, with a few exceptions such as the DDG force, reductions will come about for political and budgetary reasons, not because of aging ships as happened in the post-Vietnam period. As with the World War II buildups, the Navy can live off the Reagan-era fat for a few years, but not for long. As will be shown in Part II, after the turn of the century—tomorrow in shipbuilding decision terms—major parts of the fleet will start to reach block obsolescence. Since decreasing budgets will restrict building rates, this will require some new shipbuilding, R and D, and even fleet deployment alternatives. Before making these major changes, however, the first step is a more thorough analysis of the changing 1990 environment and missions.

Part I

The Missions

3 / The Changing Missions of the 1990s

STRATEGISTS HAVE LONG felt that mission analysis should come before discussions of force size and composition, but that has rarely happened, and for some quite understandable reasons. Following wars and entering interwar periods, the inventory is usually full from that last conflict, and there is a natural reluctance to start new projects even if changes are necessary. This reluctance, incidentally, exists not just in the military, which is then often accused of always fighting the last war, but also resides with budget cutters, including those in Congress with strong constituent interests. Building "less of the same" and moving forces into the reserves are considerably easier than changing course or closing bases. Changing directions becomes even harder when perceptions are clouded, as they are today and as they were during the first interwar period.

At the end of World War I, the U.S. Navy had many battleships and cruisers under construction and no inclination to switch direction, mainly because there was, like today, no perceived need for change. The battleship was still considered the capital ship; very few in the Navy recognized the true potential of the submarine and the aircraft carrier, just then entering inventories. It was also this surplus of ships under construction that made naval arms control more tolerable—they were really the ones restricted, not those already built.

After World War II, even though there was a recognition that the dropping of the atomic bomb signaled a new era, the fact that there were literally thousands of ships in the fleet again created a great reluctance to start even new types for which there was an obvious need, such as large-deck aircraft carriers for new jet aircraft. Some of the World War II weaponry was adaptable. For example, old gun cruisers could be converted into missile ships, CLGs. However, much was not so versatile. Jet aircraft made virtually all World War II planes obsolete, as well as most antiair weaponry. Despite this general perception of the need for change, the huge World War II inventory made justifying new types difficult.

With the major changes anticipated in the 1990s, however, a mission analysis must come first. There is, fortunately, room for careful study for two reasons. First, as at the start of the post–World War I and post–World War II interwar periods, the U.S. Navy is in fairly good shape in this new post–Cold War period due to the Reagan buildup. Second, unlike those other interwar periods, major weapon changes are probably not needed, at least not immediately. Since virtually all of the current weaponry features relatively high technology, built to fight in the sophisticated World War III scenario, it is generally adaptable to lesser threats. Thus, while the dropping of the atomic bomb and introduction of jet aircraft made much of the massive World War II inventory obsolete, such is not the case with the current inventory. There is, in short, some time for reflection.

Perhaps not too much time, however. Congressional pressure is mounting for a new defense strategy. In a series of widely publicized speeches, Senator Sam Nunn, chairman of the Senate Armed Services Committee, called for both new mission and new force analyses. Two of his points relating to missions were:

> First, although nuclear deterrence will provide the critical underpinning of our military strategy for now and the foreseeable future, it should be achievable at significantly lower levels of weaponry, and with a much higher degree of stability, that is, with reduced incentives for either side to strike first with strategic nuclear weapons.

> Second, our forward deployed forces should be reduced consistent with changes in the threat while placing greater emphasis on increased specialization among allied nations and much greater reliance on reinforcement with deployable U.S. combat forces to support our allies.[1]

Chairman Nunn also made more specific proposals such as moving more forces into the reserves and adopting a new concept of "flexible readiness." (Some of these recommendations will be discussed in Part II.) The senator further suggested that the armed services should compete among themselves to determine which is more suited for each mission. According to one press report, the Navy, undoubtedly remembering the 1949 Navy–Air Force fight, was "unsurprisingly . . . skeptical of Nunn proposals on mission competition."[2] However, Senator Nunn is not the only one calling for new mission analysis. Other senators have asked why the Navy needs fourteen carriers. And (shades of the post–World War II unification debates) some are even asking why Air Force planes cannot operate from carriers and why we have both an Army and Marine Corps.[3]

There is, of course, recognition of these changes in both the Navy and the Department of Defense. Just before retiring, Admiral Trost issued a new "Maritime Strategy for the 1990s,"[4] which is considerably broader than the old "forward strategy" concept. While one of the principles is still "forward defense," the first principle is deterrence, with a third based on alliances. The first aspect is nuclear deterrence, which he calls "the keystone on which the rest of our conventional strategy depends." He then goes into more traditional naval missions such as "presence" and "crisis response" in Third World areas, where he also noted the increase in sophisticated weaponry.

More recently, the Secretary of the Navy, the Chief of Naval Operations, and the Commandant of the Marine Corps jointly published an article entitled, "The Way Ahead." In it, they note "the winds of change blowing through the corridors of power from Washington to New Delhi, Moscow to Pretoria," where "many of our existing ground rules and assumptions will be challenged."[5] However, they also state that "our fundamental interests remain unchanged," going on to chronicle current Navy–Marine Corps missions and capabilities. This led one observer to comment: " 'The Way Ahead,' however, looked and sounded a lot like the past. Rather than presenting a carefully drawn and integrated approach, it contained the same fractured thinking—with many of the same tired and safe cliches about naval forces and sea control."[6]

There have also been discernible changes at both the national and Department of Defense levels. For example, the January 1988 *National Security Strategy of the United States* (undoubtedly written in 1987 when changes were just starting to appear) stated, "The fundamentals of our notion *change little* from year to year,"[7] while the 1990 report began with the reflection that "the international landscape is marked by *change that is breath-taking* in its character, dimension and pace."[8] (emphasis added). There are noticeable shifts of emphasis between the 1988 and 1990 reports from the Soviet to new Third World threats. While the Pentagon is still refining this new notion, according to news reports, it has also "developed a new strategy to guide U.S. military planning in the post–Cold War era that shifts the emphasis away from major confrontation with the

Soviet Union in Europe toward potential regional conflicts such as the current Iraqi crisis in the Mideast."[9]

The most significant change occurred when President Bush unveiled a new national security strategy on August 2, 1990, at the Aspen Institute.[10] The new defense policy would be based upon four major elements: deterrence, forward presence, crisis response, and reconstitution. This speech was generally ignored by the media and even much of the national security community due to the Iraqi invasion of Kuwait the same day, but the four elements have been repeated by the Secretary of Defense and the Chairman of the Joint Chiefs of Staff and could form the basis of a major defense reorganization.[11] While these broad national security statements are useful, there is still a need for more detailed mission analysis as a prerequisite to force planning.

* * *

There are several different policy levels. Many scholars accept Paul Nitze's now-classic distinctions between "declaratory" and "employment" policy.[12] Declaratory policies are those broad statements of political and military objectives, with their intended psychological effects. Such policies as defense of the homeland, containment, and more specific military strategies such as massive retaliation and flexible response—even, to some extent, the Maritime Strategy—fall into the declaratory category. Employment policy involves more concrete military objectives as well as plans employing the forces for the achievement of those objectives—where the "rubber hits the road," as one author puts it.[13] Declaratory policy is generally considered the province of the NCA, with employment policy the responsibility of the military planners, now the various area CINCs.

What is needed, however, is something in between these macro and micro levels, or what is sometimes called "mission analysis" by strategists and "force planning"[14] by military planners. That is the general purpose of this book: to look at those two middle levels of conceptual military planning. First, a mission analysis is needed to bridge the gap between the broad declaratory policies from the president and other national command authorities and the specific employment policies of the various commanders; second, decisions must be made regarding the forces needed for those missions. This section will therefore focus on the changing nature of the three more or less traditional areas of national concern: nuclear deterrence, the European (NATO) theater, and Third World operations, while Part II will look at the forces.

There will be major changes in all three areas, many already known yet still not accounted for by planners. In nuclear weaponry and deterrence, there should be at least two, and possibly as many as four, new arms control treaties in the next few years. For the first time, strategic forces will actually be reduced rather than just capped. START I has recently been signed, and a START II is already being discussed. An INF II to eliminate short-range nuclear forces is also under consideration, with some calling for a complete removal of European systems by the end of this decade. Washington and Moscow have already announced unilateral withdrawals in both tactical and strategic nuclear forces. Nowhere will there be greater changes than in the NATO theater, which has always been considered the area of greatest Soviet threat. CFE I, which restricts weapons, has already been signed; negotiations toward a CFE Ia for manpower are already under way. At this "breath-taking pace," as the national strategy statement put it, a CFE II or even III is not out of the question by the year 2000. The collapse of the old USSR into the new, shaky CIS has added other uncertainties. And, as the recent Iraqi conflict illustrates, Third World crises will continue unabated and, with the sophisticated weaponry now available, probably increase in intensity. These changing mission conditions and rationales will be explored in greater detail in the next three chapters.

4 / Nuclear Deterrence

All at Sea?

THE 1990s WILL see the first real reductions in strategic nuclear weaponry in history, and the end of a theater nuclear deterrent system that has served NATO well for over forty years. Although the Iraqi crisis delayed the arms control process a bit, the United States and the USSR finally signed the START I agreement; and both sides had agreed to begin negotiations on eliminating the remaining "third zero," theater short range intermediate nuclear forces (SNF), an INF II even before the unilateral decisions. On 27 September 1991, President Bush made the surprising unilateral offer to withdraw and destroy all SNFs overseas, remove tactical nuclear weapons from all Navy ships and place them in storage, or garrison, stand down the bomber force from alert, cease development of mobile ICBMs, and commence withdrawal of the 450 old single-warhead Minuteman II force already scheduled for elimination in START. Nine days later, on October 6, President Gorbachev met and raised Bush's offer, proposing the elimination of all tactical nuclear weapons including those in forward military tactical aviation units, cutting an additional 1,000 weapons in START I, and calling for an additional 50 percent reduction under START II.

Then, in his 1992 State of the Union address, President Bush proposed further major cuts, including eliminating the ten-warhead MX and reducing the number of warheads on MM IIIs to one if the Russians would respond in kind—in short, de-MIRVing all ICBMs. He also offered to reduce the number of warheads on sea-based missiles by one-third and ordered the Department of Energy to cease production of the new W-88 warhead for SLBMs. The president also stopped the number of new stealth B-2s at twenty and announced that a substantial portion of strategic bombers would be converted to conventional use. Both long- and short-range nuclear cruise missiles were also canceled. A few days later, President Yeltsin raised the stakes by taking some ICBMs and bombers off alert while proposing even further cuts to 2,000–2,500 strategic weapons, about a two-thirds reduction from START I limits.

While these proposals are generally welcome, especially in this new post–Cold War era, they will still cause problems and require significant changes in the U.S. strategic triad and especially in theater nuclear forces. The problems are not necessarily due to the agreements or unilateral decisions per se, but rather to the weapons choices made by the West over the past two decades. The major change should be the emergence of the Navy's "wet leg" as the predominant force in the old strategic triad of long-range bombers, land-based ICBMs, and SLBMs on SSBNs. The president's announcement on ICBMs, bombers, and cruise missiles will essentially, or at least inevitably, put the Air Force out of the strategic business. After the president's decision on SNF, naval systems could well constitute the *only* U.S. nuclear weapons remaining for theater deterrence, and these are now to be placed in garrison. These changes, however, will also challenge some old naval perceptions and attitudes, perhaps requiring the Navy to break a few traditional "sacred eggs." At the June 1992 Summit, both sides agreed to an interim measure to reduce the START I 6,000 warhead ceiling to between 3,800 and 4,250 within seven years; and what might be called START II to 3,000 to 3,500 warheads by the year 2003. New ICBM and SLBM ceilings were also added.

STRATEGIC NUCLEAR FORCES AND ARMS CONTROL

Background[1]

START will be a truly historic agreement. Though not quite the 50 percent reduction in warheads once envisioned, it will still amount to about a 30 percent cut and, depending on final weapon choices, close to a 50 percent reduction in launchers, which in many respects are more important. For example, it looks as if SSBN strength will shrink to only eighteen from the forty-one that the USN had operated for years. START will be especially significant considering that its two predecessors, SALT I and II, were (despite the impression often given by the intensity of debates

Table 4-1. SALT I Limits

Delivery system	United States	Soviet Union
ICBM	1,054	1,618
	(1,000)	(1,408)
SLBM	656	740
	(710)	(950)
Submarines	41	62
	(44)	

during the 1970s) actually only freezes on existing launchers or SNDVs (strategic nuclear delivery vehicles), as they are officially known.

SALT I, as shown in Table 4-1, simply froze ballistic systems at existing levels. (Bombers were not counted in SALT I.) Ceilings for ICBMs were 1,054 for the United States and 1,618 for the Soviet Union. SLBM limits were 656 for the United States on 41 SSBNs, and 740 for the Soviet Union on 62 strategic submarines. Some allowance was made for exchanging SLBMs for ICBMs (the numbers in parentheses), a so-called "one-way freedom to mix"—that is, SLBMs could be increased at the expense of ICBMs, but not vice versa. Although at first glance the numbers favored the Soviet Union, the disparity was in launchers only. SALT I did not count warheads, which overwhelmingly favored the U.S. At the time, the Soviet Union was just starting to place multiple independently targeted vehicle (MIRVed) warheads atop its missiles; but the United States already had the three-warhead Minuteman III and, more important, the ten-warhead C-3 Poseidon SLBM. Despite the U.S. warhead advantage of well over two to one, Congress added the Jackson Amendment, named after the late Senator Henry "Scoop" Jackson, which stipulated that future strategic accords must have "equal" limits.

SALT II was, at least for the United States, simply another freeze. Table 4-2 shows the limits of the treaty. The final 2,250 limit on delivery systems would have required the Soviet Union to retire about 300 older systems without a reciprocal U.S. move—undoubtedly the best feature of

Table 4-2. SALT II Limits

2,400 equal aggregate limit on all delivery systems (includes ICBM, SLBM, and bombers)

2,250 final aggregate limit on all delivery systems (within three years)

1,320 equal aggregate limit on MIRVed missiles and heavy bombers with cruise missiles

1,200 sublimit on MIRVed ballistic missiles (120 implied limit on heavy bombers with cruise missiles)

820 sublimit on MIRVed ICBMs

SALT II. Also, the United States still maintained a distinct warhead advantage from its MIRVed systems, mostly from the ten-warhead C-3 SLBM, by then completely deployed. Despite these advantages and the Carter administration's plea that it did represent equal limits, as required by the Jackson Amendment, SALT II was severely criticized for its throw-weight discrepancies. The Soviet Union has much larger ICBMs, the SS-19 and particularly the heavy SS-18, which has twice the throw-weight of American missiles. This throw-weight problem, which started out as a technical expert's only issue, finally doomed SALT II, with the proverbial last straw coming when the Soviets invaded Afghanistan. That forced President Carter to withdraw the treaty from consideration by the Senate (although it has been observed now for over ten years).

More important for the long run, SALT II contained some preliminary broad provisions for MIRVed warheads. For the first time, MIRV missiles were placed in a separate category, as were bombers carrying ALCMs. However, there was still no provision for limiting the numbers of warheads per se. The counting rule was still applied only to launchers, or SNDVs, with no ceiling on the numbers of warheads themselves. In short, the primary rule from both SALT I and II was that *only* SNDVs were counted, meaning that both countries were in fact indirectly encouraged to place as many MIRVed warheads as possible atop each restricted missile since there was no penalty. That penalty, and dilemma, were to be addressed in START.

START I[2]

START I will change the rules of the game drastically. As shown in Table 4-3, warheads will now be counted, and there will be real reductions. START, like its SALT predecessors, first imposes an SNDV limit: a 1,600 ceiling on ICBMs, SLBMs, and heavy bombers. However, for the first time, there is also a warhead limit of 6,000, which includes ICBM and SLBM warheads and some, but not all, ALCMs. There is a further sublimit of 4,900 ballistic missile warheads (i.e., on ICBMs and SLBMs), and

Table 4-3. START I Limits

SNDVs	1,600 ceiling on ICBMs, SLCMs, and heavy bombers
Warheads	6,000 ceiling to include ICBM and SLBM warheads, and long-range ALCMs (heavy bombers carrying gravity bombs and SRAM count as one warhead)
Sublimits	4,900 ballistic missile warheads (ICBM and SLBM)
	(1,100 implied sublimit on bombers and ALCMs)
	1,540 warheads on 154 heavy missiles

thus an implied sublimit of 1,100 on bombers with ALCMs. Finally, to solve the old throw-weight problem, START imposes a limit of 1,540 warheads on 154 heavy missiles. This means the Soviet Union will have to reduce its heavy SS-18 ICBM inventory of 308 by half.

The major problem with START is not in the agreement itself, but rather in trying to fit old and especially new weapon systems into its limits. Table 4-4 shows the current U.S. strategic inventory, with approximately 9,100 warheads on 1,750 SNDVs. Under the old SALT rules, which simply counted launchers, the new START limits would entail very few problems, considering upcoming retirements. For example, retiring the 450 quarter-century-old Minuteman IIs (already announced) would alone bring the United States into launcher compliance. In addition, by the time START phases in during the 1990s, the older Poseidon SSBNs will all be retired, as will more of the aging B-52s.

The real problem comes with the new rule—counting the warheads. The twelve Trident and twelve Poseidon SSBNs back-fitted with the Trident C-4 missile carry 3,840 warheads. Adding the 500 warheads on the fifty MX missiles brings the total to almost 4,340, leaving only 560 slots for additional ballistic warheads—186 three-warhead Minuteman IIIs, for example. But by then, more twenty-four-launch-tube Trident SSBNs will be commissioned, replacing the sixteen-tube Poseidon boats

Table 4-4. Current U.S. Strategic Inventory

System	Launcher	Number of warheads	Total warheads
ICBMs			
MX	50	10	500
MM II[a]	450	1	450
MM III	550	3	1,500
Subtotal ICBM	(1,000)		(2,450)
SLBMs			
Trident (12 x 24)	288	8	2,304
Poseidon[a] (12 x 16)	192	8	1,536
Subtotal SLBM	(480)		(3,840)
Subtotal ballistic	(1,480)		(6,290)
Bombers			
B-1B	97	1	97
B-52G (ALCM)[a]	89	12	1,068
B-52H (ALCM)	84	20	1,680
Subtotal bomber	(270)		(2,845)
TOTALS	1,750		9,135

[a]Currently being retired.

The only new systems to join the force during the 1990s will be six new Tridents with 1,152 warheads, and twenty B-2s, which will only count as "one" under START rules.

and further exacerbating the numbers dilemma. The problem would have been even more acute had the Air Force (as once planned) built a total of 100 ten-warhead MXs. While 100 MX missiles barely dent the SNDV ceiling, their 1,000 warheads would have monopolized the warhead limits. The interim measure to 3,800 to 4,250 warheads (including a new 2,160 SLBM ceiling) within seven years of signing START will add to these problems.

In short, the United States could well have problems with the new rules. This should not be surprising. After all, the new systems, the twenty-four-tube Tridents and the ten-warhead MXs, were all conceived under the old SALT rules where concentration of warheads did not matter, since they were not counted. SNDVs with very few, not heavily MIRVed warheads make sense under the new rules. While the United States may, and obviously will, squeeze through START I limits, as will be described below, going into a START II regime or even the unilateral proposals with the current weapons inventory could cause real problems.

One new START counting provision does favor the United States. The Soviets agreed to a "discount" rule whereby each ALCM bomber will be counted as carrying ten warheads, in lieu of the actual number. The older B-52Gs only carried 12 ALCMs, but the B-52Hs hold twenty and the B-1B is capable of twenty-two. Eventually, the 97 B-1Bs will switch from their current penetrator role to become ALCM carriers; had each counted as twenty-two warheads, the numbers could have quickly gone through the roof. Bombers have another decided advantage under START rules. Bombers carrying only gravity bombs or short-range attack nuclear missiles (SRAMs) count as only one warhead. Since there is no problem meeting the 1,600 SNDV limit, bombers again are favored by the rules.

The final post-START force mix has yet to be decided. For SSBNs, the numbers often heard are the eighteen Tridents with 3,456 warheads. Adding the fifty MXs with 500 warheads allows planners between 560 and 1,000 slots for more SSBNs, which the Navy might want, or additional Air Force ICBMs. It does appear certain, however, that the SSBN force will shrink by at least 50 percent from the forty-one operated for years, with the ICBM force reduced by at least sixty percent from 1,000 to around 350.

Critics of the current START agreement—ironically, on the left—have pointed out that this is not really a fifty percent weapon reduction, but only about 30 percent.[3] Since bombs, SRAMs, and some ALCMs are not counted, a few critics have even claimed that START could actually increase the nuclear inventory.[4] However, since the key to deterrence, especially for the West, has always been launcher survivability for a second strike and not first-strike capability, these reductions are significant and certainly do fall into the 50 percent category.

Future of the Triad

Except for the Navy's wet leg, the future of the U.S. strategic triad looks grim, and many are even questioning the function of the Trident. ICBM modernization is all but officially dead, and probably was even before the recent events in the Soviet Union and Eastern Europe and the president's unilateral decisions. There were three reasons for ICBM problems: costs, parochialism, and strategy. The Air Force had two proposals for ICBM modernization: a rail-mobile system with the MX mounted on railroad cars, and the single-warhead, road-mobile Midgetman. Both were terribly expensive. Cost estimates for simply relocating the current 50 MX missiles on railroad cars were over $10 billion, while those for the various Midgetman schemes ranged form $15 to 40 billion[5]—and all for just 500 warheads, less than are placed on three SSBNs. With the current budget problems, both ICBM proposals were simply too expensive; they also ran into Air Force parochialism. The Air Force, which has always favored bombers over ICBMs, would rather purchase the new B-2 stealth bomber and even offered to sacrifice both ICBM modernizations for it.

Finally, there are serious strategy problems with ICBMs. The main rationale for ICBMs has always been accuracy for a "hard target kill," with a secondary mission in quick response, "launch under warning or attack" capability. However, the new Trident II D-5 SLBM just entering the fleet now has sufficient accuracy for hard target kill, and the quick response argument never made much sense, especially in today's environment with its increased warning time. As critics have long pointed out, a quick response could be shooting at empty holes. In short, the whole strategy rationale for ICBMs went out the window when the accurate D-5 SLBM went to sea. No wonder the president made the decision to kill both mobile ICBM proposals.

Despite the Air Force's offer to sacrifice new ICBMs on the budget cutter's altar,[6] and the president's decision on mobile missile cancellation, the triad's bomber leg is also in serious trouble. The B-1B, built as an "interim" penetrator between the B-52 and the stealth B-2, cannot penetrate Soviet defenses, while the cost of the B-2 is now inching up toward $1 billion per copy. The B-1B, like any new plane, had many problems. Most were fixed or fixable, but one, inadequate electronic countermeasures (ECMs) to penetrate current Soviet defenses, will cost billions to correct, and, according to some press accounts, the system may never work.[7] Of course, the problem could be fixed overnight if the B-1B switched from a penetrator to an ALCM carrier, but that would put the B-52 mission at risk and raise a question asked all along by critics: why was the "interim" B-1B needed in the first place?

But at least the B-1B is a bird in hand. The new stealth B-2 is fighting for its life. Cost estimates for the original 132-plane request were about $500 million per plane. However, due to budgetary restraints the Air Force has cut the program to seventy-five planes—a decision that, of course, drove up individual costs, now estimated at over $800 million per copy.[8] The president's decision to stop at twenty will probably push individual costs to around $1 billion. Despite the price, after all that has been sunk into R and D costs (up to 65 percent of the total, according to some reports) the B-2 probably should have proceeded, especially since there are about fifteen now under production. However, the changing conditions in the Soviet Union and the president's decision to stand down bomber alert had placed the future of and need for strategic long-range bombers in doubt.

In short, due to rapidly changing world conditions, the president's decision on ICBMs, and budget restraints, it appears likely that the ICBM leg of the triad will simply wither away. Depending on final and reciprocal action by Boris Yeltsin on ICBMs, only the MM III force (which dates from the 1970s) will remain, and it will soon need extensive funding for upkeep—an increasingly unlikely prospect in this new era. The bomber leg will also shrink, although it will probably never quite wither away. There are programs to extend some B-52s into the twenty-first century, and the B-1Bs and the few B-2s should probably last at least twenty more years. But it will be a greatly reduced bomber force, numbering less than two hundred planes. This would leave the wet leg as the only truly vibrant limb of that old strategic triad. Besides the SSBNs and Trident missiles, to be discussed later, the Navy also has two other programs that should prove useful. But, before turning to them, one needs to look at the real strategic nuclear problem—follow-on STARTs.

Planning for START II

While the START I limits will cause problems, the United States will undoubtedly squeeze by—due in part to necessity, but also to normal retirements and changing world conditions. However, there could be major problems with the current inventory going into any START II regime. At the June 1992 Summit, Presidents Bush and Yeltsin agreed to a further reduction to 3,000 to 3,500 warheads and the elimination of all

Table 4-5. Possible START II Force Mix and Limits

System	SNDV	Warhead	Total
MX	50	10	500
Trident (18 x 24)	432	8	3,456
Totals	482		3,956
START II limits	800?		3,000

MIRVed ICBMs. SLBM warheads would be capped at 1,728 (which works out to half the current number on 18 Tridents). Imagine going into these reductions with the forces shown in Table 4-5.

Once again, the United States would have no problem meeting any SNDV limits, that is, the *old* SALT rules, but would have absolutely no flexibility with the *new* rules on warhead limits; the numbers in Table 4-5 do not even include bombers. If, by the time a START II is finalized, ninety B-1Bs had ALCMs, adding another 900 to the warhead total, the dilemma would deepen (and would be worse if, as currently being negotiated, the actual number of ALCMs—twenty-two on a B-1B—were counted instead of the discount rate of ten). It seems clear that the United States should have built weapons more in tune with the new rules, such as the single-warhead Midgetman instead of the ten-warhead MX. Even eliminating the MX as currently proposed does not solve the problem. The new stealth B-2, as a penetrator counting as one warhead apiece, also conforms to the new rules.

The Navy also has problems. As many have pointed out for years, the Navy should never have increased the number of launch tubes from the sixteen in the earlier Polaris and Poseidon SSBNs to twenty-four in the Tridents, a 50 percent increase—too many eggs in one basket, according to the critics. If, for example, the USN had remained with the sixteen-tube arrangement, the SSBN inventory under START I could have been approximately thirty instead of twenty, with a START II inventory of fifteen—still a very respectable number for vulnerability concerns. A START II regime that saw the number of Tridents cut in half to only nine or ten, with about six deployed, would seriously question the whole invulnerability rationale of the SSBNs. While no one anticipates a so-called "ASW breakthrough," only six SSBNs deployed is below many strategists' comfort levels. The other options are developing a new missile with fewer warheads or down-loading warheads from current SLBMs, which the president has proposed. A new missile, of course, costs money, and down-loading raises terrible verification problems as well as breakout concerns if the Russians also down-load. What can be down-loaded can obviously be rather quickly up-loaded.[9]

The Russians in START

Fortunately, the Russian commonwealth will be faced with similar problems in START, although it appears they understand the new rules better. Much has been made of the huge Typhoon SSBN, almost twice the size of the Trident, but the Typhoon has only twenty tubes, not twenty-four. Plus, the Russians are still building the sixteen-tube Delta IVs and, according to recent reports, have stopped building the Typhoon. Also, their new SLBM, the SS-N-23, is now credited with only four warheads. Thus, a Russian sixteen-tube Delta IV with four-warhead SS-N-23s counts as only sixty-four warheads under START rules, only one-third the 192 of an American twenty-four-tube Trident with its eight-warhead D-5 SLBMs.

The Russians have similar flexibility in their land-based systems. Their new ten-warhead rail-mobile SS-24 violates the new rules of the game, but certainly the single-warhead road-mobile SS-25 does not. Wisely, they have stopped building the ten-warhead SS-24 (while the U.S. Air Force wanted to build more MXs). They might have some problems with their heavy SS-18s, but those can be easily balanced with the single warhead SS-25s.

There could in fact be a post-START condition similar to the balance after SALT I, but with one very significant difference. As with SALT I, the Russian side could end up with more platforms; but unlike SALT I, the significant American advantage in warheads will be gone. The Russians could easily have two to three times as many SSBNs and more ICBMs than the United States and still be in START compliance. Their weaponry also gives them considerably more flexibility for any START II regimes. And what about a START III? This is now considered the SALT/START "process," and not to be forgotten is Presidents Reagan and Gorbachev's goal to eliminate all nuclear weaponry by the year 2000. While complete elimination might be too optimistic, the process will continue—and a START III is inevitable.

There are two final thoughts to consider before completely dismissing nuclear threats in this new post–Cold War era. First, with the economic collapse of the CIS and disarray in conventional forces, only nuclear weapons truly keep a Russian leader in the superpower ranks equal to an American president. Few leaders ever relinquish such power and prestige. The United Kingdom, China, and especially France all maintain nuclear systems as much for prestige as for necessity. Second is the possible breakup of the CIS into separate countries, four of which could have strategic nuclear weapons: Russia, Ukraine, Kazakhstan, and Byelarus. Since the Russians have several single-warhead weapons, a split could be accomplished quite easily while still remaining within START limits. Of course, this would be an American targeteer's dilemma.

THEATER NUCLEAR FORCES

A similar trend toward naval systems is taking place in theater nuclear forces. When NATO was originally formed, there were plans to match Soviet military strength with a ninety-six-division force goal. For many reasons, mostly budgetary, that goal was never realized, and the allies quickly fell back on nuclear weapons—deterrence on the cheap. In 1987, the so-called "double zero" INF treaty was signed, eliminating the long- and medium-range systems that were able to reach at least some targets in the Soviet Union and all in what was then the Warsaw Pact.[10] With the stroke of a pen, some forty years of NATO strategy was swept away, which was what upset the likes of Henry Kissinger and virtually all former SACEURs. While the "bean count" from INF favored the United States, Western theater nuclear strategy was all but forgotten; apparently, it still is.

All that remained was the "third zero," short-range systems. Major weapon modernizations were once planned, including a follow-on to the Lance (FOL), nuclear artillery upgrades, movement of more nuclear DCA to Europe, and a new nuclear tactical air-to-surface missile (TASM). However, in 1989 FOL was postponed indefinitely, and President Bush offered to remove the nuclear artillery; it appears that the proposed movement of F-111 fighter-bomber DCA was also dead. The only program remaining was TASM, although according to press reports its future was also in doubt. With little reluctance, the United States agreed to negotiate on short-range systems.

Thus, the president's late–September 1991 decision to unilaterally withdraw and even destroy SNF forces was not really surprising, nor did it have much effect on theater nuclear strategy. As (West) German strategists pointed out after the signing of INF, SNF warheads would only land on their soil or on the newly liberated East European countries, making their use questionable. The short-range missiles and nuclear artillery systems being eliminated added virtually nothing to the "flexibility" of NATO's flexible response strategy.

Will the recent breakup of the Soviet Union and Eastern Europe plus the CFE agreements make theater nuclear weapons and strategy unnecessary? Many Western European political leaders and virtually all military commanders still would like that theater nuclear deterrence capability. There is still the issue of European-based Air Force DCA, but it appears likely they will eventually be captured in a CFE II, or certainly in a follow-on CFE III. In his response to Bush's cuts, President Gorbachev called for the elimination of nuclear DCA weapons. Between CFE agreements and Gorbachev's offer, pressure is sure to mount for their removal. That would leave only the Navy's carrier-based DCA and nuclear SLCM Tomahawk.

Thus, the real surprise from the standpoint of theater nuclear strategy was the president's decision to also remove all nuclear weapons from Navy ships and place them in garrison. The Navy is currently planning a new stealth attack aircraft, the AX, which would have been a perfect plane for the sophisticated European area. More appropriate was the TLAM-N. Once rejected for theater operations as not "visible" enough for deterrence, the Tomahawk could have suited the new European conditions.

Serious consideration should have been given to creating dedicated submarines, SSGNs, for this theater role. But the idea ran into both Navy and Army parochialism. Army generals, used to picking up a battlefield phone for artillery support, did not want to rely on a submerged platform with all the communication problems involved. On the other hand, admirals did not want their dual-capable SSNs tethered to a land mission. These were, however, wartime and not necessarily peacetime deterrence considerations, which rely as much on declaratory policy as on weapon capabilities. In other words, since the real purpose of theater nuclear strategy is deterrence, both the general and admiral could have been satisfied. Now, both may have nothing. Besides, the use of nuclear weapons is a presidential and not service decision, and within forty-eight hours a dedicated Tomahawk SSGN could easily have been placed in position. In short, in a *very* few years, if NATO leaders still desire a theater nuclear deterrent, they will have to return to sea.

The New Navy Triad

While two legs of the strategic triad may be withering away, within the remaining wet leg a new Navy triad is slowly emerging, consisting of the D-5 SLBM, the AX, and, most important, the TLAM-N. As noted above, the new accurate D-5 SLBM makes the whole rationale for an ICBM, especially the current vulnerable silo-based modes, quite questionable. The new AX should add considerably to the Navy's, and perhaps even the Air Force's, capabilities, questioning the rationale for the more expensive B-2. The Air Force is also supposed to purchase the AX to replace their aging F/B 111s. At a reported $80–100 million apiece, the AX will certainly not be cheap *unless* compared to the billion-dollar B-2. Equally important, the AX has more flexibility. It can fly off carriers and does not come up against any proposed START or INF rules. Details on the still-"black" AX program are sketchy, but reportedly it will have a sufficient range and payload, making it quite capable for theater operations. TASMs could have given it a strategic role as well.

Perhaps most important in the future will be the TLAM-N, now going into garrison storage. The Tomahawk had long been criticized (with some justification) as "a weapon in search of a mission," but those missions could be fast approaching. If current trends continue, there will be no other single-warhead system left in a very few years. The Air Force has already announced it will retire the old Minuteman II, the only single-warhead ballistic missile currently in the U.S. inventory. The president has announced plans to down-load the three-warhead MM III to one, but that costs money and raises terrible verification problems. Strategists can, and do, argue whether limited nuclear tactics are possible, but most leaders would still like that option—and that *is* current U.S. nuclear doctrine. For theater operations, the Tomahawk could well be the only system available. The TLAM-N has long been under attack by arms controllers, and even within the naval community itself, but when the dust finally settles from START and INF it might remain as the only viable system for limited strategic strikes and all theater deterrence. Placing the TLAM-N, the sole remaining longer-range single-warhead system, in garrison might have been a major strategy blunder.

Breaking "Sacred Eggs"

A Navy captain (now senior START negotiator) has called for "passing the strategic baton" to the Navy, but questioned where it was prepared institutionally to accept it.[11] Passing the organizational baton, however, is only part of the problem. First, the Navy will have to face an old, contentious issue—the "too many eggs in one basket" problem of the twenty-four-tube Trident SSBNs. Virtually every study, both official and from think tanks, has recommended building SSBNs with fewer launch tubes in order to keep the number at sea at a "comfortable" level. As noted above, the Soviet Navy could easily have three times the numbers of SSBNs after START I and still be in compliance with the treaty. More important, the Navy will have absolutely no flexibility in a START II regime with a twenty-four-tube boat. Before the baton can pass to the Navy, more and smaller SSBNs must be built or the ICBM debate could continue, constantly draining money from strategic funds.

That brings up another point. The Navy should support Chairman

Les Aspin's proposal for a separate strategic budget within which all the services can compete. If the proposed mobile ICBM systems (which may or may not have been invulnerable) had had to compete against mobile, truly invulnerable SSBNs, there is no question in this author's mind which would prevail, especially once the D-5 was deployed. Because there was no competition, both the rail-mobile MX and the Midgetman were continually funded at low, R and D levels, draining the decreasing pool of defense funds.

The real problem, however, is that the Navy's strategic role has generally been both a strategic and an institutional orphan within the naval establishment.[12] Why, for example, does the Navy have a senior four-star admiral in charge of nuclear power, but only a junior one-star in charge of nuclear strategy, with *no* flag billets in the fleet for strategic systems per se? The Air Force does not have a full general in charge of jet engines, but they did have the four-star head of the Strategic Air Command (SAC), for years the premier command of the Air Force, and a myriad of other generals in various strategic commands.

In short, it's time to break two sets of "sacred eggs": the "too many eggs" of the Trident SSBN and the "too few eggs" of the naval strategic establishment. The Navy should consider replacing that full admiral in charge of nuclear power (which we all know is a residue of the Rickover era) and make the post into a "strategic baron." Better yet, make him the permanent head of the newly formed strategic command. A new strategic command was recently formed, which will alternate between the Air Force and the Navy. Considering the trends, the Navy probably should take permanent command. The timing could be most propitious: the Air Force has announced that SAC will be eliminated in a sweeping reorganization of the Air Force.[13] Now is the time to pick up the strategic baton.

The Navy should also consider creating two-star STRATPAC and STRATLANT billets for both naval strategic and potential theater nuclear forces. They would command the SSBNs and possible theater SSGNs. Then, within the Navy OPNAV staff should be a three-star vice admiral "strategic baron" to compete with the other Navy warfare barons and finally a four-star admiral to head a new Strategic Command reflecting the move toward a dyad. This would have the additional benefit of giving strategic-oriented submariners a clear career path up to four-star admiral.

The Navy also should support strongly the concept of a strategic budget, which would give it the funds to build those smaller SSBNs. Whether the Navy likes it or not, its nuclear role will increase, and therefore it should definitely receive both increased responsibility *and* funding—but it must also change. Before the strategic community feels comfortable moving toward a dyad based mostly on SSBNs, there must be more platforms and an increased recognition of the task within the Navy itself.

CONCLUSIONS

The 1990s will see the first reductions of strategic nuclear weapons since their inception. START I reductions have already begun, and plans for a START II and unilateral reductions are already being discussed. While a START I regime will still allow a significant inventory on both sides, a START II with another 50 percent reduction would probably end the era of massive overkill. As Senator Nunn noted, this makes issues like stability, invulnerability, and second-strike capability even more significant, meaning that remaining systems must be dispersed and invulnerable, not confined and easily detected like the stationary, land-based ten-warhead MX. Even too few SSBNs will start making strategists nervous.

The problem is not in the START or unilateral agreements per se but in current U.S. weapon systems. If the United States had built the single-warhead Midgetman instead of the MX, the land-based leg of the triad could have remained viable for many years. The B-2 stealth penetrator also makes more sense than any ALCM carrier under the new START rules. And, as critics have said for years, the Navy should start building SSBNs with fewer, not more launch tubes.

Although conditions in the European theater have changed drastically in the last few years, the Russian commonwealth will still constitute a potential threat with its massive army. CFE I and a probable CFE II should see major American-Russian troop withdrawals, but U.S. forces will move back three thousand miles, compared with only three hundred miles for the Russians. For the foreseeable future, theater nuclear deterrence could still be important.

Presidents Bush, Gorbachev, and Yeltsin have made some sweeping unilateral decisions. While many were, quite frankly, almost meaningless, others have serious nuclear strategy implications that undermine both theater and strategic nuclear policy. President Bush also might have begun a propaganda game that historically cannot be won. The Soviet Union had a long history of calling for massive reductions first and worrying about implementation and verification second, and the president's unilateral decisions on tactical systems might have fallen into that trap. Now people are concerned with hundreds of unverifiable, small tactical nuclear systems in several republics, with even some fears they could be sold for desperately needed hard cash. Some of the other unilateral decisions such as de-MIRVing ballistic missiles without proper verification should also raise concerns. Playing liar's poker with nuclear weapons even in today's more relaxed environment could be a risky affair.

In a very few years, only Navy systems such as the nuclear Tomahawk will be available for possible theater deterrence, and the Trident and new D-5 SLBM are currently the only strategic triad programs fully funded and deploying. On the other hand, it appears that the Air Force could well be out of the strategic and tactical nuclear weapons business in a very few years. It appears that ICBMs will wither on the vine, and long-range bombers will not be far behind. In short, it could well be "all at sea by the IIIs," that is, after the "third zero" theater agreement and an inevitable START III. This emergence of the wet leg, however, must be accompanied by an awareness of the changing conditions within the Navy itself.

5 / NATO

The Emergence of SACLANT

THE NORTH ATLANTIC Treaty Organization has been one of the most successful alliances in history. There have been many empires in history but very few successful coalitions. The Greek city-state alliances constantly changed; the Holy Roman Empire coalition was, as wags were wont to say, neither holy nor Roman nor an empire; and even the great anti-Napoleon alliance broke up almost as soon as the diplomats left the Congress of Vienna, leading to what many scholars see as the golden age of balance-of-power politics in the nineteenth century, with constantly shifting partnerships. NATO, on the other hand, has lasted for over forty years. Whether it lasts the decade remains to be seen.

Even before recent events in Eastern Europe and the Soviet Union, cracks were beginning to show in NATO. Former Secretary of State Henry Kissinger shocked the European allies several years ago when he suggested that the United States would not always support Europe. Others have called for reevaluations. In the United States there have been annual calls from Congress since the late 1960s for the removal of troops and more burden-sharing from allies. Europeans have also called for re-evaluations, with some of the more radical parties such as the Greens of West Germany and the so-called "loony left" of the U.K. starting to influence mainline parties. France long ago pulled out of the military side of NATO; Spain has yet to join, and Greece's status is often uncertain.

Besides these old concerns, there are the three new factors that fore-shadow major change: recent events in Eastern Europe, new arms control proposals, and the breakup of the old USSR into the CIS. The Eastern European countries, if not now actually free, are at least rapidly drifting away from Russian influence. The Warsaw Pact, a mere shell of itself for the past few years, was finally formally dissolved. The CFE I arms control agreement, bringing parity to the U.S.-Soviet military balance in Central Europe, was signed recently; CFE Ia negotiations for manpower limits are already under way. The U.S. Army has already announced major cuts. A CFE II for another round of reductions was scheduled, and East European governments are pressing for unilateral Russian withdrawals from their territories. Finally, of course, are the changes in the Soviet Union itself, the results of which may not become clear for many years.

Thus, for all these and other reasons—transformation in American attitudes and European views, decline of the Warsaw Pact, major arms control agreements, changes in the Soviet Union, and just plain old age—modifications in NATO seem inevitable. And it is certainly time for some major reevaluations. There have been many articles and recommendations on NATO's future,[1] but none have made more than a passing reference to NATO navies. It seems appropriate to ask "What is the future of NATO navies?" as well as the ancillary question, "Why?" The answer, as will be explored in depth below, is that there should be almost an inverse relationship between the anticipated changes in NATO and the need for stronger NATO navies. In fact, it would not be too surprising if the senior NATO navy commander, Supreme Allied Commander Atlantic (SACLANT) replaced the senior ground forces commander, Supreme Allied Commander Europe (SACEUR) as the most important military leader in the alliance, or at least as the most important American NATO commander. However, before turning to current and future needs, a brief look at NATO shipbuilding trends is in order.

BACKGROUND

The most discernible trend since the formation of NATO has been the drastic reduction in Western navies. On a comparative basis, the declines are probably more pronounced than similar army or air force reductions. The Royal Navy, which ruled the waves for some four centuries, is now a mere shell of its former self, and shrinking. France, for years another great sea power, has also reduced the size of its navy, although not as drastically. Canada, which had the third largest allied navy during World War II, went some fifteen years without building a warship. And there has been a similar decline in other Western European fleets. None, with the possible exception of the French Navy, has what might be considered a "balanced" fleet with adequate sea-based airpower.

A look at *Jane's Fighting Ships* over the forty-five years since World War II shows some more specific trends. Although such comparisons must be approached with a little caution since warship characteristics have changed over the years, there are still some clearly discernible changes. These are:

- decline of sea-based airpower
- decline of large surface combatants
- decline of auxiliary fleets
- decline of amphibious ships
- even a decline of mine warfare craft

Perhaps the most disturbing trend in the postwar era has been the rapid decline of navy airpower. Where once four allied countries, Britain, Canada, France, and the Netherlands, operated conventional takeoff and landing (CTOL) aircraft carriers, now only France has such ships. The Royal Navy alone operated four as recently as the 1960s. There has been somewhat of a comeback in small vertical/short takeoff and landing (V/STOL) carriers, with Britain, Italy, and Spain operating such ships; but they have serious limitations. The most severe limitation, as the Royal Navy found in the Falklands war, is the lack of long-range airborne early warning (AEW) craft. Without adequate sea-based airpower, European navies simply cannot operate in today's hostile environments, even those now found in many Third World situations.

The second major trend has been the almost complete disappearance of large surface combatants. NATO is becoming a frigate navy. True, today's frigate might be more capable than yesterday's destroyer, but then all things are relative. The simple fact remains that there is nothing like the flexibility of a multicapable large ship. Western European navies have not built a cruiser for years and (with the exception of France and Italy) have even given up on multimission destroyers. Only frigates are being built, mostly smaller ASW frigates with extremely limited AAW capabilities. Many have the point-defense NATO Sea Sparrow or its equivalent, but few have longer-range AAW SAM protection. Thus, without air support from land, these navies would be unable to operate in the North Atlantic or the eastern Mediterranean. They would also have a rough time in many out-of-area Third World scenarios.

There have also been declines in auxiliary fleets, which in many respects are what make "blue water" navies really blue: they provide the capability for sustained out-of-area operations. This, coupled with the decline of Western merchant shipping, may be the most serious problem of all, at least for any protracted out-of-area conflict. After CFE-mandated withdrawals of American forces, resupply will become even more vital.

Of similar concern is the decline in amphibious fleets. As many analysts noted, had Argentina waited a few more months the Royal Navy would have retired much of its amphibious force, making a victory virtually impossible. The Royal and Dutch marines must now rely on substitute means such as seagoing ferries! Finally, there has even been a decline in mine craft, an area once considered a strength of Western European navies.

There are a few bright spots. France intends to keep operating at least two CTOL carriers and has plans for nuclear replacements (although it desperately needs more modern aircraft than their current 1950s-era Crusaders). V/STOL carriers have proliferated somewhat, providing at least limited air support. Britain plans to buy Trident IIs, although their expense might squeeze out funds for other types. Canada at one time had a major shipbuilding program planned, including even nuclear submarines, but budget restraints have now forced cutbacks. While AAW capabilities have declined, from all reports most of the Western European frigates are good ASW platforms and, with Harpoons or equivalents, have an adequate anti-surface warfare (ASuW) capability.

Overall, though, the trends are discouraging—both quantitatively and qualitatively. The size of Western European fleets is shrinking, mostly due to budgetary restraints, with further decreases anticipated. Britain, for example, recently announced that it will retire more ships, letting the frigate-destroyer force shrink well below the Royal Navy's goal of fifty. Virtually no attempt is being made to provide adequate, long-range AAW capabilities. At the same time, the Russian navy was moving toward sea-based air capabilities; their maritime patrol aircraft now carry long-range cruise missiles. Newer Russian fighter planes with longer "legs" could threaten such areas as the Norwegian Sea, and many Third World countries now have the latest aircraft. While Western ASW is currently rated as good, the recent quietness of Russian submarines and the need for new, and expensive, ASW equipment in the future could outprice the European allies' fleets. The decline of auxiliary, merchant, and amphibious ships and mine craft, all needed in a post-CFE world, is also disturbing. In short, the present is bad and the future looks worse.

THE FUTURE: THE NEED FOR MULTINATIONAL "COMBINED" PROJECTS

The decline of NATO navies is, of course, mostly a Western European problem, and the obvious solution, increased defense budgets (which seem extremely unlikely in the new post–Cold War environment), can only be provided by their individual governments. However, there are many actions that NATO as an alliance and especially the United States can take and initiate—at surprisingly little cost, in many cases. Many involve only minor shifts of emphasis. In fact, one of the major initiatives the United States Navy could explore would cost virtually nothing. First is a look at some American programs that can help in the areas now most deficient—sea-based air and AEW capabilities.

The United States Navy is now building or developing two systems that would greatly enhance Western sea-based airpower. They are the advanced AV-8B Harrier with a joint U.S.-U.K. program to develop a supersonic V/STOL fighter, and the so-called "tilt-rotor" V-22 Osprey. Ostensibly a troop carrier for the U.S. Marines, the V-22 has been proposed as a longer-range ASW and AEW platform as well. Both these programs would make V/STOL carriers more capable and could even help French CTOL capabilities. While the French carriers operate CTOL fighters, they lack adequate AEW aircraft.

A few years ago, the United States and Britain initiated a joint project on an advanced V/STOL aircraft, but funding remains limited. Four countries, the United States, Britain, Spain, and Italy, now have V/STOL carriers, and all should be contributing to further development. Germany might also be convinced to join a NATO advanced V/STOL consortium. The original Harrier program started out as a joint West German–U.K. project. Although the FRG does not currently operate V/STOL ships, a V/STOL airplane was considered useful because of the vulnerability of German airfields. Adding wealthy Germany to any advanced V/STOL development program could help greatly. Even wealthier Japan has looked at the Harrier and Britain's "Skyhook" launch and recovery system.[2] If the "Skyhook" was fully developed for destroyers and frigates, virtually all NATO navies could have at least some V/STOL craft at sea. For the longer term, the allies should look at even more capable short takeoff and landing (STOVL) planes for ski-jump carriers.

Of at least equal importance is the lack of long-range sea-based AEW airplanes. The V-22 Osprey could perhaps fill that slot, and the program at one point was "looking for more partners."[3] Britain almost lost the Falklands war against a lesser power for lack of AEW craft. This could also be a joint project by the four countries mentioned earlier along with France, which needs AEW planes for its carriers. The V-22 was canceled by the OSD, but the Marines, the manufacturer, and Congress have kept the program alive. A potential buy by allies could help defray the costs.

While a supersonic or longer-range V/STOL plane may never replace an F-14 Tomcat and an AEW V-22 may never replace an E-2 Hawkeye, both will help considerably. Indeed, comparatively, their value would be almost immeasurable. They will give Western European naval forces the air assets they have lacked for the past two decades, allowing them to operate in higher threat areas and certainly in virtually all lower threat areas. NATO navies will no longer be dependent on their own land-based air or have to tag along under a U.S. sea-based air cover umbrella. With advanced technology, a STOVL plane might well match CTOL capabilities.

Turning to surface combatants, it is clear that if NATO is becoming a frigate navy, then it should use the best frigate available. This does not necessarily mean a "gold-plated" frigate, although unfortunately everything seems expensive these days. Until quite recently, there was a joint program, the NATO Frigate Replacement for the 1990s (NFR-90), to build such a ship; but one by one, the eight countries involved pulled out for what are often called "NIH" ("not invented here") reasons. Historically, the prospects for a common NATO frigate are dim. NFR-90 was not the first such program. In the 1970s there were proposals for a similar NATO "standard frigate," and a few were actually built. However, considering the new roles and missions for NATO navies, this program should be resurrected.

A NATO frigate for the 1990s and designed to last well into the twenty-first century must have at least a limited AAW capability. In short, at least one variant must be an FFG. There are several candidates—some American, some European—for both sensors and weapon systems. The sensor for today's environment probably should be a smaller or modified version of the Aegis system. In his survey of Western European fleets, Norman Friedman identified five such systems under development, two American and three European.[4] Even these modified versions will probably be fairly expensive, at least for most European navies. The U.S. Navy would probably have to supply most of the necessary funds, but, it would kill two birds with one stone *if* NATO navies do indeed purchase some: it would cut costs while increasing capabilities. However, if Aegis drives costs way up, it should also be abandoned. With the decreasing Soviet/Russian threat, current systems are adequate for most situations.

Perhaps all frigates need not have extensive AAW capabilities, but certain goals should be established. All NATO countries, even the smaller ones, should have a two-FFG goal. If necessary, as was proposed with the purchase of a standard frigate for Portugal, subsidies might be considered for the poorer countries. Larger countries such as Britain and Germany might commit to at least four. This would mean that each national battle group would always have at least one FFG available.

The weapons are a little easier to come by, since there are some longer-range missiles and systems, even VLS, now available. For example, the new British Type 23 frigate, weighing only 3,800 tons, has a thirty-two-cell VLS system (currently with point defense SAMs). Obviously, a cell that small would not last long, but it would help for several reasons. Even a limited capacity is better than nothing and would have a deterrent effect on enemy pilots. Also, a NATO standard guided-missile frigate would probably always be in company with others, so even a small system would have a cumulative effect. In short, Russian pilots would no longer have a free ride, and even a lone FFG would be adequate for most Third World operations.

Unfortunately, trying to assist in some of the other areas such as amphibious ships, auxiliary ships, and mine craft could be more difficult, but perhaps not impossible with a little imagination. During World War II this country helped (some might even say saved) Britain through a program called "lend-lease." There could be a similar program today for certain types of ships, with mutual benefits. The U.S. Navy is currently building two extremely flexible amphibious ships, the LSD-41 and LSD-41 cargo variants, that would be useful for the Royal and Dutch marines and perhaps others as well. The Greeks and Turks could also use this type of ship (preferably not against each other). The Dutch Marines at one point were looking for such a ship.[5] The United States could build some LSD-41s and lease them for maintenance costs to these countries. The American shipbuilding industry could certainly use the work, the marines in Britain and the Netherlands would probably like them, and they are relatively inexpensive ships. In fact, since they are for NATO, they should not even have to come out of the Navy's budget. Operations and maintenance involve some expense, but that could be part of the lease arrangement. The British and Dutch shipbuilding industries might object, but they could receive the repair and upkeep business, which turns out to be very nice revenue over the years. Today, the only work keeping many U.S. shipbuilders in existence is Navy repair and upkeep. A lower-cost common NATO LST might also be considered.

Consideration might even be given to "lend-leasing" some older but still very capable U.S. F/A-18s to the French Navy for a few years. As noted above, the French Navy desperately needs a modern plane for their carriers and did look seriously at the F/A-18 until local politics prevailed. (There was also some concern that the elevators could not handle the F-18.) Now, the French Navy has to wait until the late 1990s for a French-built plane. The USN currently plans to place some early-mode F/A-18s in mothballs, and it is unlikely that they will ever come out. These planes should be loaned to the French Navy. This would undoubtedly earn the gratitude of the French and is another example of the kinds of actions that the United States can take at little or no cost.

Since there is still a glut of merchant ships, Europeans might be encouraged to place some in ready reserve as the USN has done. And the current European lead in minesweepers should be maintained. Unlike the United States, European countries still build many patrol-type craft. These might be configured as dual-purpose ships with both patrol and minesweeping capabilities. As will be discussed in Chapter 10, there could even be some joint submarine projects—for example, a U.K.–U.S. SSN program to fill both countries' needs for a lower-cost submarine.

Of course, there are a whole host of other programs that would be appropriate for NATO-wide consortiums; many are under way, and some, such as the Sea Sparrow project, are quite successful. Britain and France recently announced a new joint frigate proposal, which the United States might consider joining. In fact, in a future of decreasing budgets, creating NATO consortiums with clear-cut goals could well be the *only* way to get anything funded. This might also present a mechanism for the U.S. defense industry to break through the forthcoming European Community (EC '92) trade barriers. There are already stories about the Europeans "shelving rivalries over big weapons contracts," with U.S. defense firms "concerned."[6] However, no projects would be more important than those focused on increasing NATO sea-based air assets and building a capable NATO frigate.

U.S./SACLANT ROLES

Finally, there is one step the United States Navy and especially SACLANT could take that would cost virtually nothing: paying more attention to the problem. SACLANT does, of course, take the role seriously, and there are contingency plans and many joint exercises throughout the year. However, according to some observers, there are really only three times when the USN pays attention to NATO navies per se. That is when the Congress asks about the lack of diesel submarines and mine craft, and about sea lift.[7] SACEUR, on the other hand, is constantly worried about and asked to comment on the state and readiness of allied armies and air forces. Several years ago this author was involved in a study of NATO standardization and interviewed both American and European military leaders. During interviews in Norfolk with SACLANT and his American staff, it was obvious that all they really wanted to talk about were their U.S. CINCLANT (area) and CINCLANTFLT (fleet) duties. Interviews with Europeans were quite different. Instead of resenting an intrusion into their business, they welcomed it. One Western European admiral mentioned that both the study and the goal of 3 percent real growth in military spending then in place gave him ammunition to use against his own budgetary officials—everyone has a number-crunching OMB. In short, NATO goals such as building a common NATO frigate or LST can be welcome, especially in this era of reduced budgets.

Attention can be directed to the state of NATO navies in several ways, most of which involve only minor modifications in emphasis. A major change actually took place about five years ago but seems to have had little visible affect on NATO. In the mid-1980s, the Navy created the additional senior four-star admiral billet of CINCLANTFLT. Prior to that time, one U.S. admiral had three responsibilities or "hats": CINCLANT, CINCLANTFLT, and SACLANT. Now that CINCLANT has been relieved of CINCLANTFLT "fleet" duties, that officer should have more time to spend on the role of SACLANT. As many SACEURs have done, SACLANT must, despite natural inclination, get more politically involved with allied countries. Generals Alexander Haig and Bernard Rogers were very successful in this manner. The occasional visit here and speech there, perhaps followed by a quiet dinner with the right people, can work wonders. This has of course always been done to some extent, but it must be increased. Generals Haig and Rogers have shown that it can be done without diminishing one's military reputation.

However, there must also be a visible increase in naval commitments that stress the multinational aspects of the alliance. To save NATO, many have suggested forming new multinational army units, yet few have proposed similar initiatives for naval forces even though one of the most successful such organizations is the Atlantic standing naval force (STANAVFORLANT) frigate squadron. Additional combined naval units could be established. Several possibilities come to mind—all, again, with virtually no cost attached. One would be for the United States to join the Channel Command's Mine Force.[8] It would be even more appropriate now that the USN is building a mine craft of European (Italian) design.[9] A permanent NATO frigate standing force in the Mediterranean, a STANAVFORMED, similar to STANAVFORLANT, which has proven very effective both militarily and politically, should be (and is) under consideration. There has been an "on call" Med force, but that should be made permanent. And there might even be a standing mine force Med, which, again, would be an appropriate use of the new American-Italian mine craft.[10] Maybe if the United States had been part of two European-based mine forces, the allies would have been less reluctant to send their mine craft to the Persian Gulf during the Iran-Iraq war—an example of the side benefits of such actions. This way, the United States would always have a couple of mine craft in forward areas for rapid deployment, avoiding the embarrassment of towing them overseas.

Standing frigate and mine forces in the Mediterranean could be built around the United States and Italy, with other countries such as Britain and even Germany (which does deploy occasionally) involved on a rotating basis. To ease interallied tensions, Greece and Turkey could alternate between the two groups, and Spain and France could occasionally "exercise" with the new units. The mine force could be stationed in Italy under the command of an Italian officer, while the frigate force command could rotate.

Consideration might even be given to donating an appropriate flagship, at least occasionally, for an embarked NATO admiral. A large *Spruance*-class destroyer could serve this purpose well. An embarked Royal Navy rear admiral in charge of the STANAVFORLANT during exercises and port visits could be extremely effective, as could an embarked Italian admiral in the Mediterranean. Finally, serious consideration should be given to making one of the retired USN battleships the flagship of SACLANT, complete with a multinational crew. One reason these manpower-intensive ships were retired is increased personnel costs, which could be offset by NATO officers and crew. There would probably be no dearth of volunteers for such duty. All sailors worth their proverbial salt want to serve on a battleship at least once in their career. Nothing would be more symbolically important than making a battleship a multinational NATO flagship.

The burden should not be placed solely on SACLANT. NATO political leaders must also recognize the changing relationships and increase their profiles. Western leaders should start pointing out the importance of NATO navies. If, for example, the president met the STANAVFORLANT the next time it made a port visit in the United States and delivered a major address, it would be carried by all the major news networks. Very few Americans, even those interested in military affairs, are aware of that important NATO navy squadron. The rechristening of a battleship as a multinational NATO flagship would similarly be a major event.

THE INVERSE RELATIONSHIP

NATO will change. It always was inevitable. The recent events in the Soviet Union and Eastern Europe and the CFE agreements will simply speed the process. What may not have been so inevitable or obvious is the relationship of that change to the importance of NATO navies. There could well be an inverse relationship between the need for NATO navies as troop strengths decline from CFE I and especially from a CFE II, which many predict as early as the mid-1990s. Considering the rapidly changing course of events, it would not be at all surprising to see a CFE III by the late 1990s. The roles and missions of NATO navies, always important, will become more crucial as U.S. and Canadian forces are withdrawn. This will come about due to new sea lift and convoy requirements. Despite efforts like POMCUS (prepositioned equipment) and the building of large cargo planes like C-5s and C-17s, the fact remains that well over 90 percent of all equipment and supplies must be sent by ship. The one tank that a C-5 can carry means virtually nothing in the European theater. Also, it is sometimes overlooked that POMCUS will be included, in some manner, in CFE. In other words, American troops cannot be simply flown back to mate up with equipment. Most of the equipment and supplies must come from sea lift. Those ships need protection (historically provided by frigates and small carriers), and that can only be accomplished with assistance by allied navies. The U.S. Navy simply does not have the resources to control enemy fleets *and* to convoy. In short, the more NATO ground forces change as a result of CFE, the more allied naval forces will be needed.

CFE and future arms control proposals could also increase the importance of other naval assets. CFE agreements encompass land-based air forces, which means that navy air could become even more important. Instead of being held in reserve as many now assume, naval air forces could find themselves very quickly on the front line, even the central front and especially on the flanks. Flank protection, always considered a primary naval mission, could increase in importance, especially if Turkish and Greek forces are included in a CFE II. While a ten- to eighteen-thousand-man U.S. Marine Expeditionary Force may not seem like a particularly large force in a historical European context, such a rapidly deployable unit, especially one with its own air force, might seem formidable after a CFE II.

And, although it is unlikely, it is not entirely out of the question that the United States might be compelled to intervene (probably as part of an international force) in some of the new conflicts in Eastern Europe to prevent wanton bloodshed. For example, there was some discussion of multinational forces actually intervening in the Yugoslavian civil war, and there are now U.N. peacekeeping forces in place. The U.S. Navy could easily have prevented the shelling of the grand old Croatian city of Dubrovnik by the Serbian-dominated Yugoslavian Navy. Navy air could also have kept the Yugoslavian Air Force on the ground. A rapidly employed, self-sustaining Marine Expeditionary Force would also be perfect for peacekeeping operations of this type.

Finally, as noted in Chapter 4, the Western promise to consider a "third zero" in short-range nuclear systems should make naval systems more important for nuclear deterrence. Depending on the final outcome from a "third zero" agreement and the recent unilateral decisions, USN intermediate naval nuclear forces (INNF), sea-launched cruise missiles (SLCM), and naval dual-capable aircraft could well become the only NATO theater deterrent force.[11] In short, NATO naval missions will increase considerably, from providing more sea lift and convoy capacity to filling various gaps created by the withdrawal of army, air force, and theater nuclear forces.

For all these reasons, the post-CFE world could well see the emergence of SACLANT as the senior NATO military commander, or at least the senior American leader. There are now calls for "SACEUR to come home,"[12] and it has long been suggested that a European general should become the next SACEUR. It was even proposed that a French general be nominated to bring France back into the alliance. Perhaps foreshadowing change, a British general has been placed in charge of a new NATO multinational army force—a force the United States vigorously opposed but was forced to accept. After CFE II or certainly III, serious consideration should and probably will be given to rotating SACEUR amongst Germany, France and Britain. (This might also be a way to keep Germany in the alliance.) This would make SACLANT the senior American NATO commander and, depending on the eventual drawdown from a CFE II, perhaps the senior NATO commander as well. (After all, SACEUR was an Air Force general during the 1950s, age of SAC predominance.)

* * *

Even if there were no major changes occurring in NATO, the decline of allied navies is still disturbing. As former Secretary of the Navy James Webb has said on several occasions, during past international crises there was often a British, French, or some other Western European fleet in the area to assist. Now it is usually just the U.S. Navy. Although the Western fleet response to the overt Iraqi invasion of Kuwait was good, even excellent, the Europeans were very reluctant to help out in the Iran-Iraq situation even though their own tankers were victims of terrorist attacks. NATO countries have generally resisted all out-of-area operations. Creation of more NATO STANAVFORs, with some under allied command, might make the allies less reticent to participate in future operations. A standing mine force Med could have quickly deployed during the Iran-Iraq war. The allied navy response to Desert Storm is a good illustration of feasibility. Even a multinational NATO battleship could have participated in Desert Storm. In the 1990s, so-called out-of-area problems could worsen with the increase of sophisticated weaponry in the Third World.

Conclusions

Even as major changes unfold in Europe, more attention must be given to the decline of NATO navies. Most of the weapon system solutions suggested are relatively inexpensive but can have lasting results. A supersonic or longer-range V/STOL plane would benefit the Marines, while at the same time being a perfect program for joint development. The V-22 is under development, and an additional AEW variant, especially if run as a joint program, would also be affordable. Eight NATO countries *were* once committed to a NATO frigate and many countries (including the United States) are researching smaller and cheaper Aegis-type systems, so no major new effort would be needed there. Many navies might be interested in a low-cost amphibious ship, or LST. In fact, if these programs were truly joint ventures, the United States could actually end up saving money by, for example, getting Germany (and perhaps Japan) to contribute to an advanced V/STOL program.

There are also many organizational changes possible, again at virtually no cost, all of which would help immeasurably. Committing one U.S. mine craft each to a channel command and to a new standing mine force Med, a frigate to a new STANAVFORMED, and an occasional *Spruance* destroyer for use as a NATO flagship are minor improvements with potentially large payoffs. Symbolically, nothing would be more important than turning an American battleship into a multinational SACLANT flagship. But these initiatives will all take changes of emphasis and leadership from both the United States and the allies.

As noted earlier, NATO has been one of the most successful military alliances in history. Despite the recent changes and the easing or perhaps even complete elimination of all the old East-West tensions, most analysts still feel that NATO will continue to have some role, at least for the rest of this decade. But there will be changes. During the 1990s, there will be a major drawdown of both NATO armies and air forces. This can only increase the importance of navies—reminding people that NATO does, after all, stand for the North Atlantic, not Central Front, Treaty Organization.

Yet another illustration of the rapidly changing times is the all but forgotten "maritime-continental" debate. During the early 1980s the Navy's new, "forward" Maritime Strategy was severely criticized by many (including some retired admirals) as a waste of money. Rather, the critics argued, the money should be spent defending against the main Soviet threat on the Central Front. This issue, which became known as the "maritime-continental" debate, was argued in several books and in the most prestigious foreign affairs journals. Once again, this illustrates the flexibility of naval forces. What an incredible waste of money it would have been to build up forces on the Central Front. Today, the U.S. Army is rapidly moving and even retiring troops and equipment, while the more flexible Navy forces can simply deploy elsewhere. In short, and with all due respect to Fred Astaire, no one is "doing the continental" today.

Finally, there are three points that should be kept in mind. First, there are simply too many missions, growing missions, for the United States Navy to conduct alone. Second, the decline of the Western European NATO navies must therefore be stopped, especially with the cuts in other forces anticipated from the CFE arms control process. Third, and most important, the United States Navy should never forget that it is a NATO navy also.

6 / Third World Operations
The Past Is Prologue

AS THE 1975 Brookings study cited in Chapter 2 first stated, "Through-out the postwar period the United States has turned most often to its Navy" for crisis response, with most of those incidents taking place in the Third World. This pattern has been reconfirmed several times. In a fol-low-up study from 1975 to 1982, another scholar concluded: "One trend that remains constant is the use of naval forces. Throughout the postwar period the United States has turned most frequently to naval units as an instrument of crisis management and political influence."[1] A report by the Center for Naval Analyses in 1989[2] once again found that naval forces have been the primary choice for crisis response since World War II, especially for actions in the Third World. The following data was used by the Navy before Congress:

Total Number of Crises	240
Number Involving USN Forces	202
Number Involving the USSR	18

There are, unfortunately, no indications that these so-called low-intensity crises will ebb. While there probably will be significant changes and some reason for optimism toward easing tensions in both nuclear strategy and NATO operations in this new interwar period, the trends in Third World operations are not so sanguine. In fact, if the recent Iraq crisis and Liberia and Somalia incidents are any indications, both the number and especially the intensity could well increase.

During the late 1950s and early 1960s, there was great optimism about the emerging Third World nations. Theorists developed the notion that these nations simply needed a little help, a boost for a takeoff, and they would be able to skip the anguish of moving though the various stages of modernization that Western countries experienced, especially the often inhumane age of industrialization of the nineteenth and early twentieth centuries.[3] Regional specialists were not so sanguine, citing tribal, border, religious, and cultural differences. Economists, especially free-market economists, were also skeptical. They noted the lack of capital, the dependence on raw material—often only one crop or mineral—economies, and the fact that virtually all Third World nations chose heavily bureaucratized, socialist governments as their models. For a while, it looked like the developmental theorists were correct. Countries like Kenya under former Mau-Mau leader Jomo Kenyatta, for example, seemed on their way to both democracy and development; strong leaders like the Shah of Iran modernized their countries. However, eventually all those cautions and problems cited by economic and regional experts became apparent. Between tribalism, old border disputes, religious fundamentalism, the corruption that unfortunately comes with many socialist governments (especially those with no democratic traditions) and the changing economic order that favors services over raw materials, many if not most of these countries are now faltering. Many economists see these Third World nations, with very few exceptions, falling farther and farther behind the West. In short, there are no lack of reasons for continued pessimism, with constant crises and conflicts to be expected.

Besides these old, continuing problems, there are two new military factors that leave little room for optimism. These are the proliferation of sophisticated weapons and the loss of U.S. overseas bases. The former will make the Third World more dangerous, while the latter could make the responsibility for crisis response fall even more to the U.S. Navy.

WEAPONS PROLIFERATION

The most alarming new trend in the Third World is the fairly recent spread of sophisticated weaponry. For years, countries with the cash have been able to buy top-of-the-line aircraft, tanks, artillery, and other more conventional munitions, but lately there has been a proliferation of missiles, chemical weapons, and even possibly nuclear weapons.

Missiles[4]

The event that has triggered the most concern is the fairly recent spread of longer-range and nuclear-capable missiles. While many countries have long had nuclear-capable, or at least adaptable, airplanes, most strategists consider sending a generally ill-trained pilot out with a bomb quite different from just pushing a button equipped with Soviet or Western software. In 1987 seven Western nations created the Missile Technology Control Regime (MTCR) to stop the spread of missiles with at least a 500-kilogram warhead and 300-kilometer range. The size was chosen as the minimum required for a nuclear warhead, while the range was reportedly chosen because it is the average distance between Middle East capitals and because it captures the most widely used missile—the notorious Soviet Scud.

Table 6-1 shows the current Third World long-range missile inventories. The Scud-B is by far the most numerous. Both North Korea and Egypt have reverse-engineered the Scud, and during the Iran-Iraq war Iraq jury-rigged one for longer range. The Soviet Union has also given the more modern SS-12 to Iraq, and China sold IRBMs to Saudi Arabia. Israel has two Jericho models, one reportedly with the range to hit the Soviet Union.

More disturbing still is the bottom half of Table 6-1 showing those

Table 6-1. Missile Proliferation

Missile	Producers	Possessors	Status
Scud-B	Soviet Union	Egypt, Libya, South Yemen	
	(North Korea, Egypt)	North Korea, Iran	
	(Iraq +)	Iraq, Syria	
SS-12	Soviet Union	Iraq	
CSS-2	China	Saudi Arabia	
Jericho	Israel	South Africa?	
M-9	China	(Syria, Iran?)	in testing
Avibras	Brazil	(with Iraq?)	in testing
Orbita	Brazil	(with Libya?)	in development
SSM (3)	Brazil		in development
VLS	Brazil		in development
Condor II	Argentina	(with Egypt and Iraq)	in development
King Hawk	Pakistan	(with China)	in development
Sky Horse	Taiwan		in development
Space (3)	India		in development
Space	Iraq		in testing

long-range missiles under development. (There are many more just below the MTCR limits.) Countries such as China, Brazil, and Argentina are developing weapons specifically for export—a good source of hard currency—and some have the backing of other nations. In short, despite the best efforts of MTCR, there will soon be many missiles on the market. Former CIA director William Webster predicted that fifteen developing nations would be producing missiles by the year 2000.[5]

Most of these weapons are fairly inaccurate, and none are antiship missiles per se. On the other hand, with a nuclear or CW warhead, you do not need accuracy, nor do you need a Cray computer for targeting such scenarios as underway replenishment, carrier flight operations, and amphibious landings. For example, a Scud-size CW warhead could contaminate an area 0.3 by 2.5 miles.[6] Also, as Iraq displayed during the recent war, the psychological effects of even an inaccurate long-range weapon can cause alarm. And these are only first-generation systems. Second generations are bound to be more accurate.

Currently there are no signs of longer-range cruise missiles, although many first-generation, shorter-range versions exist and the technology is considerably less sophisticated. There are 102 countries worldwide with cruise missiles of some type. From the ubiquitous and deadly Exocet to new Silkworms, cruise missiles are readily available on the market. Longer range and more accurate targeting could soon be available from the American Global Positioning Systems (GPS) and Soviet Glonass navigation systems, about to enter commercial use.

Chemical Weapons[7]

For years the 1925 CW non–first use treaty was considered a success despite Mussolini's operations in Ethiopia during the 1930s. After all, the argument went, even near defeat Hitler did not use CW. There were a few isolated incidents such as Egyptian use in Yemen, but these were considered aberrations.

However, during the Iran-Iraq war, CW were used fairly extensively and, to the chagrin of many, with little public outcry. CW also became a major concern for allied and American forces in the Middle East facing Iraq during Desert Storm. As shown in Table 6-2, current estimates are that some seventeen Third World nations have CW, often dubbed the "poor man's atom bomb." CW can be made by virtually anyone with a chemical or fertilizer plant. Negotiations are currently under way at the forty-nation Geneva Conference on Disarmament for a multinational ban on CW, but most observers are pessimistic.

Table 6-2. Chemical Weapons Proliferation

Producers	Possessors	Suspected Possessors
Iran	Afghanistan	India
Iraq	Burma	Pakistan
Israel	China	
Libya	Egypt	
Syria	Ethiopia	
	North Korea	
	South Korea	
	Taiwan	
	Thailand	
	Vietnam	

In addition, ten countries are believed to have biological weapons.

Nuclear Proliferation[8]

Since the dawn of the nuclear age there have been attempts to control nuclear proliferation, from Bernard Baruch's 1946 proposal to place all nuclear affairs under U.N. control, to establishment of the International Atomic Energy Agency (IAEA) in 1956 for safeguarding peaceful uses, to the 1968 Nuclear Nonproliferation Treaty. Despite the fears of the 1950s and 1960s, major nuclear proliferation has not occurred.

However, as shown in Table 6-3, thirteen regimes are considered possible candidates for nuclear status, with several on the brink. These thirteen countries have been broken down into subjective yet probably realistic groupings. The radicals include the usual suspects: Libya, Iran, and North Korea. The warriors, Iraq and Syria, are constantly fighting someone and, incidentally, do not like each other. Then there are the three isolated or pariah states of Israel, South Africa, and Taiwan. India has apparently developed the capability for prestige but also to deter China, an old adversary. Of course, if India has the bomb, then Pakistan must have it; and if North Korea has the capability, can South Korea be far behind?[9] Finally are the more benign Latin American countries, although London has second thoughts about Argentina. For a variety of reasons, these thirteen countries make up a pretty frightening group.

Table 6-3. Nuclear Proliferation in the 1990s

Radicals	Warriors	Isolated states	Deterrers	Others
Iran	Iraq	Israel	India	Argentina
Libya	Syria	South Africa	Pakistan	Brazil
North Korea		Taiwan	South Korea	

The capabilities vary widely. It has been an open secret for years that Israel possesses nuclear weapons, and many feel that South Africa might also. Both India and Pakistan are considered on the brink, capable of development within a year. Argentina, Brazil, and North Korea are all developing enriched uranium capacity. Iraq, considered a threat in the early 1980s before Israel bombed its reactor, rebuilt its program (according to recent accounts) to the point of trying to illegally obtain nuclear firing mechanisms. Although its labs were bombed again during Desert Storm, many fear that Iraq might still be hiding some nuclear facilities. The other countries are considered much further behind. Libya, perhaps the least capable, has been trying to purchase a bomb for years and is suspected of bankrolling the "Moslem bomb." There are now some fears that old Soviet tactical nuclear weapons might be sold for hard cash. Libya just might be able to purchase a "Moslem bomb" from a Soviet Moslem Republic, two of which had such weapons. Finally, there are news reports that former Soviet nuclear engineers now out of work might become nuclear mercenaries.

Other Munitions

While the recent spread of longer-range missiles as well as chemical and nuclear weapons has received the most attention, the proliferation of some other weapons has also been alarming, especially to the Navy. These weapons are mines, submarines, and torpedoes. Some forty-one countries worldwide now have mining capabilities. The mining during both the Iran-Iraq and Persian Gulf wars shows how disruptive and effective it can be—and these mines were simply unsophisticated models of World War I–era designs. There are also forty-one countries with diesel attack submarines; in the Third World alone there are nearly 250 diesel submarines. These can be particularly disruptive, as the Royal Navy found while chasing just one Argentinean submarine during the Falklands war.

For years, anyone with the cash has been able to buy top-of-the-line aircraft, tanks, artillery, and most other conventional equipment including the latest generation antiair, antiship, and antitank missiles. Now, even countries without much cash may be able to pick up some bargains. There are reports that CIS republics desperate for cash are looking for buyers for the equipment they will be pulling out of Europe. With the decrease in domestic defense building, all arms manufacturers will be looking for new customers. As the richer nations start buying second-generation systems, a "used weapon" market of first-generation systems could be open to poorer countries, furthering the spread of sophisticated munitions. In a very few years, all Third World countries could have at least a few first-generation antiship Exocets.

OVERSEAS BASES

The second major change for the United States in Third World operations is the decline in the number of overseas bases. As one author stated, "For nearly half a century, the security and foreign policy of the United States has rested on an overseas basing system that was extensive, robust, and cheap."[10] Those days may soon be over.

Over the years, the number of bases in Third World areas has dwindled to a precious few that really matter, and these were often positioned to meet only the Communist threat. Following World War II, the United States had bases throughout the world, but these have generally been consolidated in areas near Communist threats—places such as South Korea and, to a certain extent, even the Philippines. The United States still has bases in Panama and in allied countries close to Third World areas, such as Japan and Australia in the Pacific and the southern NATO countries in Europe. However, as the United States has discovered several times, these host countries are extremely reluctant to allow American bases to be used as staging areas for out-of-area operations.

The phasing out of the large Philippine bases in the 1990s has already been announced. After the eruption of Mount Pinatubo, the decision was made to close Clarke Air Force base. The long-term future of Subic Bay is also in doubt.[11] Drawdowns from South Korea have also been announced, and a complete pullout would not be surprising in a few years. The closing of the Philippine and South Korean bases could well end Army and Air Force operations in the Pacific, and greatly curtail even naval operations. Countries such as Singapore have offered to host American forces on a rotating basis, which would permit fleet visits and perhaps even an extensive upkeep period but do little for Army and Air Force requirements. This would leave only Guam and Diego Garcia for unrestricted use, and both are too far from potential trouble spots for realistic Army or even Air Force deployments.

During the Iraqi invasion of Kuwait, countries welcomed American troops and the United States displayed a great capacity to deploy troops quickly. However, such incidents are the exception; more typical was the recent crisis in Liberia, which required, indeed allowed for, only naval forces. More important is the whole question of forward deterrence.

Forces for Future Third World Deterrence

The United States has a vast array of forces, both conventional and, if need be, CW and even nuclear. No Third World country can match the United States in quality of weaponry or in forces, and only a very few in quantity. The problem is in the appropriateness of our forces for crisis response and especially deterrence in the Third World. Even some of the forces normally associated with deterrence are probably not appropriate.

Central Ballistic Systems

ICBMs and SLBMs are probably not appropriate for Third World deterrence, even for a nuclear response or second strike, for one simple reason—overkill. With the exception of the old single-warhead Minuteman II now being retired, all are MIRVed. And the Minuteman II was listed at a megaton. Also, launching a ballistic missile would undoubtedly set off CIS early warning systems. Even if forewarned, the Russians would unquestionably be uneasy, as would we if the situation were reversed. Thus, for many reasons ballistic missiles seem inappropriate for Third World deterrence, even for a nuclear retaliatory strike.

Army Forces

With the possible exception of forces in South Korea, Army forces are inappropriate for the vast majority of Third World crisis response and deterrence requirements. While the Army has mobile forces like the 82nd Airborne and new "light divisions" established for ease of movement, they have virtually no sustainability and must land in a friendly environment. Limited forced entries are possible, but only if quickly followed by logistics support. Some commentators made the point that Operation Just Cause in Panama proved the effectiveness of Army forces, which did a superb job. However, the Army used several existing forts in Panama as staging areas. While certain Army forces can be moved quickly, they still require a large logistical tail not available in Third World areas. This does not, of course, completely rule out Army responses for the "heavy" Desert Storm–type crises, but they are not the norm.

Air Force Systems

In this new interwar period, the Air Force has been touting a brief entitled "Global Reach—Global Power," which describes how it could respond to world crises. And there is no question that a five-hundred-knot plane can reach an area considerably quicker than a twenty-knot ship. But the problem is, first, "Where do they land?" And then there are those factors so important for deterrence, sustainability and presence. While virtually all Air Force combat planes are dual-capable (fighter-bomber, conventional-nuclear), with the possible exception of those in South Korea they have extremely limited range for Third World operations. The F/B-111s might be able to reach some Middle Eastern countries, but their use against Libya created quite a stir. After all the political fallout, even a good ally like the United Kingdom would probably think twice about allowing the U.S. to use them again, especially with the departure of Margaret Thatcher.

The Air Force does have a vast array of long-range bombers, but none are stationed overseas. There was a small squadron of B-52s stationed in Guam, but they are being phased out—perhaps a mistake. To save the expensive B-2 bomber, both the Air Force and the manufacturer speculated that it could have conducted the Libyan raid from CONUS with only two refuelings. Whether or not the NCA would have risked a plane costing a billion dollars each in a Third World operation, there is no question that long-range bombers with sufficient refuelings could carry out retaliatory strikes. However, the real question is *sustained, forward* deterrence and presence. Is a country deterred by a force thousands of miles away that cannot be seen and that has never been used in that manner, or by one just over the horizon that has been used before and can be used immediately? The latter applies only to naval forces.

NAVAL FORCES

Only the Navy operates throughout the Third World and thus would probably be the only force available for ongoing, sustained deterrence—as it has been for virtually all crises. This author is not suggesting that the Navy alone could necessarily respond to *all* these crises, especially major confrontations such as Iraq-type incidents. However, as the data illustrates, of those 240 crises only fifteen (about 6 percent) involved major combat, and even fewer involved large army or air forces. As study after study has shown, the Navy has been the force used most often; the first question usually asked by the NCA is, "Where are the carriers?" The carriers are still there, but they might have to change their operations —and indeed, centuries of naval habits.

The proliferation of sophisticated weaponry could well bring about a major change in naval operations and attitudes. Navies have always felt relatively safe offshore. Indeed, the historic national three-mile limit was based on the distance of cannon shot—stay beyond three miles and you were safe. For absolute safety, all a fleet had to do was sail over the horizon. This is, in fact, the way the Navy has operated since World War II. During the Korean War ships often operated within sight of land, with the biggest threat being mines. In Vietnam, the well-publicized Yankee station was only about one hundred miles offshore. During the Gulf of Sidra operations against Libya, ships operated close to the so-called "line of death," and they were deliberately within sight of land during the Lebanon crises. All of these operations are now well within new missile ranges.

The fact is, during the Cold War the Navy has operated in ways it wouldn't have dared in a "hot" war or even World War II. The famous Doolittle raid, for example, was launched about six hundred miles offshore, and until the end of the war surface ships *never* went back that close again. We have, perhaps, gotten used to "easy" operations, which is not meant to imply that those brave men in Korea, Vietnam, and elsewhere had an "easy" time. But as Adm. Roy L. Johnson, a CINCPACFLT during Vietnam, noted, "Had we faced a serious air threat or submarine threat in the Gulf of Tonkin, we might have gotten in serious trouble by operating near a fixed point."[12] This means that instead of operating from over the horizon to 100 miles or so offshore as it has done since World War II, the Navy might have to double that range to at least 200 to 400 miles.

Unfortunately, that distance is stretching the maximum safe range of most carrier-based planes. Carriers no longer carry "dedicated" tankers, and there are similar trends all in the wrong direction. There is a decided trend away from planes with longer "legs" such as the old heavy attack A-3 bomber, the medium A-6, and even the light A-7 and toward shorter-range models such as the F/A-18 and the AV-8B. The A-3 is long gone, the A-7 has recently retired, and the A-6 line has been closed (with shortages already showing up). The future of the Marines' long-range V-22 Osprey troop transport, which might be appropriate for the new conditions, is in doubt. In short, at the same time that the Navy might have to double the range, it is halving the capabilities of carrier-based planes.

The still-secret AX, successor to the A-6, might solve the problem, but in an era of reduced budgets the future of stealthy and expensive planes must be in doubt. Perhaps the follow-on A-6F that was canceled should have been built. The Navy might also take another look at stand-off weapons such as the ALCM or the Air Force's once-proposed TASM. If not captured in the recent unilateral decisions, the 300-mile TASM under consideration for "theater" use—in Europe—might be most appropriate for this role and would not come under ALCM-type arms control limits.

There are, of course, a host of other problems. Longer ranges mean more aviation fuel, a smaller ammo load, and a greater need for more reconnaissance planes and probably dedicated fueling planes. A fleet would need more oilers and support ships, which in turn would need more surface combatants; the list goes on and on. Doubling the range adds to logistic requirements at a time when such accounts might be decreased. It also brings to mind the old saw that "amateurs write about strategy while professionals worry about logistics."

Perhaps the biggest question is, would a carrier battle group be a deterrent as it has been for forty-five years, or instead a tempting target that can now be attacked by missiles rather than by generally inexperienced Third World pilots? If the latter is the case, then other ships might have to take up deterrent roles, at least for some operations.

Surface Ships: A CMC?

Surface ships have generally had limited missions in deterrence per se. Occasionally they would be used for gunfire support, but usually that role was secondary. Even during the Persian Gulf patrols, looming in the background was carrier-based airpower. The Navy's Tomahawk SLCM could change that perception and role. The TLAM, and especially the nuclear variant, TLAM-N, certainly has the range. Targeting might be limited, but that could be corrected easily.

There are several reasons for using surface ships. First, as mentioned, they would now be more capable armed with the Tomahawk. The first weapons fired in Desert Storm against Iraq were Tomahawks from surface ships. Second, they would be more visible, an important feature for deterrence, because they could operate closer to shore and, quite frankly, are more expendable than a carrier battle group. Finally, they are multicapable and could still carry out their fleet roles.

There are some cons, however. Surface combatants would be more vulnerable, and most already have other demanding roles. Although more expendable than carriers, they are still expensive. And there are other problems. If it was needed for nuclear deterrence, the TLAM-N would have to be taken out of garrison. This would possibly invalidate the Navy's "neither confirm nor deny" (NCND) nuclear policy, leading to arms control problems. The Navy could not use a surface combatant for nuclear deterrence and still follow its NCND policy although a conventional SLCM might suffice.

However, if a surface ship is deemed appropriate, the Navy might take a closer look at a completely different, dedicated vessel. Admiral Metcalf has suggested building a surface combatant specifically to carry cruise missiles.[13] This could be a relatively inexpensive ship deployed offshore just for deterrence purposes. And there would be no NCND problem since the answer would be "yes": it is probably carrying nuclear weapons. A few cruise missile carriers (CMCs) placed strategically throughout the Third World could act as a credible, visible deterrent for those theaters.

The Submarine Force: An SSGN?

A ship that might be most appropriate for this mission would be a dedicated SLCM carrier submarine (SSGN). This would be a completely new role for submarines and therefore has many pros and cons. With the Tomahawk, it would certainly be capable. Many have wondered why Tomahawks were not used in the Libyan raid; submarines did fire Tomahawks during the Iraq war. Better yet, unlike the carrier battle groups or even a more expendable (but still expensive) surface combatant, an SSGN would be invulnerable and thus always available for both deterrence and retaliation. A country could not fire at a carrier battle group with impunity if it knew an SSGN was also lurking close by. Such a ship could still conduct some ASW yet be dedicated. Finally, it might actually be faster for crisis response. For example, during the Falklands war the Royal Navy immediately sent an SSN that, after sinking the Argentine cruiser *Belgrano*, became a very effective deterrent, keeping the Argentine Navy in port.

There are again some serious cons. Since a submarine would not be visible, it would require some kind of "declaratory" statement, which is, after all, the first element of strategy. It would probably run into some of the same NCND and arms control problems of a surface combatant—but perhaps not: the Navy could still claim NCND to some extent, and arms control proposals, to date, usually involve removing such weapons from surface ships.

The largest problem may be making major changes in operations and attitudes. Submarines normally do not continually operate in Third World areas. Mediterranean-based subs could cover many Middle East hot spots, but submarines might have to start constantly deploying to Third World waters such as the Indian Ocean. This would also require significant attitudinal changes. The surface and air communities are quite used to these constant Third World operations, but submarines are not.

There is also the lack of assets. The newer *Los Angeles*–class submarines with VLS could be appropriate for this role, but they are needed for other missions. There have long been suggestions that the Navy build

SSGNs. Since their primary mission would not be ASW against frontline, quiet Soviet submarines, SSGNs could perhaps be cheaper than top-of-the-line U.S. submarines.

In short, an SSGN seems most appropriate for this role. In the future, at least for some Third World crises, the call may not be "Where are the carriers?" but "Where are the SSGNs?"

ACTIVE MEASURES

More active measures must also be considered for this new Third World environment, some not necessarily compatible with American values—measures such as preemptive strikes. Should the United States conduct first strikes, as Israel did against the Iraqi nuclear plant? For a time, it looked as though the United States was gearing up to take out the new Libyan CW site, and there are continuing vague threats by the U.S. against Iraqi facilities. Or should the United States look for "excuses" to strike these facilities?—that is, the next time a terrorist attack occurs, use that as a reason to destroy missile, CW, and nuclear sites? That might be more palatable than first strikes.

The United States has never ruled out a first-use nuclear policy, but that was during a U.S.–Soviet NATO scenario. While a bolt-out-of-the-blue first strike was always considered unthinkable, possible first use during wartime has long been NATO policy. Perhaps as a deterrent, the United States should start doing some very visible exercises off the coasts of the more radical Third World countries. Finally, some type of rollback strategy would be needed to eliminate these facilities during any real crisis. Could an amphibious operation even be contemplated before all nuclear and CW facilities have been destroyed? As noted above, only one Scud-delivered CW warhead can easily blanket any landing area.

THE NEED FOR A DECLARATORY POLICY

There is a definite need for new declaratory policies for these new Third World conditions. It is quite easy to trace U.S. strategy against the Soviets from massive retaliation, which was changed in 1962 by Secretary of Defense Robert McNamara to flexible response, which in turn was further refined by Secretaries James Schlesinger and Harold Brown in 1974 and 1980 respectively. NATO policy is similarly openly discussed from MC 14/2 (massive retaliation) to MC 14/3 (flexible response). Everyone, including both friends *and* foes, knows the right buzzwords.

However, when it comes to deterrence in the Third World, there has been almost an eerie silence, which is, perhaps, one of the reasons Saddam Hussein thought he could get away with seizing Kuwait. While some thought and effort has been given to stopping the proliferation of these weapons with the creation of major organizations and treaties such as the IAEA, the Nonproliferation Treaty, the MTCR, and a new CW proposal, few have looked at the next inevitable step—the need for deterrence. In the 1950s, strategists had a vague notion of a "nuclear umbrella" for Third World allies, but specifics were never defined. One reason was that, despite some early fears, nuclear proliferation was halted, or at least stymied. Conventional deterrence statements are even more elusive. Some scholars point to the post-Vietnam Guam or Nixon Doctrine and the anti-Communist Reagan Doctrine from the 1980s, but neither has been fully articulated. Another reason might have been the general low quality of Third World weapons, often war surplus items. Unfortunately, those days are long gone. Any country with the money can buy frontline airplanes, missiles, CW, and, perhaps in the future, nuclear warheads.

These weapons are *not* used in low-intensity warfare, a concept that has received a fair amount of study and now has a new office in the Pentagon devoted to it. While we may or may not need better coordination for low-intensity conflict, we have sufficient forces, with Marines, Army light divisions, and the new Delta force. We also have a fairly clear-cut if not fully articulated policy. For example, President Bush quickly activated the Delta force when U.S. soldiers were trapped in an El Salvador hotel. And, at the other end of the Third World conflict spectrum, troops were dispatched after Iraq invaded Kuwait. What is missing, however, is a more clear-cut policy for those hundreds of other incidents in between, events now complicated by the proliferation of sophisticated weaponry in the Third World.

All the thought and time that went into East-West conventional and nuclear strategy should now be directed to Third World deterrence. Honest people can, and do, argue about that nebulous concept called deterrence, but, looking back, it does seem to have worked between the superpowers. A carefully articulated policy must now be well thought out and discussed for conventional and nuclear Third World deterrence.

Countries have a nasty habit of using whatever weapon is available, especially when they feel threatened. During the Iran-Iraq "war of the cities," nearly five hundred ballistic missiles were fired in a short period. Despite heavy losses, Iraq emerged the winner due in some measure to its use of two weapons—missiles and poison gas—and the lessons were not lost on other Third World countries. There is some speculation that only the rapidity of the allied assault in Desert Storm prevented Saddam's use of CW.

It should also be remembered that the emphasis for both nuclear and chemical warfare has always been on deterrence, not necessarily warfare, a strategy that unfortunately cuts both ways. For example, some scholars have concluded that while Argentina might not have used nuclear weapons during the Falklands war if it had them, their presence might have prevented the British response.[14]

Finally, what about our Third World allies? Unlike NATO allies who specifically wanted a U.S. presence including nuclear weapons—the so-called "coupling issue"—Third World allies have generally been happy with that vague umbrella concept. While they wanted the protection, even the thought of nuclear weapons caused rioting in the streets. However, as advanced weapons proliferate, our allies might want more explicit guarantees.

These are only some of the questions that need answering, and at the highest level. It's bad enough that on-site commanders all too often find themselves in today's ambiguous situations; it will be much worse facing tomorrow's sophisticated weapons. And defining this new role might also help in the 1990s defense budget debates. While the traditional East-West problems might be abating (at least for the immediate future), the same is certainly not true in the Third World.

MAINTAINING OTHER ALLIANCES

As with the drawdown from NATO, the Navy could become more important as a symbol of commitment in the Third World and other areas as American overseas bases close down. The United States has forty-odd commitments overseas, including:

- Australia–New Zealand–U.S. (ANZUS) Pact
- Treaty of Mutual Cooperation and Security with Japan
- Mutual Defense Treaty with the Republic of Korea
- Mutual Defense Treaty with the Republic of Philippines
- Southeast Asia Collective Defense Treaty (SEATO)
- Inter-American Treaty of Reciprocal Assistance (Rio Pact)

Closing bases in the Philippines and Korea does not invalidate these agreements. In fact, the military and symbolic glue holding them together after the closings will probably be naval forces. Therefore, the United States might consider establishing STANAVFORs with some of these allies as well. For example, an ANZUS STANAVFOR might be a way to bring New Zealand back into that alliance, and a SEATO/ASEAN

STANAVFOR might reassure the Southeast Asian allies after the closing of the Philippine bases.

CONCLUSIONS

This chapter on Third World operations has concentrated on the new conditions such as the proliferation of sophisticated weaponry and the closing of U.S. overseas bases. However, there are enough old factors such as historic border disputes, religious fundamentalism, and regional disputes to sustain the more or less normal crisis response operations that have created the era of "violent peace," as former CNO Admiral Watkins once so aptly described it. The new conditions will simply exacerbate those old problems.

Making predictions about the future can be foolish, especially in today's rapidly changing world, but there are some that feel fairly safe. Despite the MTCR, the 1990s will undoubtedly see the spread of longer-range missiles, with inevitable new generations meaning that even conventional warhead systems will be more deadly. There is also a good chance of CW and even nuclear proliferation, which all leads to an irony: both the United States and the Russian commonwealth could actually find themselves outgunned. With INF, the two superpowers eliminated longer- and medium-range theater missiles (both nuclear and conventional), and each has unilaterally agreed to eliminate shorter-range systems. They are also working on a bilateral CW agreement. Without similar multilateral accords, the two superpowers could find themselves outgunned in both missiles and CW. There have been calls for a world-wide INF agreement, and a proposed CW treaty would eventually be multilateral *if* other countries agreed to join (which seems unlikely at this time). It would truly be ironic if U.S. forces, especially ships, had to start carrying CW and ungarrison the TLAM-N for Third World deterrence. Since the Russian navy seldom ventures far from home, it could perhaps live with this situation. But the same cannot be said for the U.S. Navy.

Proliferation of sophisticated weaponry could well surpass nuclear superpower relations as the most important problem for the 1990s. Since only the Navy operates throughout the Third World, it is the most affected branch of the services and therefore the most appropriate for handling new deterrence concerns. However, this could well signal a major change in naval operations, perhaps even necessitating a look at new systems such as longer-range airplanes with stand-off weaponry, surface combatant cruise missile carriers, and SSGNs. One thing seems certain: the days of sailing rather casually off the shores of Third World adversaries are definitely over.

7 / Maritime or National Missions?

WHILE THE WORLD might be entering a new era, at least on the surface, it appears the Navy is still using the old (Maritime) strategy. As a result, even though by most objective measures the capabilities that the Navy and Marine Corps bring should predominate in this new era, they could end up losing in the anticipated post–Cold War roles and missions debate of the 1990s, sure to follow once the dust from the Iraq crisis and 1992 elections subside. Senator Sam Nunn, powerful chairman of the Senate Armed Services Committee, has called for such a debate, even suggesting that the services compete among themselves for roles and missions. Some disturbing signs are already evident in proposed CINC changes. For example, according to one report on possible major command reorganizations, the Army may be placed in charge of a new Atlantic Command. Although the rationale for such a decision escapes this author, the real culprit might be the Navy's continuing concentration on traditional maritime, rather than national, missions. It could, in short, well be the classic example of winning the Maritime Strategy battle and losing the mission responsibilities war.

The Navy has been very proud of its development of the Maritime Strategy, as well it should be. As all strategies should, it set the tone for its period. Although the Maritime Strategy is sometimes associated with the "600-ship Navy" from the Reagan-Lehman-Watkins administration of the 1980s, its roots actually go back to the 450-ship (and declining) Navy of the late 1970s.[1] During this period, when the Soviet Navy was finally starting to build first-rate ships including sophisticated surface combatants and especially quiet submarines, CNO Admiral Thomas P. Hayward developed the notion of forward deployments to meet that new threat.[2] This was then developed further by the Navy during the early 1980s.

While the Maritime Strategy was appropriate for the 1980s, it may not suffice for the new interwar period and the new mission requirements outlined in the previous three chapters. There were two problems with the presentation of the Maritime Strategy, one more traditional (and in some respects semantical), and the other pertaining to the future interwar period.

MARITIME MISSIONS OR STRATEGY

One of the problems with the Maritime Strategy was that, at least on the surface, it ignored more traditional naval missions such as naval presence, including crisis response, sea control, and projection ashore.[3] At the top of any list of Navy priorities should come the oldest naval mission in the world, presence—what one author correctly called "the misunderstood mission."[4] Often derogatorily called "gunboat diplomacy," presence is mainly aimed at keeping the peace, especially in today's environment. While in the past gunboat diplomacy was intended to intimidate the natives, today it is usually meant to protect one's own nationals from those natives as well as to enforce freedom of the seas. In other words, traditional gunboat diplomacy has been turned on its head. It is also, as Admiral Turner and Commander McNulty explained in their articles, an extremely complex mission, yet one that is seldom thoroughly analyzed. Admiral Turner breaks the presence mission down into "preventive" and "reactive" deployments, with the latter often falling into the crisis response situations. Commander McNulty lists seven contributions of naval presence, from acknowledging international commitments and providing humanitarian aid to coercion.

The second, more traditional naval mission is sea control and all its variants, from complete control of the seas—as the Royal Navy maintained during its heyday and, to a certain extent, the USN had at the end of World War II—to local control and everything in between. Finally comes projection ashore, which in many but not all cases means amphibious operations. Carrier operations against the shore could also fall into this category, as could even surface or submarine Tomahawk land attack options.

In many respects, this concentration on maritime missions rather than strategy is simply a semantical difference. The three phases of the Maritime Strategy, "Deterrence or Transition to War," "Seizing the Initiative," and finally "Carrying the Fight to the Enemy," could have been expressed in more traditional terms. For example, the first phase could have been listed in the language of naval presence as either preventive or reactive deployments; seizing the initiative was nothing more than traditional sea control; and even parts of carrying the fight to the enemy such as moving the Marines to Norway were simply projection ashore. Had the tenets of the Maritime Strategy been presented as traditional maritime mission concepts, it probably would not have raised such a storm of criticism.[5] But more important, it would have fit into current and future national missions, remaining useful for the new interwar conditions.

THE CHANGING NATIONAL MISSIONS

Another problem with the original Maritime Strategy was that it generally overlooked national strategy even though, somewhat ironically, the Navy's role had always been crucial in at least two national missions. Indeed, it was often described as "the maritime component of national military strategy."[6] The two national missions ignored were nuclear deterrence and crisis response, with the latter particularly a naval mission. The Navy did not, of course, completely overlook either. CNO Admiral Watkins often talked about the era of "violent peace," which, considering the constant crises and incidents, was a most appropriate phrase. Yet the Maritime Strategy did neglect those day-to-day naval operations in Third World areas that, as noted in Chapter 6, are mostly naval responsibilities. And, as noted in Chapter 4, the Navy has always had an important if often unrecognized role in nuclear deterrence. However, neither of these two crucial roles ever received more than a passing mention in the original Maritime Strategy statements.

European defense was the main thrust of the Maritime Strategy, although even here there was a problem. It was an effective strategy for bottling up the Soviet Navy and for flank protection, particularly on the Northern flank, but it probably contributed little to the Central Front, which was then the main concern. Now, however, as detailed in Chapter 5, the importance of the Central Front may be diminishing, with more traditional naval missions such as sea lift becoming important.

THE IMPORTANCE OF MISSION ANALYSIS

Strategists have long searched for a grand, overriding strategy. However, it is more realistic to think in terms of specific missions. Concentrating on maritime missions rather than on strategy offers many practical advantages. Missions, for example, involve those day-to-day operations that frame the frequent crises. Mission analysis also helps establish the political-military parameters; finally, missions really define the importance of the Navy's role in national security. As noted in Chapter 3, mission analysis is one of the two important midlevel steps between macro, broad declaratory policy and micro, detailed employment policy. Mission analysis is also crucial in advance of the second midlevel step, force planning. Mission analyses like the three that follow can serve to clarify future force needs.

Nuclear Strategy

While the trend seems to be toward a dyad of sea-based systems and long-range bombers, there are problems. For strategic deterrence, most analysts see a need for more SSBNs with fewer launch tubes, which probably means a completely new and much smaller SSBN—a major force decision for the submarine community. With the eventual changes in theater nuclear deterrence, there also seems to be a need for an SSGN, or at least for some current SSNs to be specifically designated for that role. The TLAM-N might have to be taken out of garrison. There might also be a need for SSGNs for certain Third World deterrence situations if, as many predict, nuclear proliferation becomes a reality in the new interwar period. In short, looking at the nuclear deterrence mission requirements, it appears that the submarine community might have to make some serious future force decisions, none of which are currently planned; these will be discussed in Chapter 10. However, one trend seems clear. That is an even greater reliance on Navy nuclear systems, indicating a new role and responsibility for the Navy in any new Strategic Command.

NATO and European Defense

As noted in Chapter 5, there will be a host of changes in Europe with major effects on naval forces. These changes could make SACLANT the major American (if not NATO) commander. Indeed, in a very few years NATO navies could be the only glue holding NATO together. Missions like sea lift, SLOC, and convoy protection will grow in importance. Naval air forces could also become more important, as well as rapidly deployed Marines with their full capabilities.

For force planning, this means that merchant ships, convoy escorts, frigates, and perhaps smaller V/STOL (ASW) carriers could become more important; the Navy is not currently building any of these. Fortunately, this is not just an American but rather a multinational NATO problem, which means that combined efforts might be most appropriate across the board, in surface, air, and submarine initiatives. Combined efforts could also help stop the decline of NATO navies, allowing them better out-of-area capabilities.

Third World Operations

By all indications, Third World operations will continue unabated, while probably increasing in complexity—witness the sophisticated array of equipment held by Saddam Hussein of Iraq. This sends a mixed signal to force planners. While in the past less sophisticated ships were sometimes considered adequate for Third World patrols, that may no longer be the case. On the other hand, considering the many places the Navy must cover, there have to be some trade-offs. Most crises are minor, involving only naval presence. The decline of American bases overseas will also mean that floating bases (i.e., aircraft carriers, combat logistics ships, repair ships, and the like) will now be needed in these remote areas. Once again, the Navy's role will increase, meaning that the Navy should at least be placed in charge or at least in rotation for any new Readiness Command.

The Pacific

Finally, a brief word about a mission area not specifically covered in this section: the Pacific. Naval analysts have long complained that a major theater, the Pacific, has often been neglected, even ignored, and there is some truth to that claim. There are several reasons for this. One is the assumption that the Pacific is obviously an area of naval responsibility. While analysts can argue over who should control a Strategic Command, or who might better be placed in charge of a new Atlantic Command that might have to fight land battles, few question the Navy's predominant role in the Pacific. Another reason is that the Pacific requirements more or less get thrown into that "Third World" crisis response mission where, once again, the Navy has played the major role.

Perhaps the main reason for neglect is that during the Cold War concerns over nuclear deterrence naturally came first, followed by Soviet threats to the European theater. At the time, even the Korean War was considered by many as simply a feint away from the real threat in Europe. For many years the Soviet Pacific fleet was second rate and never considered a serious threat. There is no question that despite the major wars in

Korea and Vietnam, the Pacific mission was always considered a secondary concern after nuclear and NATO strategy.

That will undoubtedly change in the new post–Cold War era. Many even feel that the true future of the United States is in the Pacific. However, what will not change is the assumption that the Navy will, and should, always remain in charge as the area CINC for the Pacific. This section and the chapters on roles and missions has emphasized the changes in the post–Cold War era, and certainly did not mean to ignore this vital area of national security concern.

* * *

In sum, a mission analysis is vital in advance of the next step, force planning. Only by going through the various missions can the stage be set for deciding what forces are actually needed, a process that will be detailed in Part II. There are, however, two other reasons for mission analysis.

THE FORTHCOMING MISSIONS DEBATE

Many senators and analysts are calling for an interservice missions debate. All services, but particularly the Navy, have been most reluctant to engage in such debates. The precedents of the 1949 Navy–Air Force fight and the McNamara era are not encouraging. However, with the changes in missions and the declining budgets, they seem inevitable. And, in this author's opinion, the Navy has nothing to lose and much to gain. One reason the Navy does not want to challenge the Air Force on, for example, strategic command is that funds would come out of current Navy budgets. If, on the other hand, there was a strategic budget, as Les Aspin, chairman of the House Armed Services Committee, has suggested, the funds for smaller SSBNs would be available.

There are similar trends and arguments in the other mission areas. As savings are realized from European drawdowns, at least some of those savings should go into a major sealift program, which the Air Force and particularly the Army will also need. As overseas bases are closed, at least some of the money saved should go into Navy support funding which, in turn, actually helps the other services. In short, the Navy should not hesitate to take part in a new missions debate because of old funding fears.

Finally, there is another reason the Navy should not hesitate to challenge old mission jointness assumptions. There are suggestions to pare the current CINC command structure from ten to only four—Atlantic, Pacific, contingency, and strategic forces. While the Navy would retain the Pacific Command, the Army would probably assume the new Atlantic Command with the Air Force still in rotation for the strategic force.[7] Presumably, the Army and the Marines will remain in rotation for the new Contingency Command. The Navy should also be in that rotation. Why the Army should assume an "Atlantic" command is unclear, as is why the Air Force should be in rotation for a new Strategic Command, considering the force trends. Yet that might happen *unless* a more thorough missions analysis and debate takes place. This author, incidentally, is not concerned with traditional Navy parochialism but rather the sound organizational principle that the one who controls the most, and especially the preponderant, forces should be placed in charge. The whole issue of jointness and the Goldwater-Nichols Act requirements from the mid-1980s should be reexamined in this new post–Cold War period. They could well be simply another relic of the old Cold War era. Whether that particular reorganization plan is implemented, charges are bound to occur in this new interwar period, and the Navy must be prepared to enter the forthcoming fray, even challenging pre-era jointness assumptions.

THE NEED FOR NEW DECLARATORY POLICY

Another advantage of mission analysis is that it points up the need for new declaratory policies as well. While the primary purpose of mission analysis is to go from declaratory policy to force planning to eventual employment policy for the CINCs, it can also be used to move the other way. This need for new policies is most evident for the new situations in the Third World. All the thought and study that went into both nuclear and conventional strategy for fighting and deterring Soviet forces must now go into policies that address the changes in Third World operations. Maybe if Third World deterrence policy had been clearer, Saddam Hussein would not have invaded Kuwait. The ambassador to Iraq, April Glaspie, was severely criticized in some quarters for sending the wrong signal to Saddam and implying that the United States had no position on any invasion of Kuwait. No American ambassador to a European country would have sent such a signal.

There are similar needs for a new declaratory policy debate over both nuclear deterrence and NATO policy. If, as trends seem to indicate, the United States moves toward a dyad of just a few long-range bombers and mostly sea-based systems, this should be recognized in some manner by the NCA. Moving most if not eventually all Army and Air Force units out of Europe will also require new thinking.

In short, a Maritime Strategy for the new interwar period is needed, but the building blocks are missions—both traditional naval missions such as naval presence and, more important, national missions and priorities. These mission analyses are needed for force planning, for new declaratory policies, and finally for the possible upcoming defense debates of the new interwar period.

Part II

The Forces

8 / Concepts for the New Interwar Period

The Need for Alternatives

WHILE MISSION ANALYSIS is a crucial first step, eventually the issue becomes the forces—type, quantity, and building plans, including R and D; possible new deployment concepts, since they will become increasingly important; the role of the reserves; and finally, reconstitution when and if the interwar period ends. This section will look at these questions and their problems, prospects, and alternatives, which, unfortunately, are not always compatible. For example, the main "problem," a declining defense budget and a smaller fleet, does not square with the "prospect" that the Navy's roles and missions will increase during the 1990s. Although there appears to be some consensus that the Navy should get the largest slice of the future DoD budget pie, that will still be a much smaller pie.

Current building plans can be described as "less of the same," and there is some thought being given to moving even more ships into the reserves. For example, it appears that instead of building two SSN-21s a year, only one will be built; instead of five to six Aegis DDG-51s a year, only three to four. Similar delays or stretch-outs are planned for other forces. There are a few new concepts: for surface forces, the Navy has proposed a "flexible transition" plan, or what might more properly be called "transition-down," which calls for building high-level sophisticated ships and moving them to less demanding missions as they age. Surface forces are being classified as battle force combatants (BFCs) or protection of shipping (POS) escorts. Ships will be built and deployed as BFCs, moving into POS roles as they age. For example, the DD-963 ASW destroyers and even CG-47s now classified as BFCs will, as they get older, be reassigned to POS missions. There is some question, however, over how flexible this plan really is, since it still requires (perhaps even justifies) building only expensive, high-level ships.

Other plans are also in the works. Two future carrier studies are under way by the Center for Naval Analyses and the National Research Council. The David Taylor Research Center has conceptual building plans for future ships, recommending only one or two basic types and using them for different missions. For example, it suggests building a carrier dock multimission (CDM) ship and using variants for everything from the next generation of amphibious ship to aircraft carriers and even a carrier dock guided missile (CDG) ship. There are preliminary plans for low-cost destroyers and nuclear attack submarines. Many have suggested moving forces into the reserves. Former Secretary of the Navy John Lehman has recommended moving up to two-thirds of some forces into the reserves. The administration has announced a new acquisition program that emphasizes R and D, perhaps limited to building a few prototypes. And, as noted, there have been other suggestions over the years—the high-low mix, transition to V/STOL, construction of only nuclear ships, and the like.

While there has been no lack of ad hoc suggestions, there does not seem to be a complete spectrum of alternatives available for the new interwar period, just when they might be needed the most. That is the purpose of this introductory chapter—to offer many different shipbuilding, R and D, reserve, and even fleet deployment alternatives. There are, for example, well over twenty different shipbuilding and R and D alternatives that should be considered, not just one or two; not one method of moving forces to the reserves, but eight; and at least five different deployment and fleet concepts. In short, there is a whole menu of choices that should be considered.

BUILDING AND TRANSITION CONCEPTS

As shown in Table 8-1, there are a range of twenty different building and transitional concepts that can be readily identified. While all are distinct, they are not necessarily mutually exclusive (e.g., while a dreadnought might be a prototype, all prototypes need not be dreadnoughts). They can be further broken down into four basic building concepts, a few miscellaneous concepts, and some eleven different modernization and transitional notions.

Table 8-1. Building and Transitional Concepts

Basic building	High level
	Medium level
	Low level
	Multiple mix
Miscellaneous	Dual use
	—service
	—joint
	—combined
	—civilian
	Modular
	Training ships
Transitional (time/improvements)	Less of the same
	Modernization
	Conversion in lieu of production (CILOP)
	Transition-down
	Transition-up
	Phase-in/phaseout
	Skip a generation
	Hop a generation
	Silver bullets
	Prototype
	Dreadnought

Basic Building Concepts

High Level   Ideally, the best option (and one that the Navy appears to be following today) is to build the best, most sophisticated ships and aircraft possible. While commanders have always wanted the best, there are four additional reasons to prefer this option. First is the need to counter a sophisticated enemy, which the Soviet Navy was becoming in the late 1970s. Therefore, in this author's opinion, the Navy was probably wise to build sophisticated ships during the 1980s. Second, during a period of rapidly expanding budgets like the late 1970s and early 1980s, "Why not the best?" Third, high-level weaponry can usually also be used for low-level threats, but not necessarily vice versa. A final reason for building only high-level weaponry is in some respects contradictory: during a time of decreasing budgets those few ships built should be the best available, with cost savings coming from cuts in quantity, not quality. The problem, however, is when you need both quantity and quality.

Medium Level   An obvious compromise is to build what might be considered medium-level ships, both in size and sophistication. In size, this appears to be what the David Taylor Research Center is recommending: a few standard ship types adaptable for many missions. Some medium-level sophistication could perhaps be achieved by using only current off-the-shelf technology and waiting for normal modernization.

Low Level   There is also the low-level alternative; however, building *only* smaller, less sophisticated ships does not appear to be a real option for the U.S. Navy. That does not mean that the USN cannot build some of this type for certain missions.

Multiple or Modified Mix   An obvious compromise is to build some mix of each, what used to be called the high-low mix of balancing a few large, sophisticated ships with many more lower-level, less costly craft. This author prefers the term "multiple or modified mix" for two reasons. First, even though the high-low mix was not really new (there have always been balances throughout history), the phrase became such a pejorative phrase during the 1970s that it is best left to the historical dustbin. However, there is another, more important reason. A "multiple mix" concept would also encompass medium-level ships. Some medium-level systems might be most appropriate for the new interwar conditions with the emphasis on Third World threats, yet provide a hedge against more sophisticated threats. Modified mix might be more appropriate when costs are a consideration.

Miscellaneous Building Concepts

Dual Use: Service, Joint, Combined, and Civilian   More serious consideration and planning must be devoted to possible dual-use capabilities. Again, it appears that the David Taylor Center is seriously proposing this concept, using certain basic designs for many different naval purposes. This might also be most appropriate for both joint (i.e., U.S. interservice) and combined (i.e., multinational) projects. For example, there have been suggestions for a joint Coast Guard–Navy cutter-minesweeper. Joint Navy–Air Force plane projects make sense in an era of limited budgets. Multinational or combined projects such as a NATO frigate, LST, V/STOL, and weapon systems should also be approached more vigorously. In the past, parochialism or "not invented here" attitudes, both service and national, have always killed these projects, but in this new era they should be reconsidered. In fact, joint and combined efforts could well end up being the only way to fund new programs.

Not to be forgotten, especially in this post–Cold War period, are some possible dual-use military-civilian projects, especially in electronics. The largest procurement items in the defense budget are not ships, planes, or tanks, but electronics. Many civilian fields from meteorology to medicine also use sophisticated electronics these days. The Navy recently announced that it would purchase a civilian computer for shipboard use rather than developing a military mode. This military-civilian cooperation could become crucial in the upcoming war for markets.

Modular   Another old concept is to use more modularity in shipbuilding. Using this approach, whole ship sections can be switched around; or one basic type can be built initially, with different weapon systems inserted as needed. This also eases improvements and modernization.

Training/Reserve Ships   Finally, since training and reserve forces could become a larger factor, consideration should be given to building ships and planes for just these purposes. Many other countries build training ships. Ships, planes, and weaponry that require less upkeep and maintenance for training and have some dual-use capability would be useful for the reserves.

Transitional Concepts

Less of the Same   One option would be simply to build less of the same, or to stretch out current purchases. This is not necessarily a bad idea. During times of doubt when the future is unclear (which seems to be the case today), building less of the same makes a certain amount of sense. Of course, quantity reductions and stretch-outs do usually drive up per-unit costs.

Modernization Only   An option that navies have always followed is simply to modernize current systems. Electronic suites, weaponry, and the like can be replaced as new technologies are developed.

Conversion in Lieu of Procurement (CILOP)   Rather than build completely new systems, the Navy has often remanufactured older modes using a concept called CILOP. Currently, some early F-14A planes are being converted to the more sophisticated F-14D in this manner. During the 1950s, World War II–era light gun cruisers (CLs) underwent a similar conversion to CLGs.

Transition Down   One option the Navy is currently pursuing and which, to some extent, has always been Navy policy is to build a fairly high-level, sophisticated ship and, as it gets older, move it to less demanding tasks. This is the plan for current cruisers and destroyers; being built as first-line BFCs, they will move to less demanding POS escort duties as they get older.

Transition Up   The opposite approach would be to "transition up" with what are usually considered major, planned block or flight improvements. This has been done in a somewhat ad hoc way with the FFG-7 frigate and SSN-688 attack submarine programs going through distinct block upgrades, but it is being planned more carefully for the new DDG-51-class destroyer, which will go through three distinct blocks. By Block III, the DDG-51 will have a larger VLS capacity and, most important, full helicopter facilities. Transition up differs slightly from modernization in that major, usually shipwide capabilities are upgraded rather than just individual electronic and weapon systems. Initial use of modular concepts would help considerably in the transition up to major improvements.

Phase-In/Phaseout   It has been suggested that a more coherent plan be developed for phasing in and out systems. For example, the Navy once had plans to replace its complete spectrum of older planes with new advanced modes. As a result, they all are in trouble. A better phase-in might have saved at least some of them. This could also be a good proposal for joint production. For example, the Air Force and Navy both built their top-of-the line planes, the F-15 and F-14, at approximately the same time. Had they been phased in, there might have been some incremental improvements. Consideration should also be given to switching the lead for joint projects so that service parochialism could be kept to a minimum. That is, let one service take the lead for the first generation, and another for the second.

Skip a Generation   Many, such as Richard Perle, have suggested that all the services "skip a generation," since there will probably be a gap before sophisticated World War III–type threats once more become more a concern. That is, just go on to the next generation of systems for the true twenty-first-century environment. There is an interwar precedent for this suggestion. After World War I, Winston Churchill suggested using a ten-year gap for planning. His, however, was a floating ten years, with the result that building decisions were constantly put off.

Hop a Generation   Rather than completely skipping a generation, it might be better to just take a "hop"—that is, start production, but perhaps build only a few. This might be most appropriate for weaponry that has been under development for years or where no substitute currently exists.

Silver Bullets   The Congressional Budget Office (CBO) has suggested building just a few sophisticated systems such as stealth aircraft and using them as special "silver bullets" for difficult missions. The Air Force's new stealth F-117s were used in this manner during Desert Storm.

Prototype Only   Another plan might be to build only a prototype or two for testing. The Navy has done this in the past, as have the Soviets. Building a prototype is usually not inexpensive, even for low-end systems, but it is considerably cheaper than series production. This allows for full testing, which might be most appropriate for the interwar period. It could also make possible rapid production and reconstitution with state-of-the-art equipment if world conditions start to change, while enabling some excellent R and D companies to function only in that mode.

Dreadnoughts   A final approach would be to build some very sophisticated prototypes with the latest technology—dreadnoughts, or systems that make all else obsolete. Building a series of dreadnoughts in all areas could in fact be the best deterrent against future threats. It could also be a testing ground for the latest R and D project.

RESEARCH AND DEVELOPMENT CONCEPTS

Research and development *must* be continued, and in fact a robust R and D program might be the best deterrent. Many Sovietologists, for example, are convinced that President Reagan's decision to proceed with the Strategic Defense Initiative (SDI) finally convinced Soviet military leaders that their society had to change. The Soviet general staff realized that they were falling further and further behind the United States.

R and D must also be continued to maintain a robust industrial base. However, as with everything else, R and D is expensive. Some tough choices must be made, and this requires a spectrum of options. Table 8-2 lists eight possible R and D alternatives.

Less of the Same   The first alternative would be simply to continue all current research, but at lower levels. Again, this is not necessarily a bad thing, since all research probably should be continued at some level.

Skip a Generation, the "D"   Another alternative is skip current projects and go on to the next level. In other words, after completing the preliminary research, the "R", drop the "D" of current programs and go on to the research and full development of the next generation.

Table 8-2. Research and Development Concepts

Less of the same
Skip a generation, the "D"
Capability without production
Build prototype only
Joint
Combined
Civilian
Drop systems
—areas (ASW, etc.)
—weaponry (e.g., lightweight torpedo)
—components (e.g., microchips)

Capability Without Production   Going just one step further, it has been suggested that the United States should develop certain capabilities, but not necessarily go into production. That is, go through the complete R and D cycle, perhaps even build some production capabilities, but do not proceed with full-scale production. This was done to a certain extent with binary CW weapons.

Build Prototypes Only   Similarly, another alternative is to build prototypes only, especially in some kind of black, "skunk works" environment. The early U-2 Blackbird and even to some extent the Air Force's F-117 were built in this manner. The U.S. Navy has also done this with some success in the past. Some early nuclear submarines and surface ships were built as prototypes. Some worked, some did not. All prototypes, incidentally, need not be top-of-the-line dreadnoughts.

The administration recently announced a new acquisition strategy that will focus on R and D and the building of prototypes. This has come under some criticism because it appears that only prototypes will be built. Construction of prototypes must be balanced with some actual series production.

Joint R and D   Joint R and D projects between the services are nothing new, although in the past, many if not most have been resisted due to service parochialism. With decreasing budgets, that parochialism must end. Another option is joint research but not necessarily development in cases where true differences, not just service parochialism, do exist.

Combined R and D   Similarly, multinational projects must be pursued more vigorously, especially in areas where the U.S. has not always taken the lead. The V/STOL Harrier improvement programs are a good example of combined development, and other potential combined efforts include lightweight torpedoes and a smaller Aegis system. This approach could be particularly helpful in some areas of limited interest to the U.S. The V-22 Osprey tilt-rotor plane might have been a good project for combined development.

Dual-Use Civilian-Military R and D   More effort must also go into possible civilian-military dual-use R and D. As noted earlier, the largest procurement item in the defense budget actually involves electronics. There are bound to be some possible dual-use capabilities. This could perhaps become a top priority for the dozens of military (and Department of Energy nuclear) laboratories that are now looking for work. Although the topic lies beyond the scope of this book, it is clear that the next immediate war will be over leadership in high-tech research—and there is no reason the Department of Defense cannot join that effort.

Drop Certain Areas   Finally, the United States could simply drop certain elements of R and D, especially where another friendly country might be ahead (e.g., Japan in some types of electronics). This *might* be appropriate for certain equipment or components, but not for a broad area such as ASW or AAW. The United States cannot militarily afford to abandon research in whole areas—although, as noted above, some combined projects might be considered, especially where another country has taken the lead. This could be done for complete weapon systems, or just for certain components.

RESERVE OPTIONS

Reserve forces have always been important, and during the next few years their importance will undoubtedly grow. One of the most frequently suggested alternatives to save forces and funds has been to move them into the reserves. The "total force" concept, incorporating reserves with active forces, has been accepted for years in theory although often ignored in practice. Ignoring the reserves may not be an option in the 1990s, and new situations require new concepts. A list of reserve options follows—four old basic ideas, with some new fleet concepts—and is summarized in Table 8-3.

Basic Concepts

Ready Reserve   When most people refer to the reserves they usually mean the ready reserve, those "weekend warriors" who drill once a month and for two weeks each year. Ready reserve ships and plane squadrons usually have a few active duty personnel but are mostly manned by reserves. The reserves have been called up on occasion, such as during the 1961 Berlin crisis, Vietnam, and more recently the Iraq

Table 8-3. Reserve Concepts

Basic	Ready reserve (active reserve)
	Inactive reserve (mothball fleet)
	Inactive "Ready Reserve" (Thirty-day notice, etc.)
	Sectional reserve (e.g., all minesweepers)
	Navy National Guard
Fleet	"In Reserve" (active held "in reserve")
	Flying squadrons (reserve battle group)
	Reserve fleets (First and Second Reserve Fleets)

crisis. In certain areas reserves are crucial; for example, virtually all the minesweepers are reserve ships, as is most of the Navy's logistical air support. Placing too much in the reserves, however, can be a mistake. The Navy has found this out with minesweeping capabilities. Virtually all of the Army's logistical tail is in the reserves, necessitating call-ups in times of crisis.

Inactive Reserve   The other major reserve component is the inactive reserve, the mothball fleet. Mothballed warships have seldom been called up for emergencies, although the merchant fleet has been very important. There are also inactive personnel who in theory are subject to recall, but they have never been utilized.

Inactive Ready Reserve   Another concept could be an inactive but ready reserve, subject to recall on short notice. There are currently some merchant ships kept in standby ready service for rapid breakout, but this status could be expanded to cover some warships and even perhaps personnel, especially recently retired personnel or those with special skills. The Navy does, for example, have a program for convoy commodores, which consists mostly of retired Navy captain volunteers. These "old salts" train occasionally, and most love it. It has been suggested that a merchant marine inactive reserve also be established.

Sectional Reserve Units   Another possibility is to place certain sections or units in reserve. As noted, virtually all the Navy's minesweepers are in the reserves; much of its intelligence units are also reserves. This practice could be expanded. The Army has put much of its logistical tail into the reserves, requiring a massive reserve call-up for any major contingency. One reason for the Army decision was to force civilian leadership to call up the reserves to avoid "another Vietnam." But placing too much into the reserves can be a problem, and it certainly reduces flexibility.

Navy National Guard   Since there are Army and Air Force National Guards, why not a Navy National Guard? During the Revolutionary War the first navies belonged to the states. State navies existed up to World War I, with three still operating. This concept could be expanded and formalized into a Navy National Guard. This could be particularly useful for maritime states and those with maritime academies and large NROTC units (both college and high school).

Fleet Reserve Concepts

Active "In Reserve"   Still another concept would be to place active duty ships "in reserve" at lower manpower levels. The Navy used to have a squadron of old LSTs in this status. During the Cuban missile crisis it was discovered that the Navy did not have adequate sea lift for Army troops. A squadron of old World War II LSTs was commissioned and kept manned at about one-third strength. These ships were active duty, not reserve, so they could be utilized more easily. They later proved useful for other incidents such as the Dominican Republic crisis and especially Vietnam, where most were eventually sent. This concept could be useful again.

Reserve Battle Groups Nothing would be more appropriate for a rejuvenated, larger reserve force than the creation of reserve battle groups (RBGs). During the 1970s interwar period when the fleet numbers were going down, one author suggested creating "Flying Squadrons for Flexibility" built around older carriers and reserve escorts. Currently, the Navy, the Department of Defense, and Congress are in a struggle over whether deployable carrier strength should be maintained at twelve, or slip to ten. As a compromise, the creation of two reserve carrier battle groups (RCVBGs), one for each coast, might be considered. There are two other RBG concepts that should be considered: a reserve amphibious ready group (RARG) and a reserve battleship battle group (RBBBG).

Reserve "Fleets" Finally, the home fleets might be considered semireserve fleets, or even specifically designated as such. For many years, the Second and Third Fleets (and especially the old First Fleet in San Diego) were considered de facto reserve/training fleets for the forward Sixth and Seventh Fleets in the Atlantic and Pacific, respectively. It was with the advent of the Maritime Strategy that the Second and Third Fleets started to act as true battle fleets. There were always exercises, but generally the ready fleets were (and still are) the Sixth and Seventh Fleets.

The Navy could return to that informal concept, or perhaps even create new semireserve fleets—for example, a new First Fleet for the West Coast and a Second Fleet for the East that would be considered more or less the reserve fleet. This could more formally ease transitions. A ship would move from the First Fleet, kept mostly in upkeep and maintenance with only limited operations, to the Third for more vigorous training and even some fleet exercises, to the forward Seventh Fleet deployment,

Table 8-4. Deployment Concepts

Less of the same
Reduced OpTempo
Substitution
Alternative deployments
New fleets
Joint operations
Combined operations

returning eventually to the First. This is, in fact, how things used to be done (and still are, to a certain extent), but making it more formal would help in this new era. This might fit in with Senator Nunn's call for more flexible operational concepts.

Deployment Concepts

Finally, there must be some new deployment concepts. With fewer ships, and probably fewer operations and maintenance funds, some new deployment alternatives must also be examined. Seven alternatives are discussed below and are summarized in Table 8-4 on page 99.

Less of the Same   Once again, one alternative is simply less of the same: fewer ships in the forward fleets, fewer exercises, etc. This is nothing new. During the 1970s interwar period the Sixth Fleet went from having two carrier battle groups always on station to having just one.

Reduced OpTempo   Another quick fix would be an overall reduced operations tempo, with fewer days at sea. This would keep all the fleets at the same general level but reduce operations by spending more time in port and maybe even lying at anchor overseas in secure havens as the Soviet fleet did.

Substitution   Another option is substitution. The battle groups and fleets since World War II have always been built around carriers, but they could also be built around large amphibious assault ships, especially those with embarked V/STOL Harriers. Battleship surface action groups (SAGs) have operated alone in some environments. The new sophisticated Aegis-class cruisers and a couple of appropriate ships with helicopters could be a substitute in many cases.

Alternative Deployment Concepts   With the new world situation, serious consideration should be given to completely new deployment concepts. Do we really need a fleet in the Mediterranean on a continuous basis? It appears that more than just the normal token Middle East force might be required. Will a permanent African squadron be needed to protect American lives, as it was in Liberia? What will the pullout from bases in the Philippines and South Korea mean—more or less deployments?

Alternative Fleet Concepts   As noted earlier, another alternative is the creation of separate fleets for reserve/upkeep, readiness/training, and forward deployment, one for each coast. This is simply in keeping with the old "rule of three": for each ship deployed you need three, one for each of the functions noted above. Formalizing the concept into coastal fleets would simply recognize this tradition. It might actually increase readiness and training and improve morale.

The fleets could be redesignated First and Second for reserve, Third and Fourth for ready, and Seventh and Sixth for forward for the Pacific and Atlantic, respectively. The new reserve/upkeep First and Second Fleets could act as a bridge between a type commander and the readiness fleet. It would end the fiction of every ship always being "ready," with crews on more liberty sections improving morale. Ships returning from heavy forward deployments would move into these reserve fleets, allowing time for crew leave as well as much-needed upkeep. With warning time now increased considerably, there is no need to keep these ships at constant alert; such a stand-down would also improve morale. The backbone of the reserve First and Second Fleets would be reserve carrier (RCVBG) and amphibious ready (RARG) battle groups.

The Third and Fourth Fleet readiness and training commander could then focus on battle performance. Readiness would be increased, watch sections decreased, and the like. These training fleets would also be battle fleets, their ships ready for deployment to the forward fleets. The roles and missions of the Sixth and Seventh Fleet commanders would change little.

Joint Operations   Consideration must be given to more joint operations. The Navy might transfer some land-based naval missions to the Air Force, but these could be more than made up for by increased naval air responsibilities in forward areas as air bases close overseas. The Navy and Coast Guard could also work together more closely for national security as well as drug concerns.

There might also be more cross-fertilization among the services. For example, each Coast Guard officer could be required to have one overseas deployment on a Navy surface combatant before he or she is made a lieutenant commander. While a Coast Guard officer cannot take time out of his or her career for a complete two- or three-year tour, a six-month deployment to the Sixth or Seventh Fleet will teach lessons that will never be forgotten. Similarly, at least some Navy officers should deploy with Coast Guard cutters.

Combined Operations   More consideration must also be given to combined operations such as the NATO STANAVFORLANT squadron. Similar combined squadrons could be established for the Mediterranean, the Channel, and even in certain Pacific areas with ANZUS and ASEAN multinational squadrons.

RECONSTITUTION/INDUSTRIAL BASE

If history is any guide, the capability for quickly reconstituting forces could well be the most important concept for the new interwar period.

During World War I, the United States started building battleships but had to switch to destroyers. Had it not been for the Vinson-Trammell and similar acts of the late 1930s, which were as much anti-Depression public works measures as Navy programs, the Navy would have been in considerable trouble during World War II; the ships built in that period really won the war. It was not until late 1943, when the issue was no longer in doubt, that the World War II–era ships started to join the fleet. Reconstitution for the Korean War involved simply recommissioning World War II ships, which then had enough life for the Vietnam War. During the post-Vietnam era, building ships like the FFG-7 from the low end of the high-low mix kept the numbers up until the Reagan administration increased sophisticated shipbuilding programs.

Today, the building of "less of the same" expensive ships has lowered warship building rates to around ten a year, adequate to maintain only a 300-ship Navy. Worse, the industrial base needed for reconstitution is shrinking. If current trends continue, there will only be a few shipyards and plane manufacturers remaining by the end of the decade. Using some of the concepts listed above could help maintain that base. For example, a multiple mix building program would keep more yards open, while building prototype dreadnoughts could help maintain the important R and D industrial base. Current less of the same building plans will allow the industrial base needed for reconstitution to continue to deteriorate.

COMMENTS AND CONCLUSIONS

During the 1980s, with growing budgets and an increasingly sophisticated Soviet threat, it was appropriate to build mostly high-level ships and develop the battle-ready, forward Maritime Strategy, making the home Second and Third Fleets truly "ready" fleets. But the 1990s, with decreasing budgets and a diminishing Soviet threat that allows for more warning time, require new strategies. While there are no lack of conceptual alternatives—some new, some old, with many variations—they have generally been presented in an ad hoc manner.

What is needed is a complete spectrum of choice, from high to low and everything in between. There are other values. These concepts also set certain standards and touchstones for evaluation and illustrate to OSD, OMB, and Congress that the Navy is truly looking at alternatives. The next four chapters will look at the various forces using these basic concepts for evaluation and comparison.

9 / Naval Air Forces

"Where Are the Planes?"

AIRCRAFT CARRIERS HAVE been the "capital" ships of the Navy for the past fifty years, and there is no reason to believe that will change anytime soon. Some argue that submarines have now assumed that role, but while that might have been the case during a World War III between the United States and the Soviet Union (although even that is open to debate), that particular scenario is fading further into the background. Submarines simply do not have the naval "presence," flexibility, or utility required for most foreseeable incidents. Others have speculated that with long-range missiles and better surveillance, surface action groups (SAGs), especially those built around a battleship or Aegis cruisers, could replace carrier battle groups. BBBGs have operated independently and might have been able to substitute in some limited situations. However, there is still no real alternative to sustained air superiority. And the United States has *never* fought a war or even been involved in a crisis in the era of flight without assuming absolute control of the skies.

In short, there is simply nothing comparable to the flexibility of carriers, with their long reach and ability to remain on station for long periods of time, which has led to that now-familiar question asked by all national command authorities during any crisis: "Where are the carriers?" The Brookings study on crisis response bears this out; carriers were involved in a majority of those incidents. With the changing world conditions, the importance of carriers will undoubtedly increase for several reasons. First, as noted in Chapter 6, is the inevitable loss of air bases overseas, including those in the Philippines and probably South Korea over the next decade. In the western Pacific, this could leave only Japan for land-based air operations, or faraway places like Guam or Diego Garcia. Second, the CFE talks include air forces and will eventually lead to their elimination or at least relocation, with the latter proving quite complex, as the Air Force has already discovered. After being thrown out of Torrejon Air Base by the Spanish government, the Air Force is now trying to locate just one wing to Italy, but Congress is balking at funding for a new base (as are NATO allies, who must share the cost). In sum, by the end of the decade it would not be at all surprising if most U.S. overseas bases were closed, leaving only those floating airfields called aircraft carriers available for *any* overseas response. "Where are the carriers?" will continue to be the call for many years.

AIRCRAFT CARRIERS

Current Forces

CTOL Carriers   Since the end of Vietnam, the Navy's goal has been fifteen carrier battle groups. During the Carter administration that dropped to twelve, but it rose again during the Reagan administration to fifteen "deployable" carriers—which, considering long overhauls, really meant sixteen or seventeen carriers. Starting in the 1980s, the postwar large-deck conventional powered carriers (CVs) underwent extensive shipyard overhauls called a Service Life Extension Program (SLEP). The work added fifteen years to their operational life, taking them out of commission for approximately eighteen months during the process. At one time, all eight conventional carriers were slated for SLEP, but it appears the program will stop with five although Congress once added some funds for a sixth. Nuclear carrier overhauls and refueling can take them out of commission for almost two years.

As shown in Figure 9-1, at the start of 1990 the Navy did, in fact, have seventeen carriers, but that included the old training carrier *Lexington* AVT-16, which did not have any storage facilities, and the *Independence*, out of commission in SLEP. Then, just when it was about to make its fifteen-carrier-group goal with the commissioning of the *Abraham Lincoln* CVN-72, the Navy was forced to retire the World War II–era *Coral Sea* CV-43 for budgetary purposes—keeping the total at fourteen deployable carriers, where it had been for most of the 1980s.

While the Navy would still prefer fifteen carriers, according to press reports, it will settle for fourteen. OSD, however, wants to cut the num-

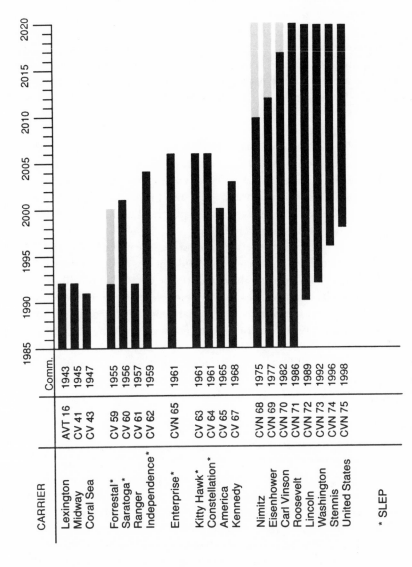

Figure 9-1. Aircraft Carrier Retirement Schedule

ber to twelve, which the Navy has reluctantly accepted.[1] Some in Congress are recommending eight to ten or even six by the end of the decade. Based on the normal thirty-five-year life for these large ships (approximately forty-five for those undergoing SLEP), the Navy could remain in fairly good shape during the 1990s, with only three going out due to normal life-cycle retirements: *Lexington* AVT-16, *Midway* CV-41, and *Ranger* CV-61. The training carrier *Lexington* was retired in 1991 (replaced by the *Forrestal*), as was the last World War II–era carrier, USS *Midway.* According to current plans, since the *Ranger,* commissioned in 1957, did not undergo a SLEP, she will be retired in 1992 after thirty-five years. Counting the *Constellation* in SLEP, that would still give the Navy thirteen carriers (fourteen counting the *Forrestal,* which unlike the *Lexington* does have some emergency surge capabilities), with the *Stennis* CVN-74 joining the fleet in 1996 and the *United States* CVN-75 in 1998. However, the Navy has announced that the *Saratoga* CV-60 will be decommissioned in fiscal year 1995 and the *America* CV-65 in 1996, even though both could have lasted until 2000 according to normal life spans. In short, the Navy should have some twelve active duty carriers during the 1990s and could have had fourteen without the early retirements.

The major crunch will come after the turn of the century. Around the year 2005, all the conventional carriers should be retired, with the single-class *Enterprise* CVN also nearing the end of its life cycle. There will still be the eight *Nimitz*-class carriers; seven will be deployable, with one always in extensive overhaul/refueling. Current plans for the *Nimitz* class are for an approximately forty-five- to fifty-year life (which may be too optimistic), with refueling about every dozen years. Had the *America* and the *John F. Kennedy* undergone SLEP as once planned, the Navy could have had ten deployable carriers through 2010. Thus, based on normal retirements and without building replacements, the Navy could have had twelve to fourteen deployable carriers through 2000, about eleven to twelve through 2005, and about seven through the year 2020.

Helicopter, V/STOL Carriers   Although not normally listed under "carrier air," there are also thirteen large amphibious assault ships, with more being built. Often referred to as "minicarriers" in the press, with some at 40,000 tons, they are actually the size of World War II flattops. There are three classes of amphibious assault ships: seven 19,000-ton *Iwo Jima*–class LPHs (often, although wrongly, called "landing platform helicopters"), built in the 1960s; five 40,000-ton *Tarawa*-class LHAs, built in the late 1970s; and a new class very similar to the LHA designated the *Wasp*-class LHD, currently under construction with the first, the *Wasp* LHD-1, recently commissioned. Current plans are for six LHDs, although the number was once as high as eleven.

All three classes have helicopters and varying degrees of V/STOL capabilities. During the early 1970s, the *Guam* LPH-9 operated as an experimental SCS to evaluate Admiral Zumwalt's concept of a smaller V/STOL and ASW helicopter ship for convoy defense. She operated AV-8A Harriers and SH-3 Sea Kings from 1972 to 1974 before reverting to an amphibious assault role. Although designed for helicopters, the much larger *Tarawa*-class LHAs have operated often with small Harrier squadrons and even on occasion with OV-10 Bronco STOL aircraft. The *Wasp*-class LHDs, however, were specifically designed for V/STOL operations with increased support capabilities for a full Harrier squadron.

While all of these large amphibious ships have operated V/STOL Harriers at one time or another, none of these minicarriers has a ski-jump bow ramp structure to facilitate takeoffs, which has now become standard in all other navies of the world. Ski jumps would even give these ships limited CTOL and STOL capabilities, increasing payload and flexibility. The ski-jump concept has in fact become so refined that the latest Soviet carrier is even able to operate high-performance CTOL aircraft with them. "Why don't we have any ski jumps?"[2] on the new LHD class (and back-fitted on the LHAs), giving them a true dual capability? Although there are some good, legitimate reasons, the real reason might be Navy–Marine Corps parochialism. Once again, what might have been appropriate for the past may not be for the new interwar period.

Future Plans

While future plans for surface and submarine forces are well known, long-range plans for carrier forces are "under study." The Navy currently has plans for one *Nimitz*-class CVN in their shipbuilding program for FY95. While anything in the "out-year" projections must be considered a wish list (especially in today's environment), it is still considered an important first step. There was once even some press and congressional speculation on rescinding funds for the *Stennis* and particularly the *United States*—always considered an ominous name. Twice, carriers called the "United States" have been canceled or renamed, the most famous being the 1949 ship that precipitated the Navy–Air Force fight and "Admiral's revolt." There seems no question that the Navy's preference would be to simply continue building *Nimitz*-class carriers. With an estimated forty-five-year life, only one new start every three years is required to maintain current force levels.

Further complicating future plans is the fact that SLEP modernizations for the remaining three conventional carriers have been canceled. There were once plans to modernize all eight large-deck postwar carriers, but that might end at five or possibly six depending upon final congressional and administration negotiations; some advance funds for SLEP to the *Kennedy* were once added by Congress, and it appears the ship will now undergo a complex overhaul. The Philadelphia shipyard, which had performed the SLEP work, is now slated for closing. While other shipyards could undoubtedly do the work, much experience would be lost. There were many problems with the first SLEP, but subsequent work has proceeded smoothly. In lieu of SLEP, some have now proposed "complex overhauls" for these carriers.

Plans for more amphibious LHD carriers seem to be changing almost daily. Final numbers have varied from the five already authorized to as many as eleven. They have been listed as replacements for the seven LPHs, which will start reaching their thirty- to thirty-five-year life cycle around the turn of the century. There was also consideration given to building four more to compensate for the four LHAs never built due to shipbuilding and then budgetary problems. According to the latest plan, however, the LHD program will reach at least six. And although the LPHs could last longer, they are now slated for retirement during the 1990s.

Alternatives

CTOL   Although several future carrier studies are under way, with one recommending looking at a 200,000-ton "stretch Nimitz" and floating islands,[3] the alternatives are limited and probably boil down to about four—either large- or smaller-deck nuclear and/or conventional carriers. During the Carter administration, three CTOL alternatives were considered: continue building *Nimitz*-class CVNs, return to *Kennedy*-class large-deck conventional-powered carriers, or design a smaller conventional-powered ship of about 55,000 tons then designated a CVV. This author in an article also suggested that the United States and France jointly look at building smaller CVNs, which the French Navy was then just exploring and has since begun.[4] There is another CTOL alternative that might be considered for the longer term. The David Taylor Research Center has suggested some carrier alternatives based on their common Carrier Dock Multimission (CDM) ship concept. They have proposed a 31,000-ton CDV of approximately 730 feet with a 90-foot plug or extension for a CDV-long variant. Both would have ski jumps with limited CTOL capabilities.

There is, however, a question of real or at least realistic near or even midterm affordability, especially in today's environment. During that 1970s carrier debate, only two CVNs had been authorized, not eight, and the World War II flattops were retiring at an alarming rate. The main rationale for alternatives was saving money for a *large* buy. Critics of large-deck *Nimitz* nuclear carriers argued that similar-sized conventional *Kennedy* types would be considerably cheaper and that two or three CVVs could be built for the price of one CVN. However, after more careful analysis it was determined that building another *Kennedy* versus a *Nimitz* would save little and that the CVV:CVN cost ratio was not 3:1 or 2:1 but about 3:2—and only if CVVs were built in quantity. The Carter administration finally decided to build some six to eight CVVs, which undoubtedly would have saved some funds over the long run. On the other hand, building only one or two today may not.

In fact, if history is any guide, building just one or two of *any* completely new carrier design will be very expensive no matter what the size. Also, savings of over $600 million were realized by authorizing two *Nimitz* CVNs at the same time, which became the practice during the 1980s. Since twelve large attack carriers can be maintained at a building rate of only one every three to four years, there is some question as to whether switching to a completely new design in an era of reduced budgets really is an affordable alternative. To save money, building two CVNs concurrently would be better. That could be done every five to six years. There is a further question as to whether smaller designs would be able to handle large twenty-first-century stealth planes. In short, while some improvements to the basic *Nimitz* design should not be ruled out, starting a completely new design seems unlikely in today's budget environment.

Two other CTOL alternatives might be considered. The first is to conduct a complex overhaul of the *Ranger*, commissioned in 1961, and particularly the *America* and *John F. Kennedy*, commissioned in 1965 and 1968, respectively. That would definitely keep the numbers up through 2010, allowing time for a proper study and evaluation of the twenty-first-century environment. It would also maintain a conventional carrier through 2010 for home porting in Japan. (Japan might not accept the permanent presence of a nuclear ship.) The other alternative is to seriously consider the David Taylor Center's CDM carrier *if* that basic design is also used for several types of ships. As will be noted in Chapter 12, a CDM variant proposal has been suggested to replace some five different amphibious types. If built in series, CDV and CDV-long modes might prove cost-effective and should probably be considered.

V/STOL   While there might not be realistically affordable alternatives for a new midterm CTOL carrier design, the same does not hold true for V/STOL options. Over the years, there have been four suggestions. Admiral Zumwalt wanted to build a small SCS of about 14,000 tons to carry a few Harriers and ASW helicopters for convoy duty. Others have proposed even smaller V/STOL ships. Senator Hart suggested using the large DD-963 hull for a V/STOL variant—and in fact, such a ship was once authorized, only to be reprogrammed at a later date. There were also proposals for a 22,000-ton VSS during the Carter administration, including plans for the transition to V/STOL. Most of the foreign navy V/STOL ships are in this 20,000-ton category. Finally, as has been noted, all the amphibious assault ships have operated Harriers at one point, with the current LHD specifically designed for their operations. Ski jumps could be added to the current LHD (with LHA back-fits), making it more dual-capable. There might even be some multinational possibilities. At one point Australia looked at using the LHA design as a V/STOL carrier to replace their small CTOL carrier, the *Melbourne.*

The most obvious and cheapest alternative would be to add ski jumps to the LHA and LHDs, almost doubling forward air presence (although certainly not capabilities). Currently, besides the forward carrier battle groups, there is also an Amphibious Ready Group (ARG), although just how "ready" that group is remains open to question. For example, it often carries only helicopters, not Harriers, and thus has an extremely limited air presence. And, it very seldom operates with surface combatant escorts. With the new-generation AV-8Bs finally being outfitted with radar and better communications capabilities, a ski-jump LHD or LHA with its embarked Harriers would be truly ready for most of the kinds of contingencies and crises that have occurred during the postwar period.

Although almost completely overshadowed by Desert Storm, the Navy conducted two crucial operations in 1991, interesting for one aspect—they were two of the very few naval crisis response incidents where carriers were not detached. Instead, both were readily handled by ARGs. These were Operation Sharp Edge, to remove U.S. citizens caught in the

Table 9-1. Aircraft Carrier Modified Mix Alternatives

Level	Class	Concepts/Comments
High	CVN+	Improved *Nimitz*
	CVN	Continue building *Nimitz* class
	CV	Modernize (SLEP)
Mid	CDV long	Dual use/study
	LHD CTOL	Ski and arrest gear/prototype
	LHD+	Add ski jump/transition-up
	LHA+	Add ski jump/modernize
	LPH+	Add ski jump/SCS-VSS prototype
	CDM variants	Dual use/study
Low	VSS	Combined/study
	DD-963 V/H	Prototype/with Sky-Hook
	SCS	Combined/study

civil war in Liberia, and Operation Eastern Exit, to conduct similar evacuations from Somalia. One could argue that carriers were not required in either the Liberia or Somalia crises, but then neither were flattops needed in most Third World crisis response situations; yet they were sent for effect, flexibility, and possible contingencies. Due to the Iraq situation, carriers could not be sent, but ARGs with Harriers and surface combatant escorts did just fine. And it is the Liberian and Somalian crises that are the norm, not the Iraqi incidents.

Why don't LHAs and LHDs have ski jumps? The more-or-less official answer is that they would take away helicopter spots,[5] but there are other, more subtle reasons involving both Marine Corps and Navy air parochialism. While the Marine Harrier pilots would undoubtedly favor the ski jumps, the Corps as a whole fears "their" ships would soon be taken over for minicarrier operations. On the other hand, the Navy air community fears it will then be forced into building only V/STOL airplanes. While there might be these temptations, the LHAs and LHDs with their well decks will undoubtedly always remain amphibious ships for the Marines, and (as the Soviets have shown) CTOL planes can be used with ski jumps. Operating high-performance CTOL planes off ski jumps would probably require arresting gear for recovery. Therefore, as a prototype, one of the LHDs still under construction should be fitted with arresting gear (and perhaps even an angled deck) as well as a ski jump.

The United States might have missed an opportunity for some multinational combined building programs. During the 1970s when not just U.S. but Western naval air was disappearing, this author suggested combined building programs for both larger and smaller V/STOL carriers, which were then just starting to emerge. Since that time, NATO allies Spain and Italy have joined the V/STOL carrier club, and the Royal Navy has added two more to complement its initial "through-deck" cruiser, the *Invincible*. Spain actually used the old American design. There still might be some opportunities left. Brazil and Argentina are reportedly considering replacing their small, aging CTOL carriers with V/STOL ships, and Australia once looked at the concept. Japan's name keeps coming up as a country interested in acquiring a carrier. If some combined efforts can be negotiated, building a 20–30,000-ton VSS might become cost-effective. However, for the USN to go it alone at this point seems to make little sense in light of the current LHD/LHA ski-jump option.

There are a few less expensive prototype options that might be considered. First would be to refigure one or two of the aging LPHs, add ski jumps, and operate them as V/STOL ships. As mentioned, the *Guam* did operate as an SCS in the early 1970s. The *New Orleans* and *Inchon* (commissioned in 1968 and 1970, respectively) should have at least ten years of life remaining for such experimentation. Since the LPHs do not have well decks for landing craft, the Marines should not complain too much about loss of assets, especially since both ships are now slated for early retirement. Another prototype project might be using the DD-963/CG-47 hull for a small SCS, as was once actually authorized. This is only suggested because the hulls for the CG-47s are still being built. Again, starting a completely new type would probably be expensive, even for this smaller ship, but using an existing hull currently in production might be considered. This could also be a good size on which to test the sky-hook concept. It has been proposed that V/STOL planes could be recovered by smaller, even frigate-size ships using a crane, or sky-hook, that would snag the plane while it hovers and swing it onto the deck.[6] Both the Japanese and Royal navies have explored this option, making it perhaps another candidate for combined development. One DD-963H/V could be built and sailed around to various countries and air shows for demonstration purposes.

For the longer term, the David Taylor Center's CDM proposals should be considered for V/STOL variants. As currently designed, virtually all its proposed amphibious CDMs would have V/STOL capabilities, some with ski jumps. The old Arapaho concept for converting merchant ships into V/STOL carriers could be revisited. Others have suggested more futuristic designs such as large SWATH carriers, but these new types seem unlikely with today's budget restrictions. However, the development of advanced STOVL planes could open up many more options in the twenty-first century.

AIRPLANES

Nowhere is there a clearer example of the problems of building only high-technology systems—at virtually the same time, for a threat that might not currently exist or has at least diminished greatly—than in Navy airplane proposals. At one time the Navy had five brand-new "advanced" airplanes on the drawing boards; one by one, they have all been canceled. There were once plans to replace the old attack A-6 Intruder with a new stealth Advanced Tactical Aircraft (ATA), later designated the A-12; the still top-of-the-line F-14 Tomcat with a new stealth Navy Advanced Tactical Fighter (NATF); current ASW, AEW, and EW aircraft with an Advanced Tactical Support (ATS) plane; and the venerable P-3 with a P-7. The Marines also had a proposal for a new, very advanced plane, the "tilt-rotor" V-22 Osprey, which takes off like a helicopter then tilts its rotors forward to fly as a normal fixed-wing craft.

There was not a low-technology or even a normal "modernization" upgrade in the whole bunch, nor much of a phase-in. The result, not surprisingly, was that something had to give—and something did. One by one, all these new advanced planes were canceled or indefinitely postponed. Only the V-22 has been kept alive by traditional congressional pork barrel interests, although OSD still urges its cancellation. Adding to the problem, some of the old production lines have been closed down, or are about to close. Former Secretary of the Navy John Lehman has stated that if Navy air were a business it would be headed for Chapter 11 bankruptcy.[7] In short, this seems to be an area ripe for some major conceptualization decisions such as skipping generations, modernizing, or at most conducting a transition up with some major block upgrades as well as both joint and combined programs—especially for V/STOL or STOL modes which might be the true wave of the future, not stealth.

Current Planes

Attack   For most of the post–World War II period, the Navy operated either a complete multiple mix spectrum of bomber or attack planes from high through middle to low, or a mix of just medium and low (or light) aircraft. At the high end was the heavy A-3 Skywarrior, in the middle was the medium attack A-6 Intruder, and at the low end was the reliable A-4 Skyhawk (first developed in the early 1950s and still being flown by some air forces including the Navy's own "aggressor force") followed by the A-7 Corsair, which became the workhorse during Vietnam. Although the A-3 retired as a heavy bomber in the early 1960s it continued to operate as a reconnaissance plane until recently, illustrating the flexibility of large planes. The A-3J Vigilante (later designated A-5) was developed in the late 1950s as a medium-heavy attack aircraft. Changing mission requirements doomed a A-5B, but the Vigilante also operated for several years as the RA-5C reconnaissance version. However, while the heavy A-3 and then the A-5 were retired by the mid-1960s partially because ICBMs, SLBMs, and longer-range bombers had taken away their old strategic mission of the 1950s, the Navy still continued to operate a mix of middle and low or light forces through both Vietnam and Desert Storm. In short, until the mid-1980s decision to place all its attack eggs in the expensive stealth A-12 basket, there was nothing new about a modified mix of Navy attack aircraft.

The backbone of the Navy's attack force today is still the venerable A-6 Intruder. The A-6, whose design can actually be traced to the late 1950s, has of course been upgraded several times. The latest mode, the A-6E, was first flown in 1971 and last produced in 1986, although there were many modernizations in between. There were once plans for a new mode A-6F with major upgrades, but it was canceled to make room for the A-12. The low or light A-7 Corsair developed for Vietnam for both the Navy and Air Force and used as recently as Desert Storm was finally retired last year.

There are actually two other attack planes in the force, although their utility has been questioned. First is the dual-mission fighter/attack F/A-18 Hornet, which in sophistication probably falls into the "medium" category but which has a notoriously short range that limits its attack capabilities. Then there is the Marines' AV-8B II, which despite the "A" designation is usually considered a "close air support" (CAS) plane due again to range limitations. With the cancellation of the A-12 and the retirement of the A-7, the venerable A-6 remains the Navy's only classical attack aircraft.

Fighters   Although there was never the complete three-level mix of fighters, throughout most of the Cold War era there was at least some mix. By today's standards, all the early post–World War II and Korean War–era fighters would probably be classified as "light." But this changed in the late 1950s. The first new plane developed was the F-8 Crusader, a fairly sophisticated medium-level plane; it was soon followed by the very sophisticated F-4 Phantom, one of the most successful planes ever built. Developed by the Navy, it was soon adopted by the Air Force and then purchased by many foreign air forces, where it is still flying. Although never formally given the "F/A" designation, the Phantom was always considered a fighter-bomber so it also had attack capabilities.

In the 1970s, the Navy formalized their fighter mix—building the high-level, very sophisticated F-14 Tomcat, still considered one of the world's premier fighter airplanes, and balancing it with the lower-level F/A-18 Hornet. With the retirement of the F-4s a few years ago, current Navy fighter air wings consist of F-14s and F/A-18s. Both are in a second generation and are considered extremely capable planes, although that was not always the case.

While the F-14A first deployed in 1974 had an extremely sophisticated electronics suite, it was notoriously underpowered by the TF 30 turbofan engine. It could track up to twenty-four targets simultaneously and guide up to six longer-range Phoenix missiles to six different targets, which gave it a good long-range capability, but the underpowered engine limited its maneuverability for close-in dogfighting. This changed in the mid-1980s when the early F-14As were upgraded to F-14A+ with the installation of General Electric's F 110 engine, which the Air Force had recently selected for its F-16 fighters. At about the same time, the Navy announced an F-14D mode that, besides the F 110 engine, includes a new, more reliable radar and improved avionics. Currently, the Navy is in the process of upgrading all F-14As to F-14A+ and/or F-14D modes, with a few new F-14Ds also being built.

The F/A-18 has similarly been upgraded. The initial modes introduced in 1978 had only a daytime fighter/attack capability, the F-18A with a single seat and the F/A-18B with a two-seat attack mode. The upgraded F/A-18 C (single) and D (two-seat) began flying in the late 1980s; later modes were given some all-weather and night attack capabilities. Although the F/A-18 began life as the YF-17 as part of the low-cost fighter competition of the 1970s, by most measures it would not be considered a light aircraft except in one category—range. With two engines and fairly sophisticated avionics, electronics, and weapons capabilities, it probably qualifies for the high side of the middle of the spectrum, and with unit costs of about $40 million it is certainly not cheap. But its main limitation is its extremely short range. According to one report, it "sucked up gas" during Desert Storm. Its main attributes are ease of maintenance and much increased readiness over the F-14.

While the F-14 and F/A-18 now constitute the Navy's fighter inventory, the Marines' Harriers also have some fighter capabilities. As the British displayed during the Falklands war, the Harriers can perform quite well in many Third World situations. The latest AV-8B II with radar and better communications should enhance this capability, giving amphibious assault ships a much wider range of protection.

Other Planes   There are, of course, a host of other planes that must be mentioned. It could even be argued that at least some of the missions delegated these other planes are more important than those performed by the attack or fighter aircraft. These important missions are AEW, EW/ECM, and ASW. As was noted by virtually every observer of the Falklands campaign, the Royal Navy almost lost that war for lack of a sea-based AEW airplane. The U.S. Navy currently operates the AEW E-2 Hawkeye, often referred to as a "mini-AWACS" and still considered a quite capable plane. EW and ECM planes are now essential for virtually any kind of strike, even in most Third World situations; the Navy operates, and is still procuring, the EA-6B Prowler. Finally, there are both land- and sea-based ASW craft. The land-based plane is the P-3 Orion; the sea-based force includes S-3 Vikings and various ASW helos. Although usually considered an ASW plane, the P-3 performed other missions during Desert Storm and is currently used by the Coast Guard for drug interdiction. The Navy also uses the LAMPS III helicopter for other missions as well as ASW operations.

Future Plans

With the cancellation of the advanced planes on the Navy's drawing boards, future plans were thrown into "disarray"—now a favorite term of naval commentators. And there appears to be some truth to that description. It seems as though every issue of *Inside the Navy, Navy Times,* and similar naval news journals brings forth yet another proposal. One newspaper account derisively referred to the Navy airplane "plan du jour."[8] Although there is still considerable infighting among manufacturers, OSD, the Navy, congressional interests, and others, some trends are starting to emerge.

Attack   Within weeks of cancellation of the A-12 Avenger, the Navy announced plans for a new stealth "AX" with an IOC target date of around 2003 and full deployment by 2010. Although details are still sketchy and probably will be for many more years, reportedly it will be a less capable plane than the A-12 with a slightly shorter range, a smaller payload, and fewer stealthy characteristics although still "low observable." Its combat radius will be 700 nautical miles versus 785 for the A-12, its maximum weapons load will be 12,000 pounds versus 16,000 for the A-12, and apparently the AX will incorporate less costly stealth characteristics.[9]

Despite the fact that the AX will be less capable than the A-12, there are currently debates over whether the AX should have a multirole fighter/attack capability—or, as one commentator put it, "an f/A with a big A."[10] Once again confusion seems to reign. One news account says that Navy leaders doubt the plane can have such a capability,[11] while another cites this possibility.[12] Current unit cost estimates for the AX are $65 million in 1991 dollars. However, since A-12 estimates were about $165 million when it was finally canceled, one can only speculate on what the final costs for an AX will be in turn-of-the-century dollars, especially if it is built as a multirole aircraft.

This leaves the venerable 1950-era A-6 as the Navy's attack backbone for another decade. There are plans to rewing some of the later-mode A-6Es, but it appears that shortages will start to show up as early as the mid-1990s with no clear-cut solution in sight. Canceling the A-6F was probably a mistake. The F/A-18 and AV-8B give the Navy some flexibility—although, considering their limited range, not much.

To take up the gap, there are proposals to procure either an F-14D Tomcat modification called "Quick Strike" or an "extended" new upgraded F/A-18 E/F mode. According to news accounts, the Navy prefers the Quick Strike (F-14Q), while the OSD budget cutters prefer the F/A-18

E/F option. Proponents of the Quick Strike cite availability in that the F-14Q is only a slightly more costly modification of the current F-14D and considerably more capable than the F/A-18, including much greater range. Proponents of the extended F/A-18 E/F claim that it can match the range of the F-14Q while they cite eventual lower unit costs, although it will take some $3–4 billion to develop.[13] Secretary Cheney also points out that the F/A-18 E/F "is three times more reliable, twice as easy to maintain, has a safety record which is 50 percent better, requires about 25 percent fewer maintenance personnel, and costs about 25 percent less to operate per flight hour" than the F-14.[14] If the F/A-18 is ultimately chosen, it will probably doom the F-14 and perhaps even Grumman as an aircraft manufacturer, leaving an all F/A-18 Navy attack and fighter force after the turn of the decade.

Fighters   The future Navy fighter situation is similarly in "disarray," with both internal and external fights among the Navy, the OSD, and the two manufacturers. The main issue concerns the future of the F-14 and, if continued, whether the F-14D should consist of remanufactured F-14As—that is, conversions in lieu of procurement (CILOPs)—or new construction. Secretary Cheney and OSD budget officials want to cancel the F-14 program and proceed with an all F/A-18 force, moving to the E/F mode. Again, according to news reports, the Navy prefers the Tomcat, and Congress has at least to date kept the line open, funding a few new-mode F-14D and F-14A CILOPs. If the F-14 does continue, OSD prefers conversions rather than new construction, citing cost differentials of about two to one.

Regardless of the F-14's future, F/A-18 production will proceed at the fairly substantial rate of about forty per year. While well below the initial annual production rate of over eighty, this is still considerably more than the dozen or so F-14s produced or converted each year. The only major question for the F/A-18 is when R and D and then production will start on the E/F modes. In short, if OSD has its way (and it usually does), in a few years the Navy's fighter inventory will consist of the medium-level F/A-18. Research on a high-level stealth NATF is still being given minimal funding, but there are no current plans for procurement.

Others   There are somewhat similar problems in future plans for other planes, although there is one relative bright spot that illustrates yet another advantage of multinational "combined" production. The Navy had canceled P-3 production when it announced plans for the P-7, but the line was opened in order to accommodate some foreign purchases. With the P-7 now canceled, the Navy plans to take advantage of that open line by purchasing new P-3s with Update IV electronics, a high-speed computer processor, improved communications and navigation systems, a new radar, and electronic support measures equipment to detect hostile radars.[15] The EW/ECM Prowler production line is similarly open.

However, both the ASW S-3 Viking and AEW E2C Hawkeye lines are closed, and shortages are already developing in the S-3s. The decrease in the Soviet submarine threat has made this situation less critical, although some S-3 planes are still required for Third World threats. To ease the S-3 problem, squadron size has been reduced from ten to eight and now to six. Eventually, a follow-on S-3 will be needed.

Alternatives

Perhaps the main problem with Navy airplane proposals—the factor that partially explains the "disarray" and "plan du jour" comments—is that there are not too few but too many alternatives. Both major Navy airplane manufacturers, Grumman and McDonnell Douglas, have a family of upgrades or "transition-up" proposals that cut across the traditional attack and fighter categories; both are also fighting for their very existence. Added to the problem is the intramural fight between the Navy and OSD budget cutters, complicated by decreasing budgets and increasing confusion on future missions requirements.

The most detailed modernization plans are Grumman's "advanced F-14 family," which proposes a transition-up concept using the F-14D as a baseline. Next would come an F-14D enhancement with limited attack capabilities known as "Quick Strike," which would capitalize on F-14D/A-6F/F-15E commonalities and add some air-to-surface missiles and radar modes to make it a near-term attack force multiplier. For the longer term Grumman has proposals for a "Super Tomcat-21" with an "Attack Super Tomcat-21" alternative. The Super Tomcat 21 would be an evolutionary upgrade with improved engine, cockpit, sensors, lift, and fuel capacity and would address some of the vulnerability, reliability, and maintainability issues. At the end of the chain are proposals for an ASF-14 that would combine some ATF stealth technology.[16] McDonnell Douglas has similar plans for the F/A-18: first an extended F/A-18 E/F and then a Hornet 2000 proposal.

The costs and capabilities of these proposals are, quite frankly, somewhat elusive—adding to the "disarray." According to some studies by the Navy and Grumman proponents, the F-14Q could be developed for $100–200 million, with a fly-away cost of about $55 million. The F/A-18 E/F would take at least $3.3 billion to develop, with a fly-away cost of about $40 million. While some advocates of the F/A-18 claim that an extended version could match the range of the F-14, most analysis disputes this.[17]

Adding to future uncertainties is the whole question of stealth. No wonder there is confusion and "disarray." But the more the confusion, the greater the need for major reconceptualization from top to bottom. Navy air must have an overall plan for a realistic and affordable modified mix.

At the high-technology end, tough decisions must be made on the question of whether to proceed with stealth aircraft. Advocates of stealth point to the F-117A Desert Storm experience, citing the fact that although the planes conducted only 3 percent of the strikes they accounted for 40 percent of the damage—a truly remarkable statistic in favor of stealth. On the other hand, stealth aircraft are terribly expensive and, with the demise of the sophisticated Soviet threat (and despite the unique Desert Storm experience), probably not needed for the immediate future. In short, it might be best to skip a generation in stealth aircraft.

There are, however, two other important reasons for the Navy to postpone building stealth aircraft. The first is that the Air Force is proceeding with, and therefore testing, a trio of different stealth systems; the second is that stealth technology is still evolving rapidly.[18] This could readily be seen at a recent air show at which the current stealth planes, the F-117, the B-2, and the YF-22, were shown side-by-side. The first-generation F-117 with its sharp angular sides looks like something straight out of an old Buck Rogers or Flash Gordon movie; the second-generation B-2 flying "bat wing" is quite different, with more rounded edges; but what is most surprising is the latest-generation YF-22, which, although apparently made out of composites and painted black, looks surprisingly like an ordinary new-generation aircraft. With the latest advances and studies, there are now discussions of simply adding some stealthy or low-observable features to all planes. With the Air Force testing, stealth still evolving, and sophisticated threats diminishing, at least for the more immediate future, the Navy might consider placing stealth on hold, or simply building on current Air Force programs. In the interim, two Navy stealth prototype/dreadnought alternatives could be considered.

According to some reports, enough parts were completed to build a couple of the now-canceled A-12s. If so, and if costs are reasonable, at least two A-12s might be built as prototype dreadnoughts. The Congressional Budget Office has recommended spending funds to "capitalize" on the initial investment and building two A-12s, one for flight and the other for equipment testing.[19] There are also reports that the Air Force's YF-22 could be adapted for carrier operations;[20] a few F-22N prototype dreadnoughts might also be built for similar testing purposes. Both the future AX and NATF could then be placed in a study or a joint program. There are continuous questions about the AX program and eventual mission needs. For example, with the B-2 program greatly curtailed, the Air Force

Table 9-2. Airplane Modified Mix Alternatives

Level	Attack	Comments	Fighter
High	AX/AX+	Study/joint A.F.	NATF
	A-12	Prototype/dreadnought	F-22N
	F-14Q	Transition-up F-14	F-14D
Mid	A-6F	Study open line	
	F/A-18E/F	Study/prototype	F/A-18E/F
	F/A-18C/D	Continue	F/A-18C/D
Low	A-7+	Study/joint A.F.	
	AV-8B III	Combined	ASTOVL
	A-L, MRF	Study/joint/combined	F-L, MRF
	Miscellaneous Concepts		
Joint	Attack stealth	Navy-1990s	Air Force-2000s
(lead)	Fighter stealth	A.F.-1990s	Navy-2000s
Combined	Harrier III (supersonic?)		
	ASTOVL		
	V-22 (AEW, ASW, EC/ECM modes)		
	P-3 follow-on		
	Common Tactical Support (CTS)		
	—AEW		
	—ASW		
	—EW/ECM		
	—tanker		

might now become more interested in a medium-level stealth bomber. This would make an AX+ a likely candidate for a joint Navy–Air Force program, but this may not become clear for several years. Testing a few prototype A-12s would also help to clarify the true needs and requirements for a twenty-first-century joint Navy–Air Force AX. Similarly, testing a few F-22Ns would clarify future Navy fighter needs.

The Navy and Air Force should—and with decreasing budgets, probably must—continue joint projects, especially for advanced technology. There might be better phase-in and perhaps some transfer of leadership roles. For example, for the next generation the Air Force could take the lead on medium bombers (attack aircraft) and the Navy on fighters. This will ensure that each can maintain necessary characteristics while keeping one eye on their service brothers—as children do when one splits the candy bar while the other chooses first. Services do have different priorities. The Navy, for example, does have special requirements for carrier operations. On the other hand, these legitimate service requirements should not be used as excuses, as they might have been in the past. Switching generational leads might help solve that problem.

Although future mission needs may not be entirely clear for some time, the Navy cannot go a decade without improvements in its aircraft programs, including some high-level capability. Perhaps not as many sophisticated planes are needed as once were required for Soviet threats, but there is still a need for a few "silver bullets" for certain missions. This probably means proceeding with the F-14 family: continuing to build or CILOP the F-14D fighter and then developing the F-14Q Quick Strike attack mode. Proceeding with the F-14 also has the additional advantage of keeping another line open. Then, depending on how the stealth question is finally resolved, keeping the F-14D and F-14Q lines open would leave the Navy the option of making the transition to the Super Tomcat proposals or proceeding with stealth.

Some consideration might also be given to reopening the production line for the canceled A-6F if it is not too expensive. The costs for all these options, the F-14D, the F-14Q, and the A-6F, could be partially offset by not spending the $3–4 billion dollars needed to develop the F/A-18 E/F mode. Development of eventual F/A-18 follow-ons should not be completely ruled out, but since the F/A-18 C/D line will be kept open for some time anyway, that decision can be delayed. However, the idea of trying to jury-rig what was initially designed as a low-level aircraft to meet all Navy fighter and attack needs should be carefully reevaluated.

There are some lower-level options that could also be explored. Several years ago LTV Corporation offered to upgrade the Air Force's A-7 to a "strike-fighter" for some $8 million, which included a new engine. That option might be revisited for both the Navy and the Air Force. An advanced, re-engined A-7 strike-fighter would probably be more than adequate for most Third World situations. Carrier-based A-7s participated in Desert Storm.

Finally, both the Air Force and Navy should take second, and honest, looks at new light attack (A-L) and fighter (F-L) airplanes for both themselves and export. The Air Force, which is proceeding with the very expensive B-2, F-22, and C-17 airplanes, desperately needs some low-cost alternatives to maintain its numbers. There are plans for an F-16 successor, the Multirole Fighter (MRF), but it will be built after the B-2, C-17, and F-22. Such a plane would also help the Navy. While low in technology and lightweight, these airplanes could be fairly advanced, especially if built in large numbers. It should also be kept in mind that some of the latest sophisticated weaponry such as AMRAAMs are so-called "fire and forget" or "launch and leave" systems that do not need sophisticated platforms. The Navy's new stand-off SLAM is 98 percent autonomous. These light attack and fighter planes could still pack quite a wallop with the right "fire and forget" stand-off weapons. Besides, pilots love hot airplanes.

The A-L and F-L might also make perfect planes for export. All countries are now desperately looking for lower-cost alternatives. Even nations such as Sweden and France, which for years produced indigenous models as much for pride and prestige as for need, are now finding it too expensive to produce advanced planes. The U.S.–developed F-5 for export was an extremely successful plane that is still in use by some foreign governments and U.S. aggressor squadrons. The F-20, developed during the early 1980s for export, was reportedly a good plane produced at the wrong time—when U.S. defense budgets were expanding. Now the F-20 might be needed. The United States certainly has the capability to develop such planes, *if* the Air Force and Navy would also commit to buying some. Rather than have five consortiums bidding on an AX that may never be built, the U.S. aircraft industry should be set loose on designing F-Ls and A-Ls or an MRF, which could be built in great quantity to maintain the industrial base.

For the longer run, the whole question of V/STOL and STOL/STOVL should be pursued, especially considering allied navy trends. This could be an ideal area for some multinational development. The United States is currently in combined programs with Britain, Spain, and Italy, who all operate V/STOL carriers. Britain has asked the United States to assess common needs for a STOVL aircraft. The British estimate they might need about 100, and the U.S. Marines would need about 200–300.[21] Even Navy air is looking at advanced STOVL concepts to replace the F/A-18 and AV-8B.[22] A newly designed STOVL aircraft should have no difficulty operating off large ski jump–equipped ships. The Harrier started out as a combined U.K.–German project and has since been a combined effort between U.S. and British companies. Japan has eyed the AV-8B and might be persuaded to join a consortium.[23] All these options should be pursued and expanded. A supersonic V/STOL and especially an advanced STOVL should be top priorities; the Soviets have reportedly already developed a supersonic V/STOL.[24] It has been suggested that the V-22 be used for sea-based AEW and ASW, capabilities that allied navies desperately need for their V/STOL carriers. In sum, for the long term the whole question of V/STOL, STOVL, STOL, tilt-rotor, etc., might actually become more important than stealth.

The other planes for the important ASW, AEW, and EW/ECM missions should not be ignored, but rather than developing an *Advanced Tactical Support* (ATS) aircraft it might be better to look at a less expensive *Common* Tactical Support (CTS) using current technology. A CTS might also be used for a tanker, which would become necessary if the Navy does move to an all F/A-18 force. More advanced, even stealthy, characteristics should not be ruled out, but they should be dropped if costs become prohibitive. Once again, a CTS might have some export possibilities.

RECONSTITUTION/INDUSTRIAL BASE

Currently only one shipyard, Newport News, has the capability to build large-deck, nuclear-powered carriers. If that industrial base was ever lost, it would be extremely expensive, and perhaps almost impossible, to reconstitute. That alone might be reason enough to proceed with at least one more CVN while conditions in the former Soviet Union and Third World threats are finally sorted out. Putting the three remaining conventional CVs through a SLEP or at least a complex overhaul would keep alive other shipyards for a few more years, allowing for future flexibility.

Adding ski jumps to the LHDs, and back-fitting them on the LHAs, would undoubtedly keep the Litton/Ingalls shipyard in Pascagoula, Mississippi, open for several more years. It would also maintain an industrial base for building follow-on V/STOL or STOVL carriers, which could well become the wave of the future. One of the future carrier study recommendations was to investigate building "LHA/LHD-size" carriers.[25]

However, the most critical reconstitution and industrial base problems lie with airplane manufacturers. If current trends continue and the F-14 is canceled, the Navy might find itself with only one source of planes, McDonnell Douglas, which may itself be heading for Chapter 11 bankruptcy for other reasons.[26] Indeed, most commentators feel that the whole American airplane industry is heading for rocky times and that many of the current companies will go out of business by the turn of the century. Even the supposed "good news" in military aviation is now being reevaluated. For example, last year a Lockheed-headed consortium won the "deal of the century" to build the Air Force's new stealth F-22; but already some are questioning if the plane will ever be built, or at least in the numbers once mentioned.[27] Five consortiums are currently starting preliminary design work on the Navy's AX, but again many insiders in the press, Pentagon, and Congress are wondering about the AX's future. There will undoubtedly be some F-22s and eventually an AX, but between their increasing costs and decreasing defense budgets, neither may qualify as "deals of the century."

To maintain the industrial base the United States must build in quantity, which probably means both joint and combined (export) programs. Nothing would seem more appropriate than to build A-L and F-L aircraft that would not only keep Air Force and Navy numbers up but also be affordable for foreign buys. Such planes should be more sophisticated than some of the very light export models currently on the market for Third World countries—probably more in the F-16 range, or the once-proposed F-20 range. Building A-Ls and F-Ls for the Navy, the Air Force, and especially for export should keep at least a few more plane manufacturers in business for several years.

Other options already mentioned would also help maintain the industrial base for any reconstitution. These include keeping the Grumman F-14 line open for at least one more generation with the F-14D and F-14Q, and building combined V/STOL and STOVL aircraft and a less expensive CTS for AEW, ASW, EW/ECM, and tanker modes. Many foreign countries also operate the P-3 and could probably afford a reasonable follow-on, although not the expensive P-7. And there are undoubtedly many more options that could be pursued to help maintain the industrial base. One thing does seem certain: moving to an all F/A-18 force is not one of them, nor is building just a few expensive stealth aircraft. Aviation is one of the few remaining areas where American industry still has a distinct lead, and it should not be cavalierly treated. The choice might be survival or stealth.

RESERVE/DEPLOYMENT OPTIONS

There are several reserve and new deployment options that should be considered. Using the old rule of three, the Navy needs *at least* twelve deployable carriers to maintain four forward. Constant deployment in the Indian Ocean–Persian Gulf area probably requires at least fourteen. (Even these numbers might be too low. Counting transit time, the Navy calculates it that takes 5.1 carriers to maintain one in the Mediterranean, 5.2 in the Western Pacific, and 7.2 in the Indian Ocean.)[28] If the decision is made to go below these numbers, consideration should be given to placing one or two of the conventional carriers "active, in reserve" as RCVBG "Flying Squadrons"—one for each coast, for both reserve training and Desert Storm–type call-ups. They could probably be manned with one-third to one-half the normal crews, filled out on weekends and during crises with reserves. This would also give reserve air wings their own training flattops. Reserves often have problems obtaining carrier flight time for training, but these two ships should eliminate constant scheduling conflicts with the active forces.

The same consideration should be given to placing two of the retiring amphibious LPHs "active, in reserve," one for each coast for similar contingencies and for training of Marine Corps (Reserve) air. With a reserve LST and LSD, the Marines would have Reserve Amphibious Ready Groups (RARGs). These RCVBGs and RARGs would then form the backbone of the new First and Second Reserve Fleets. Finally, if LHDs and LHAs were equipped with ski ramps and the new generation of all-weather Harriers, the forward-deployed ARGs could probably "substitute" for CBGs in many situations.

COMMENTS AND CONCLUSIONS

Navy air forces should consider a multiple-mix approach for carriers, and it must do so for airplanes. At least for the near term, it is cheaper to continue building *Nimitz*-class (or slightly improved) carriers about every three years to maintain that high-level capability. Actually, authorizing two every five to six years would be considerably cheaper, but politically such a proposal would never get through Congress. Serious consideration should also be given to modernizing the three conventional-powered large-deck carriers that have not undergone a SLEP with either a SLEP or a complex overhaul. That would definitely keep the numbers up through the early years of the twenty-first century, so that new threats can be properly evaluated. If the number of carriers falls below twelve, retiring CVs should be placed in reserve forces as the backbone for RCVBGs.

For the medium level, ski jumps should be added to large LHAs and LHDs, giving them a true dual capability. With advanced Harriers, they would be able to substitute for CVBGs in certain situations. To properly test the use of CTOL planes, at least one of the new LHDs should be built with arresting gear. There are many V/STOL ship prototype and study options that could be explored—from adding ski jumps to LPHs and operating them as SCSs for a few years, to using the large DD-963/CG-47 hull for a smaller V/STOL ship that might also test the sky-hook concept, to looking at some multinational combined projects.

Nowhere, however, is there a greater need for building and transitional conceptualization than in Navy airplane plans and programs. There is no clearer example of "disarray" than the utterly unprecedented firing of three admirals over the handling and subsequent cancellation of the A-12 program.[29] Often an admiral has been quietly retired for some reason or another; but never three, and never in such a public and well publicized manner. The current admiral in charge of Navy air, in a rare, fresh breath of candor, now describes his own programs as in a "complex dilemma" and a "modernization crisis."[30] While the early retirement of carriers may ease the immediate airplane shortages, shortages will still show up after the turn of the century. In short, unless the Navy airplane programs are sorted out, and soon, the call may not be "Where are the carriers?" but "Where are the planes for those carriers?"

* * *

Carriers will continue to be the capital ships of the Navy for the foreseeable future. Like all capital ships throughout history, they are large, expensive, and very symbolic. While the NCA may still ask "Where are the carriers?" so, unfortunately, will the budget cutters. Ideally, it might be best to keep building *Nimitz*-class carriers to reach a twelve- to fifteen-ship goal, maintain the large amphibious assault ships for the Marines' operations, and build all new types of advanced stealth-type airplanes across the board. But that will not happen. There simply are not the funds. Therefore, a spectrum of alternatives must be considered, and some tough choices eventually made.

10 / Submarine Forces

Transition Time?

ALTHOUGH MANY NOW consider submarines to be the capital ships of the fleet (citing the old submariners' saw that there are only two types of ships today—submarines and targets), their use, at least in visible operations, has been extremely limited since World War II. There have been only two or three specific military uses of submarines since 1945, and neither involved the USN or even the Soviet Navy. Ironically, these uses have generally been overlooked by many naval strategists, yet these incidents may give the best clue to the future of submarine operations. These two incidents were the Pakistani sinking of a Indian frigate and the use of submarines by both the British and Argentineans in the Falklands war. The Royal Navy's sinking of the aging cruiser *Belgrano* sent a strong message to the Argentine surface navy to stay in port, which it did. The Argentineans did have a light carrier that, with proper use, tactics, and planes, might have caused problems for the Royal Navy task force. However, one Argentine diesel submarine did venture forth and proceeded to drive the British commanders crazy. British ships expended a considerable amount of ASW weaponry, all to no avail. There is some speculation that, with a better torpedo (or training), that single Argentine submarine could have sunk several ships, forcing the complete withdrawal of the British invasion force.

The lessons seem clear. First, as shown by the Royal Navy's SSN, a fast nuclear submarine can play an important role in conventional deterrence, even in Third World operations. It can be sent alone, quickly, and be the first ship on the scene. A surface ship is not only slower: no surface combatant, no matter how powerful, would dare to operate alone in a hostile environment. Thus, despite its invisible "presence," a submarine in the right place at the right time can contribute to deterrence. Second, and perhaps more ominous for the future, submarine operations by Pakistan and Argentina illustrate that Third World countries are fully prepared to use them. As noted in Chapter 6, there are now some 250 diesel submarines in Third World inventories. The days of operating on a fixed Yankee station may be over.

Despite these very few overt uses, no one has ever suggested that submarines are not needed. They probably were the capital ship of the Soviet Navy. As many have noted, Hitler started the war with only sixty-two submarines and never had more than a hundred at sea; yet Germany almost won the Battle of the Atlantic. The Soviet (now Russian) submarine fleet has numbered well over 300 for years, with its latest classes now quite capable and very quiet. The approximately eighty-five attack submarines now maintained by the USN seem the bare necessity to counter that vast Soviet submarine force—even during this new post–Cold War period.

Although less publicized, submarines were also used for many other missions including crucial intelligence gathering and special operations. For example, Vice Admiral Roger F. Bacon commented on how forward-based submarines were used during a July 1989 Middle East hostage situation: "The unseen capability during this contingency is our forward deployed submarines. I can think of no other recent real world event that illustrates our submarine strengths more than the hostage crises. . . . The fundamental characteristics of a nuclear submarine—covertness, mobility, endurance and offensive firepower—are ideally suited for support of U.S. policy in most Third World crises."[1] Although the admiral did not go into details, that statement was undoubtedly a recognition that the main roles and missions of the submarine force may be changing from an anti-Soviet, primarily ASW and deterrent posture to possible Third World operations including even some projection ashore missions using either special operations forces or land-attack Tomahawks.

These changing roles and missions can be seen from the mission analysis of Part I. The primary role of submarines in the Cold War period was ASW, normally concentrated in northern waters against Soviet bastions. That could change with the new conditions in NATO as ground forces are withdrawn. Sea lift requirements will increase, meaning that possible open-ocean SLOC interdiction, which used to be a low Soviet priority, could well increase. Soviet SSNs could wreck havoc on sea lift without an adequate American ASW submarine force to challenge them both north and south of the G-I-UK gap and in the Pacific. Thus, despite all the changes, anti-Russian ASW capabilities must remain as a deterrent.

However, more likely for at least the immediate future will be a shift to new Third World ASW operations. As the Falklands and Indo-Pakistan wars indicated, Third World nations are quite prepared to use their diesel submarines. While this indicates that traditional submarine ASW may be needed, it will be in a completely new area, one where American submarine forces seldom operate and where conditions are quite different. As a commentator at a recent conference stated, the USN has designed submarines for ASW operations in deep, cold water and not the warm, shallow waters found in many Third World areas. These shallow-water ASW capabilities are now a major concern of the U.S. Navy.[2]

There could also be some entirely new mission requirements. As Admiral Bacon commented, for using submarines for Third World operations as the Royal Navy did in the Falklands war or (more likely) in antishore operations, an SSGN might be appropriate, especially against those countries with sophisticated weaponry. For the first time, submarine-launched Tomahawks were used during Desert Storm against Iraq. As noted in Chapter 6, with the proliferation of long-range missiles, CW, and even nuclear weapons, the new call may be "Where are the SSGNs?" for Third World crises. An SSGN would also be most appropriate for new theater deterrence requirements in Europe. In short, while potential anti-Russian ASW operations will undoubtedly remain a top priority of the submarine force as a deterrent, similar operations in Third World areas may be increasing in importance, and a completely new class of submarines may be required for both nuclear and new Third World deterrence requirements.

CURRENT FORCES

Attack Submarines (SSNs)

The Navy currently has three different classes of SSNs with a fourth, the SSN-21 *Seawolf*, being built. (The last fleet diesel submarine retired in 1990, leaving only one experimental boat.) These are the SSN-594 *Permit*, the SSN-637 *Sturgeon*, and the large SSN-688 *Los Angeles* classes. As shown in Figure 10-1, the thirteen *Permits* built in the mid-1960s will soon be reaching the end of their normal thirty-year life and are already being retired. While the thirty-seven SSN-637s built in the late 1960s and early 1970s could probably last into the twenty-first century with refueling, they are also currently slated for retirement to free up funds for the

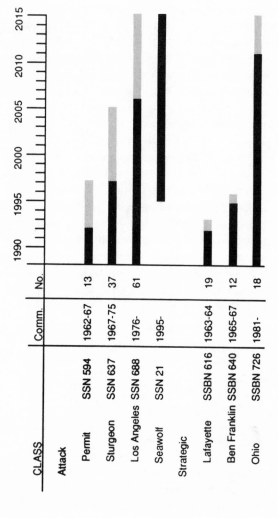

Figure 10-1. Submarine Retirement Schedule

SSN-21. As the *Sturgeons* come up for refuelings and refits they are instead being retired. With the cancellation of the *Seawolf* program, that might—and should—change. Finally is the huge, sixty-two-ship *Los Angeles* class, started in 1976 and still being built. These sixty-two submarines will not start to be retired until well after the start of the twenty-first century.

The 688s are a good example of "transition up," with two major block improvements. The SSN-719 *Providence* and all subsequent units are of an "improved" design, sometimes designated the SSN-688I class. The improved SSN-688s have better electronics, an advanced sonar and fire-control system, and better under-ice capabilities. Most important for the future, they also have a twelve-capacity VLS for Tomahawks. The earlier *Los Angeles* could launch Tomahawks (and Harpoons) from torpedo tubes but took up valuable torpedo space. The VLS capacity of the 688Is could almost give them an SSGN designation. From SSN-751 *San Juan* onward are even further improvements in electronics.

Strategic Submarines (SSBNs)

Until recently, there were three SSBN classes. These included the nineteen SSBN-616 *Lafayette* class and the twelve only slightly different SSBN-616 *Benjamin Franklin* class, which together were usually referred to as the "Poseidon" (missile) SSBNs. Then there are the new SSBN-726 *Ohio* class, usually referred to as the "Trident" (missile) SSBNs. Many of the nineteen *Lafayette* boats built from 1963 to 1964 have already been retired. Although they could last until 1994, the Navy recently announced that all will be retired by 1992.[3] Similarly, even though some of the *Benjamin Franklins* could last until 1997, the Navy announced that all will be retired by 1995.[4] Thus, in a very few years, the important SSBN "wet leg" of the triad will consist solely of Tridents. The Tridents should not need replacing for age reasons until 2010, although as pointed out in Chapter 4 there might be a need for small SSBNs to comply with future START agreements. There are twelve Tridents now in commission with six more currently planned. At one time the Navy planned to build at least twenty but now has stopped production at eighteen.

* * *

In short, in a very few years SSN strength, which now stands at around eighty-five, will shrink to approximately seventy-five with the retirement of the *Permits* and then to sixty-two by the end of the 1990s as the *Sturgeons* go out. The large sixty-two-ship SSN-688 class will soon be completed and will not need replacing until 2005, by which time work on a new SSN class should have begun. In this new interwar era, sixty-one-odd sophisticated SSNs might be sufficient for the foreseeable future. SSBN strength will drop drastically from thirty-six to only eighteen by 1995, remaining stable through the year 2010 (depending upon any new START requirements).

FUTURE PLANS

Until 1992, all plans for the submarine force could have been summed up in one word—*Seawolf.* Everything else in the submarine community was being sacrificed to fund the new SSN-21. This effort includes retiring submarines earlier than necessary and, in the case of the *Sturgeons*, not refueling them when needed. The Navy had originally planned to build the SSN-21 at a rate of three per year, then two, but that had recently been cut to one. With a thirty-year life expectancy, this meant an eventual thirty-ship submarine force—pre–World War I numbers. But now the size of the force might shrink even further, since cancellation of the *Seawolf* program includes the two previously authorized (although Congress might save them).

Quite frankly, the cancellation of the *Seawolf* should not have come as any surprise. The SSN-21 had long come under some severe criticism, with many in Congress calling for its complete cancellation. These criticisms were cost, current building problems, capabilities vis-à-vis the Soviets, and finally the numbers. Some of these criticisms were probably unfounded. The lead ship will cost approximately $2 billion—or, counting development costs, $5 billion, according to the Navy.[5] Once under series production, however, costs were expected to be in the $1.5 billion range, although that depended on the final shipbuilding rates. While certainly not cheap, in an era of billion-dollar destroyers *and* bombers these costs should not be too surprising.

The *Seawolf* was also experiencing some serious building pains, most involving the new AN/BSY-2 combat system. The combat system has run into a "variety" of problems, including "software development, finding enough programmers familiar with the Ada computer language, getting the fiberoptic data distribution system to work properly and meeting delivery schedules."[6] The BSY-2 combat system combines the roles of sonar and fire-control systems and was being developed concurrently with the submarine itself, a practice that many have criticized. These combat system problems have come under the close scrutiny of two watchdog committees in Congress. There are also serious welding cracks in the *Seawolf.* While these were troubling problems, they are also probably (and unfortunately) the normal, excruciating growing pains of any new system. While it is tempting to criticize concurrent development of the weapons and submarine systems for a new class, the alternative also seems questionable. That is, why develop a completely new, supposedly sophisticated class of submarines using old equipment? As the Navy has pointed out, virtually every new weapons system, including the Trident SSBN program that is now cited as a model of shipbuilding, initially had problems.

Some of the other criticisms of the *Seawolf* were, in this author's opinion, a little more troubling. These are the capabilities vis-à-vis the latest Soviet submarines and the numbers. Many commentators such as Norman Polmar have criticized the *Seawolf* for not being good enough.[7] Polmar notes that the USN has steadily lost the lead in twelve of fourteen key submarine technologies over the past thirty years. While in 1960 the Soviet Union had the lead in only two areas, with one about even, today they are ahead in seven and even in three others. By the year 2000 Polmar estimated that those 1960 ratios will be almost completely reversed, with the United States ahead in only two areas.[8] Others are disturbed by Soviet press reports of their developing 100-knot submarines capable of diving 8,000 feet.[9] Polmar claims the *Seawolf* "never should have been started."[10]

The *Seawolf* would have been a great improvement over the SSN-688 *Los Angeles* class. The 688, whose design can be traced back to the 1960s, had reached its capacity for growth. While there have been two 688I block improvements with better electronics, under-ice capabilities, etc., there was only so much room for further expansion in that old design. The SSN-21 will be ten times quieter than the 688I and thirty times quieter than the original 688s.[11] It will also have a greater weapons capacity, and the AN/BYS-2 will be a major improvement over the BYS-1. And there are many more advantages. This author has also been told that at least some of the items on the Polmar list indicating Soviet leads in submarine technology were wrong, and that talk of 100-knot Soviet submarines is just that—talk. With the turmoil in the CIS, new submarine construction has apparently ceased. However, while the SSN-21 will be an improvement and the United States might not be as far behind in certain submarine technologies as claimed, nevertheless the trends seemed disturbing, indicating that an SSN-21 follow-on, not cancellation, might have been warranted.

Perhaps the most disturbing problem was the eventual numbers. The Navy originally wanted to build three a year, which would have maintained an attack submarine force of ninety. Due to increasing costs and decreasing funds, this was later cut to two a year, then three every two years, and finally the one. With decreasing budgets, the one-per-year rate would have meant an eventual strength of only thirty SSNs. While the large sixty-two-ship *Los Angeles* class gives the Navy some breathing room for the next five years or so, when those submarines reach block obsolescence the numbers could drop precipitously.

There are currently no public plans for a new SSBN. While from an aging standpoint a new SSBN will not be needed until 2010, that completely ignores the arms control process—which by all indications will soon necessitate a new, smaller SSBN with considerably fewer launch tubes in order to meet future START requirements.

ALTERNATIVES

The cancellation of the *Seawolf* program now has added another Navy community to the "disarray" category. However, while Navy air does still have some readily available options, no such alternatives currently exist for submarines—and the Navy might have only itself to blame. Despite all the criticisms, for many years the Navy held the line on building the *Seawolf*. For example, a few years ago there was a newspaper account that the Navy was looking at an SSN-21 follow-on,[12] but the leadership "flatly" denied the existence of a *Seawolf* successor.[13] Some in Congress have suggested continuing to build 688Is in lieu of *Seawolf*, but that proposal was killed in committee. Finally, after it became obvious that *Seawolf* building rates would not increase, the Navy reluctantly gave in and announced it was looking at a "low-cost" SSN alternative tentatively named "Centurion." Although low cost, according to the Navy, it will have a full range of mission capabilities. The chairman of the seapower subcommittee, Representative Charles Bennett, and others have questioned whether a "cheaper, equally able submarine can be produced."[14] The real problem may be timing. Design on the Centurion has just started, with production slated for the late 1990s. This could leave a three- to five-year gap between the *Seawolf* and the Centurion, with the industrial base decimated in that period. Alternatives must be found.

Besides the Centurion, there are a host of alternatives across the complete building spectrum, from high to middle to lower levels—a multiple mix, with many relatively inexpensive options. The most obvious, immediate mid-level alternative (which would also keep the numbers and the industrial base up throughout the 1990s) would be to refuel and perhaps even modernize the SSN-637 *Sturgeons*. Refueling costs about $50–100 million, with another $100 million for modernization. Thus, for the cost of one or two *Seawolfs*, all *Sturgeons* could be refueled—or more likely, twenty of the later SSN-637s could be both refueled and modernized. While listed as a "mid-level" alternative, these are still very capable submarines with better under-ice capabilities that the early 688s.

The real issue, however, is the future of a truly sophisticated submarine to meet a twenty-first-century threat. Some analysts and congressional critics felt that the *Seawolf* should simply be terminated and a follow-on begun immediately. That would be a foolish, and extremely expensive, mistake. You simply do not switch on and off major programs. The SSN-21 is now into the eleventh year of a thirteen-year development plan, and as Vice Admiral Daniel Cooper, then assistant chief of naval operations for undersea warfare, stated, to think that the Navy can "immediately, like magic, build this other submarine . . . is an unrealistic scenario."[15] The SSN-688 has probably reached capacity, a follow-on is needed, and the SSN-21 will be an improvement.

While completely skipping the *Seawolf* generation would have been a costly mistake, it does seem a candidate for a "hop"—the Navy could build fewer than originally planned, work out the current problems, learn some lessons, and start developing that next-generation submarine. When the *Seawolf* program started in the early 1980s, the new, quiet Soviet submarines were starting to enter the fleet. An SSN-688 follow-on was needed—and by old Cold War standards, quickly. However, while the Russian commonwealth can still build first-rate submarines, that immediate threat has greatly diminished. With recent events in the former Soviet Union, no one anticipates a threat from that quarter for several years, at least. There is, in short, time for a respite, a transition, and the SSN-21 program can probably be slowed; but complete termination and especially recision of the two already authorized *Seawolfs* seems a waste. At least four to six SSN-21s should be built for three reasons: as prototypes, as possible "silver bullets," and, more important, as a way to maintain the nuclear submarine industrial base until a follow-on SSN is ready for production.

In short, three high-level alternatives should be considered. These are, by level of sophistication, an SSN-21 follow-on dreadnought, a small number of SSN-21s, or, only if necessary, more SSN-688Is as some in Congress want. The real need is an SSN-21 dreadnought follow-on or at least a prototype for evaluation. One author has suggested that the best approach might be a "submarine design competition."[16] Another has suggested:

> The United States should be continuously designing a submarine for production, in addition to the concept designs. The lead shipbuilder perhaps should be alternated between the two remaining submarine yards. Each yard would be on a ten-year design-and-build

Table 10-1. Submarine Modified Mix Alternatives

Level	Class	Concept/Comments
High	SSN-21 (Follow-on)	Prototypes (dreadnought)
	SSN-21	Hop a generation
	SSN-688I	Continue if needed
Mid	SSN-688	Modernize/transition-up SSN-688I
	SSN-637	Refuel/modernize
	SS(G)N	Dual use/combined/study (Centurion?)
Low	SSn	Combined/U.S. lead
	SSBn	For START II & III
	SS (AIP)	Combined/U.S. build one type
	SS	Export mode/FMS

cycle, with a five-year overlap. This way the builder would have a manageable production problem, and the Navy would benefit from a *new* class of submarine *every five years*. Follow-on ships of competing classes could be put out for bids for production at either yard.[17] (emphasis added)

A design competition between the two yards might be a better candidate for some of the R and D concepts such as capability without production or having both yards build prototypes. Since this will be a truly sophisticated ship, it might even be a candidate for a black program.

Building an advanced SSN dreadnought would be *very* expensive, potentially drying up shipbuilding funds. Thus, other alternatives are needed. Two mid-level alternatives seem possible. One already mentioned would be to simply refuel the still quite capable *Sturgeons*. Another would be to modernize the older, first-block SSN-688s as they come up for refueling and even to upgrade them (if possible) to 688I capabilities. While these two mid-level alternatives could help maintain the force for a time, eventually numbers and budgetary considerations would still become a problem. The only other obvious alternative is to build some low-end submarines, which leaves the Navy with only one realistic choice—nonnuclear boats.

For years, many naval analysts have suggested, and the Navy has steadfastly resisted, looking at nonnuclear (diesel) submarines. Diesel submarines are quieter, but their main attribute is cost, with current modes about $150–300 million—one-third the cost of current SSN-688s and one-sixth the cost of the SSN-21. There were several reasons, many legitimate, why the Navy opposed diesel submarines. The main military problem was that, although quieter when on batteries, while snorkeling to charge those batteries diesel submarines were detectable. However, the more practical and political reason was the Navy's fear that, once such a program started, Congress would force it to buy *only* diesel submarines. Both arguments are quite legitimate and understandable. However, these are changing times, and some exciting new submarine developments are being totally ignored by the Rickover-trained nuclear submarine force.

These new developments involve the emergence of so-called "air-independent propulsion" (AIP) alternatives now under R and D, with a few prototypes actually being built by European countries. These AIP alternatives would allow nonnuclear subs to remain submerged for long periods of time without snorkeling. They are called "air independent" because the air is recycled within the sub instead of being vented by snorkeling, which, as noted, was rather easily detectable by ASW methods. Thus, the primary military rationale for not building non-nuclear subs soon will disappear. Table 10-2 lists the different AIP alternatives under various stages of R and D. These are the Stirling engine, fuel cells, closed-cycle diesels, and closed-cycle gas-turbines.[18] In addition to these four "conventional" AIP alternatives, there is a "combined" engine proposal, sometimes dubbed SSn, that uses a small reactor to charge batteries.[19]

As shown in Table 10-2, all countries interested (with the exception of Sweden) are NATO allies, indicating that this might be a good area for multinational R and D and perhaps even eventual production. Different countries could take the lead, with others promising purchases. The concept that seems most appropriate for the United States to take the lead in is the SSn, the small reactor type. At one point Canada was interested in the SSn alternative but appears to have dropped out due to budget problems. However, to fully capitalize on the nonnuclear aspects the United States should also become involved in one of the other AIP alternatives, with some U.S. production.

There are many side benefits from developing the SSn and building SSs. The main benefit would be regaining some export possibilities that have been lost. The lack of a nonnuclear building capability meant that when U.S. Foreign Military Sale (FMS) funds were allocated to build some Israeli submarines, the money went to German instead of American ship-yards.[20] Egypt asked the United States to build a European-designed SS

Table 10-2. Air-independent Propulsion Concepts

Concept	Countries
Stirling engines	Sweden, France, the Netherlands, Germany
Fuel cells	Germany
Close-cycle diesels	U.K., the Netherlands, Germany, Italy
Close-cycle gas turbines	Germany
Small nuclear reactors	Canada

using FMS funds but the Navy intervened, citing national security problems! Several countries have expressed an interest in an SSn, including Canada and Turkey. The "small n" project might also help solve the large SSBN problem. A few six- to eight-tube SSBns could be built to keep strategic submarine numbers up. SSBns would also maintain strategic submarine community "commander" C.O. billets. The retiring Poseidon boats were skippered by commanders, but Tridents have full captains.

While other NATO countries might assume the lead on the nonnuclear SS developments, the United States should start building under license at least one of the most promising AIP proposals. The Navy should also drop its rather silly opposition to building current European modes under contract, especially those being built with U.S. FMS funds. As noted, this would give the United States a conventional-sub export capability; but there would be many other benefits. SSs could be placed in the Ready Reserves. Because of safety concerns, placing a nuclear boat, even an SSn, in the Ready Reserves might be impossible, but the same would not be true of nonnuclear boats. Finally, it would once more give the sub community some lieutenant commander skipper billets, which they desperately need.

There is one other lower-level option that has often been suggested and might be considered. That is, build a truly low-cost SSN with perhaps a (VLS) SSGN variant. There have been many suggestions over the years for building low-cost nuclear submarines,[21] and, as mentioned, the Navy has started another model called Centurion. Quite frankly, in this era of rising costs for virtually *anything* new this author would be surprised if starting a completely new SSN program, no matter what the intent, would save money. Any new SSN would probably fall into at least the high end of a mid-level category. However, it might be worth an expert's "summer study" to review all the low-cost proposals, old and new. There have been twenty-two different submarine studies since 1970 that could be reviewed.[22]

A better approach for a low-cost SSN might be a combined multinational SSN program with the Royal Navy, which will need a new SSN in a few years. Due to a lack of funds, the Royal Navy has had to scrap plans for a new submarine.[23] Perhaps France and even Canada might join a consortium. Allies would make sure the U.S. Navy kept costs down. Finally, a low-cost SSN might be a good candidate for a dual-use program as an SSGN needed for both theater and Third World operations.

As shown by Table 10-1, there are realistic submarine alternatives. Many fall into the "study" or "prototype" category, but that seems most appropriate for the submarine community for several reasons, not the least of which is lack of funds. While slowing the SSN-21 would free up some money, it would not be enough for major new programs. But there is another good reason. Although carriers will continue to be busy with Third World operations, as will surface combatants, the next few years could be a transition period for the submarine community. The sixty-two *Los Angeles* boats and few *Seawolfs* should be more than adequate for this transition period. Although the Soviet Union was building new, sophisticated submarines at old Cold War rates, that has apparently ceased and the overall CIS threat has dissipated for at least the next few years, allowing time for study and prototypes.

RECONSTITUTION/INDUSTRIAL BASE

Nowhere will there be a greater problem in reconstitution and maintaining a continuing industrial base than in nuclear submarine capability. Although the aircraft manufacturer base will undoubtedly shrink throughout the 1990s, between Air Force, commercial, and Navy requirements, there will probably always be at least a few aircraft manufacturers for some competition and redundancy. Similarly, most larger shipyards can build surface ships. However, there are only two nuclear submarine-capable shipyards—at Newport News, Virginia, and Electric Boat in Groton, Connecticut. But if the Navy builds only one or even two submarines a year, only one yard is likely to survive. Realizing their predicament, both shipyards have taken the issue of who will build that one sub in and out of court.

Now that the *Seawolf* has been canceled both yards could end up going out of business, especially if the Centurion project is delayed. Some commercial base might be maintained with refits, although most are now done in Navy yards. Groton is currently building six *Los Angeles* and finishing six Tridents, but all will be finished by the mid-1990s. Even one *Seawolf* per year cannot take up the slack of twelve boats.

The original Navy desire was for the Centurion to cost half as much as the *Seawolf* but have almost as much capability. Even if that is the case, Centurion will not hit the blocks until the late 1990s, probably too late to save both yards. The only realistic way to maintain a nuclear submarine-capable shipyard is the quick construction of a cheaper multinational design.

More realistic is maintaining one nuclear-capable yard, with another for AIPs. If the Navy had not vetoed the Egyptian request, there might have been a third yard—in Mississippi. The United States now should be able to maintain two, but only if some kind of multiple-mix scheme is followed. Building two Centurions a year might have kept both yards open, but by the time it is ready one will undoubtedly have already closed.

In short, in order to maintain some redundancy, another yard should be used to build nonnuclear or SSn modes. The Israeli and Egyptian requests might have given one yard several years' work. By that time, the conditions in the former Soviet Union and Third World threats should be sorted out.

RESERVE/DEPLOYMENT OPTIONS

There are several reserve/deployment options that should be considered, one of which was already mentioned—that is, building some nonnuclear AIP submarines for the Reserves. There has not been a reserve submarine for years because of safety concerns. Current safety rules preclude placing nuclear boats in the Reserves, but that would not necessarily be the case with SSs. This might also help with the sensitivity of building SSs in the current nuclear (active) Navy. But there are some more practical reasons. Submarine-trained reserve personnel often have no place to go for further training. An extremely large investment of time and money is wasted on those who quit the service after their initial obligation yet want to remain in the Reserves. The Reserves could probably sustain four or five SSs on each coast.

There are two other changes that should be considered. First are more operations in the Third World and the possibility of building, or at least designating, some submarines as SSGNs (or even SSGs). There seems little question that submarines will now have to be constantly deployed in Third World areas such as the Indian Ocean where they normally do not operate. Third World operations could present a multitude of new challenges to the submarine force. Since some countries have problems with nuclear-powered ships, this is another area where an SS or SSG might be useful. One problem often cited against SSs was the overseas distances involved, but that could easily be resolved by forward basing. Some U.S. SSs could even use the old SSBN Holy Loch anchorage recently abandoned. And a multinational NATO AIP SS could easily be maintained in foreign shipyards.

Then there is the whole question of nuclear deterrence. As noted in Chapter 4, in a few years the TLAM-N could constitute the only theater nuclear deterrent. The *Los Angeles* class with VLS could easily fulfill this function. Whether it should be a tethered SSGN just for theater deterrence or a multicapable SSN does not really matter for peacetime deterrence, but could during times of tension. If missile, chemical, and nuclear proliferation continues in the Third World, an SSGN might be appropriate for deterrence. An SSG might also be considered for this role.

Finally, the undersea community should probably be more forthcoming on its missions and capabilities, such as Admiral Bacon was in his references to submarine operations during a Middle East hostage situation. Submarines do have a role to play in many different situations, but their commanders' penchant for secrecy has often left that role unrecognized. That could be self-defeating in this new era of decreasing budgets. In short, it might be time for the old silent service to go public.

COMMENTS AND CONCLUSIONS

Submarines are vitally important to the security of the United States, and during major confrontations there could well be just two types of ships: submarines and targets. It is imperative, therefore, that the Navy maintain both the quality and quantity of the force—a goal that, unfortunately, is not compatible with current funding plans. It also may not be compatible with the current threats. While the SSN-21 is a major improvement over the SSN-688 class, it may not be, as former Under Secretary of the Navy Jim Woolsey said, that "quantum leap" needed for the new threats.[24] Therefore, work probably should begin on a follow-on. Then, in order to keep the numbers up, some medium- and even low-level options must also be considered. The most obvious would be to develop, in conjunction with our allies, some of the new AIP alternatives. A low-cost SSN should not be ruled out, but, if history is any guide, unless constrained by a multinational program a U.S. Navy–built SSN will be too expensive no matter what the intent. The options seem reasonable and, most important, relatively inexpensive. By using some type of multiple-mix scheme, the U.S. Navy can maintain the submarine force at adequate levels in both quantity and quality.

11 / Surface Combatants

Quantity Versus Quality

WHILE THE NATIONAL Command Authorities might like to ask, "Where are the carriers?" during a crisis, and while submariners argue about what will be the new capital ship for a World War III scenario, the most versatile and therefore numerous warships by far throughout history have always been the surface combatants—the real, "black shoe" navy of cruisers, destroyers, and frigates useful for crises, wars, and especially day-to-day naval presence missions. There are fourteen carriers and about eighty submarines, but the traditional surface navy totals approximately 150. Surface combatants have many different roles, ranging from screening carriers for both ASW and AAW, to vital SLOC protection (still important, as witness the recent events in the Persian Gulf, especially during the Iran-Iraq War), to those constant "show the flag" presence patrols also still needed in this continuing era of violent peace.

The reasons for such large numbers of surface combatants are not hard to fathom. No aircraft carrier battle group would dare operate without a screen of at least eight to ten surface combatants during wartime. This would include two to three AAW Aegis cruisers, two to three more guided missile destroyers (DDGs), and then an ASW screen of at least four ASW destroyers (DDs) or frigates. During intense operations in wartime, this screen would probably be increased to twelve. The Amphibious Ready Groups (ARGs) would similarly need extensive ASW escort protection and, closer to land, AAW screens as well. Once ashore, the Marines need gunfire support, which is always available from surface combatants.

Depending on their size and paths, merchant convoys would need anywhere from three to seven escorting frigates and, if operating within reach of enemy air power, probably some AAW DDGs or even CGs as well. Finally, underway replenishment ships—including both the combat logistic forces operating with the fleet as well as shuttle ships bringing supplies from home bases to forward operating areas—would require at least ASW frigate escort protection. Many, if not most, strategists feel that Japan made a crucial mistake on submarine use during World War II, especially immediately following their Pearl Harbor attack. Unlike the Germans, who did use their submarines for SLOC merchant ship interdiction, the Japanese campaigned only against warships. There was not a submarine "Battle of the Pacific" requiring hundreds of escorts to guard supply ships from the continental United States to forward areas in the Pacific to match the Battle of the Atlantic. Had the Japanese used their submarines first around Hawaii and later to interdict supplies to the forward American forces, they might have at the very least delayed defeat.

In short, there are numerous roles for surface combatants, many of which have been almost completely ignored in the fifty years since World War II. For example, Amphibious Ready Groups rarely operate with escorts. During the 1950s and 1960s, ARGs always had at least some old modified destroyer escorts (DEs), redesignated APDs (for fast amphibious assault), as token protection. APDs carried some Marines or Navy frogmen for reconnaissance and special operations; but under way, they were the amphibious groups' only escort, although they contributed little protection because they were equipped with old, obsolete sonar. The APDs could also provide limited gunfire support, usually from a single five-inch gun. Now, except in emergencies such as the recent Liberian crisis, amphibious groups generally operate without escorts.

Combat logistic ships rarely have screens. During so-called "realistic" naval exercises, there is a break every few days as a combat logistic ship comes steaming over the horizon, alone, to join the battle group for refueling and replenishment; then it departs, again alone, and the exercise resumes. Shuttle ships that actually bring supplies from the United States to forward areas similarly have no escorts. They are, in short, extremely easy targets for submarines. Even a Third World country willing to make a point could sink a USN combat logistic ship rather easily.

In sum, there is no dearth of missions for surface combatants. Therefore, *both* quality and quantity are important, and until recently this wide range of mission requirements has been the primary rationale for surface combatant shipbuilding. Throughout history there has always been a modified mix of different-sized surface combatants. In modern times, this has been a mix of high-level cruisers, mid-level destroyers, and lower-level destroyer escorts, now called frigates. The current force still reflects this traditional mix, but there is some question about the future.

CURRENT FORCES

Cruisers

As shown in Figure 11-1, the Navy currently has about thirty-five cruisers. These include three older, single-class nuclear cruisers and the nine-ship *Leahy* and the nine-ship *Belknap* classes, all commissioned during the 1960s. Service life for cruisers has been calculated at thirty to thirty-five years, which means that these twenty-one ships will probably be retired sometime during the 1990s. However, their numbers will be more than made up for by the new twenty-seven-ship CG-47 *Ticonderoga*-class guided missile cruisers, which have been entering the fleet since the mid-1980s. These sophisticated Aegis cruisers with phased array radar are the world's most capable AAW ships, developed to provide protection against both aircraft and antiship missiles. The CG-47s also have good ASW capabilities with two LAMPS helicopters and a sophisticated active-passive sonar. Finally, there are six nuclear-powered cruisers (CGNs) of the *California* and *Virginia* classes, built during the 1970s.

While the large *Leahy* and *Belknap* classes and older CGN cruisers will reach block obsolescence by the turn of the century, with the six *California*- and *Virginia*-class CGNs and the twenty-seven *Ticonderoga*-class CG-47s, cruisers should number well over thirty for the next twenty years. According to current estimates, that should be an adequate cruiser fleet. The Navy's goal was 1.5 Aegis cruisers per carrier, or three for each two-carrier battle group in high-threat areas, and then one for each independent battleship group. Thus, for fifteen carriers and four BBBGs the 27 CG-47s were needed. However, with fourteen or soon probably only twelve carriers and no BBBGs, the Navy only needs eighteen or so cruisers. Requirements might dictate at least one cruiser for each ARG, which again would push the number up to around twenty-seven. Regardless, the twenty-seven CG-47s should be more than adequate for the forseeable future, with the six CGNs providing even more flexibility.

Destroyers

The Navy has approximately sixty destroyers, about half primarily ASW DDs and the other half AAW DDGs. The ASW DD force consists of the relatively new thirty-one-ship *Spruance* DD-963 class. While the cruiser

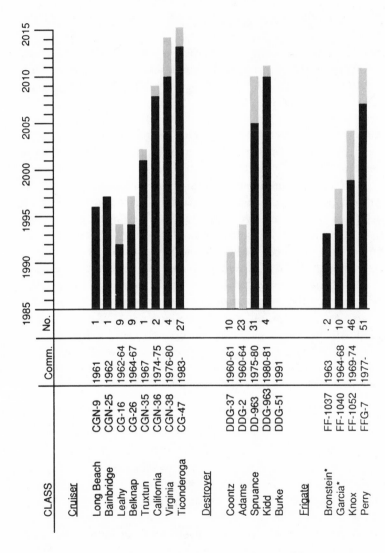

CLASS	Comm.	No.
Cruiser		
Long Beach CGN-9	1961	1
Bainbridge CGN-25	1962	1
Leahy CG-16	1962-64	9
Belknap CG-26	1964-67	9
Truxtun CGN-35	1967	1
California CGN-36	1974-75	2
Virginia CGN-38	1976-80	4
Ticonderoga CG-47	1983-	27
Destroyer		
Coontz DDG-37	1960-61	10
Adams DDG-2	1960-64	23
Spruance DD-963	1975-80	31
Kidd DDG-963	1980-81	4
Burke DDG-51	1991	
Frigate		
Bronstein* FF-1037	1963	.2
Garcia* FF-1040	1964-68	10
Knox FF-1052	1969-74	46
Perry FFG-7	1977-	51

* Already retired.

Figure 11-1. Surface Combatant Retirement Schedule

situation might be stable for the next two decades, there will be an apparent "DDG gap" in a very few years. Using the normal thirty-year life for destroyers, as shown in Figure 11-1, both the ten-ship *Coontz* class and the twenty-three-ship *Charles F. Adams* class, both built in the 1960s, are reaching block obsolescence; many have already been retired. This will leave only the four *Kidd-* or "Ayatollah"-class DDGs, built in the early 1980s. (These ships, built for the Shah of Iran, were taken over by the USN when he fell and are known sarcastically as the "Ayatollah" class.) Some consideration was given to modernizing the old DDGs, but costs proved to be prohibitive, especially for ships already near the end of their normal thirty-year life. To fill the DDG gap, the Navy has started building the DDG-51 *Arleigh Burke* class, with the first ship commissioned in 1991.

Traditionally, destroyers have been multimission ships used to complement and, in some cases, supplement other requirements. That is still their role. The DDGs are needed to complement the cruisers. Current estimates of screening requirements call for approximately two DDGs per carrier or four per carrier battle group, which means a force of about thirty for fifteen carrier battle groups. In addition, estimates call for two per ARG in high-intensity areas, and, again depending on their path, one or two for each merchant convoy. Thus, the Navy probably needs at least thirty-five to forty DDGs. Current estimates for ASW DDs are again about two per carrier, four per two-carrier battle group, and a couple for each ARG, for another total of thirty-five to forty. The thirty-one *Spruance*-class destroyers should meet the minimum ASW requirements through at least the early years of the twenty-first century, but with the retirement of the thirty-three-ship *Coontz* and *Adams* classes DDG numbers will rapidly shrink to only the four of the *Kidd* class until sufficient DDG-51s start entering the fleet in the late 1990s.

Frigates

The Navy has approximately one hundred frigates: the forty-six-ship *Knox* FF class, built primarily for ASW operations, and the newer fifty-one-ship FFG-7 *Oliver Hazard Perry* class, which has some limited AAW capabilities. Fifteen other frigates with some life remaining have been leased to foreign governments or retired. According to current plans, all the frigates except the FFG-7s will either be sold, placed in the reserves, or retired during the 1990s. There was some debate over whether the *Knox* class, commissioned in the early 1970s, should be modernized, but at best such ships would still have to be retired around the year 2000. Thus, it appears that only the FFG-7 *Perry* class, those much maligned "low" ships of Admiral

Zumwalt's high-low mix, will remain into the twenty-first century. Even with the retirement of the other frigate classes, the *Perrys* will still constitute about 40 percent of the surface combatant force. Smaller ships, DEs and now frigates, have usually been the most numerous for one simple, obvious reason—cost. There are, however, also many role and mission rationales for these lower-level ships. Their primary role has always been escorting merchant convoys and amphibious groups. Since convoys and even amphibious groups normally operate outside the range of enemy air envelopes, escorts need only limited AAW capabilities, their primary role being ASW. (Once in hostile areas, they would normally come under carrier battle group protection.)

The numbers for escorts vary, but if the Battle of the Atlantic is any guide literally hundreds of escorts would be needed to meet any major threat. In addition, frigates are extremely useful ships for showing the flag. Finally, they are quite frankly more expendable. In World War II the DEs were usually placed on the outer perimeter. This author suspects that during the Iran-Iraq War, one of the reasons FFG-7s were chosen for escort duty in the closed, dangerous, and mined Persian Gulf waters was their expendability. As tragic as the Exocet attack on the *Stark* FFG-31 and the mining of the *Samuel B. Roberts* FFG-58 were, they would have been considered worse had they happened to a cruiser. The mining of the *Princeton* CG-59 during the Iraq crisis, for example, was played down by the Navy.

Many have argued that for all these reasons, frigates have today overtaken the destroyer as the Navy's primary multipurpose ship. The *Perry*-class FFG-7s, built for convoy escorts, are now with the front-line carrier battle forces, and while it might be a "marriage of necessity," they are performing quite well.[1] Between their lower cost and general flexibility, they have replaced the once-ubiquitous general purpose destroyer in most navies. NATO navies have essentially become frigate forces, with some quite capable. Frigates have allowed the foreign navies to maintain both quantity and quality to some extent.

FUTURE PLANS

Building plans for the surface warfare community currently revolve around only one ship, the DDG-51, and a concept called "flexible transition."[2] The DDG-51 will be (or at least was to be) built in three distinct blocks or "flights," each incorporating new war-fighting and other improvements. In other words, there is a planned "transition up." Under current plans, the first two flights will total thirty-nine ships, replacing the thirty-three *Coontz-* and *Adams-*class DDGs. Flight II will have only modest upgrades, primarily in warfare and command and control.

Flight III, however, was to have major transition-up improvements to answer two of the three major criticisms of the DDG-51: lack of full helicopter facilities and limited magazine space. The current *Burkes* will have landing capabilities only, with no indigenous facilities for their own embarked helos. Their lack of full helicopter capabilities has come under severe criticism both from Congress and within the Navy itself.[3] The DDG-51 flight III, once scheduled for the 2000s, will have complete helicopter facilities. The *Burkes* have also been criticized for having only a ninety-missile magazine capacity versus the 122 in current CG-47s. Flight III upgrades will increase that capacity to 120. To add the helicopter facilities and increase magazine capabilities, the DDG-51 will be lengthened by twenty-three feet. If history is any guide, flight III DDGs will probably be designated as cruisers, CGs, which they probably should be according to current standards.

The third and final criticism leveled against the DDG-51 has to do with its cost.[4] The lead ship will cost about $1 billion. Critics pointed out that for about the same price the Navy could have continued to build CG-47s, which have both helicopter facilities and a much larger magazine. The Navy once estimated that follow-on DDG-51s would cost about $750 million, but that is now up to approximately $870 million. The effects of increasing costs and decreasing budgets are already being felt. The Navy originally planned to build the DDG-51 at the rate of up to ten per year, but that has been reduced to four to five per year with further cuts probably inevitable. To further save funds, the fully capable DDG-51 flight III has been put on hold.

Between "prospects for continuing budget cuts and changes in future warfare missions," the Navy has announced a Destroyer Variant Study (DVS) and is currently looking at some six to ten different alternatives. Construction of the follow-on DDG-51 type is tentatively scheduled to begin in 1998. According to some reports, the destroyer variants range from having limited ASW capabilities, to reevaluating the old eight-inch gun proposals to support amphibious groups. Cost estimates are approximately $600 million per copy, but that is sure to escalate. To save money, the Navy was looking at variants with no sonar, which has not happened since the old flush decks from World War I.[5] Since the Navy's goal is still a 150-ship surface combatant force, other alternatives might be required.

Flexible Transition

The Navy has also announced a new concept called "flexible transition." According to this plan, instead of the traditional cruiser-destroyer-frigate modified mix, ships will be classified as either front-line "battle force combatants" (BFC) or "protection of shipping" (POS) escorts. Henceforth, ships will be built as multimission BFCs with phased array radar, Aegis-type battle management systems, a vertical launch system (VLS) of 60–120 cells, advanced surface-to-air missiles, and an SQQ-89 antisubmarine combat system. Then as they get older and their "battle" capabilities degrade with the onward march of technology, they would be moved into the POS escort role.

There are some obvious advantages to flexible transition. First, there would be only one basic ship type instead of the current dozen different classes. Today's present surface combatant force lineup under the new concept is:

- **BFC:** CG-47, CG-16/26, CGNs, DDG-2 & 37, DDG-993, DD-963
- **POS:** FFG-7, FF-1052, FF-1098, FF-1037

These twelve classes were all to be replaced by the DDG-51 and subsequent flights. With similar combat, hull, mechanical, and electrical systems, this should be both a shipbuilder's and a logistician's dream come true. And there are other benefits. Instead of spending millions, if not billions, of dollars modernizing old ships to maintain their capabilities, it does make a certain amount of sense to simply move them to less demanding missions. As mentioned earlier, there were once plans to modernize the DDG-2 *Adams* class, but expenses became prohibitive, many times their original cost.

There are, unfortunately, some rather obvious disadvantages. This concept could be used as a rationale—perhaps even a justification—for building *only* high-level ships. The Navy's goal was once an approximately 200-ship surface combatant force (now lowered to 150). Even assuming the rather optimistic forty-year life for the new *Burkes* requires that the original building plan be followed. And if history is any guide, building low-cost or stripped DDG-51s or a destroyer variant will save little. To truly solve its problem, the Navy must return to a modified mix.

As the force evolves, the Navy will—for the first time in modern history—not have a traditional modified mix of cruisers, destroyers, and frigates. As shown in Table 11-1, during the 1950s the Navy built the large *Norfolk* and *Mitcher* "destroyer leaders" that today would be considered cruisers, *Forrest Sherman*-class destroyers and three different classes of DEs. During the 1960s, there were two cruiser and destroyer classes and, again, three frigate classes built. Even in the 1970s post-Vietnam interwar period there was a modified mix of two CGN classes, the *Spruance* ASW DDs, and two frigate classes, first the large *Knox* FF class in the early 1970s and then the larger *Perry* FFG-7 class in the late 1970s and throughout most of the 1980s. The major change came in the 1980s, when traditional simul-

Table 11-1. Surface Combatant Modified Mix: 1950–2000

	1950s	1960s	1970s	1980s	1990s
Cruisers	Norfolk, Mitscher	Leahy, Belknap	California, Virginia	Ticonderoga	
Destroyers	Sherman	Countz, Adams	Spruance	Kidd	Arleigh Burke
Frigates	Dealey, Courtney, Jones	Bronstein, Garcia, Brooke	Knox	Oliver Hazard Perry	

taneous building ceased. Instead of building the three traditional levels, only one was built: the CG-47 *Ticonderoga* cruisers, now being followed by the DDG-51 *Arleigh Burke* class.

Besides the crucial cost issue, there is a question as to whether the current DDG-51 is the right ship for *today's* environment. When conceived in the early 1980s, with the upcoming block obsolescence of the DDG-2 and DDG-37 classes, a DDG was "urgently needed," as this author once wrote;[6] and it appeared the *Burke* was indeed the right ship for the twenty-first century.[7] However, that was at the height of the Cold War, when the Soviet Navy was the major threat and the Maritime Strategy envisioned wide-ranging, open-ocean global warfare. The DDG-51 was envisioned as part of a layered defense for a carrier battle group.

Times have changed. Third World operations are now the top priority, and the DDG-51 may not be the right ship for Third World operations for one specific reason—lack of helicopter facilities. While one reason the *Perrys* were chosen for Persian Gulf operations was that they were more available, another was their flexibility, with both AAW and especially helicopter capabilities allowing Marine and even Army helicopter operations off them. This became crucial for the Persian Gulf and would be important for most Third World operations. Ships with helicopters allow tremendous flexibility; witness the *Mayaguez* rescue off Cambodia in 1976. Without helicopter capabilities, the DDG-51 could not (or should not) operate independently. If this author were commanding an operation in a typical Third World crisis, he would prefer the flexibility of a helicopter-capable FFG-7 over a DDG-51. In short, for several reasons from cost to mission flexibility, it appears that alternatives must be considered.

ALTERNATIVES

With only two classes currently being built, the CG-47 and the DDG-51, both of which are sophisticated and expensive, there are few immediate alternatives for building a smaller, less costly ship to maintain the numbers. Until quite recently, there was an option that could have solved the quantity-quality dilemma as well as other problems. That was the common NATO Frigate Replacement for the 1990s (NFR-90) program, which, according to the original schedule, would have begun soon. One by one, the eight countries involved all dropped out for what are often called "NIH"—"not invented here"—reasons. While the U.S. Navy was never wholeheartedly enthusiastic about the program, it was at least committed to building a few of these ships. That would at least have opened up a production line. A new NATO frigate is one alternative that should be resurrected.

Something has to be done to maintain the numbers of surface combatants. During the 1990s, the fleet will probably lose over one hundred surface combatants: twenty-one cruisers, thirty-three DDGs, and over fifty frigates. About one-third that number will come on line: the remaining ten-odd CG-47s still being built and perhaps ten to twenty DDG-51s, probably less. While an alternative could be to increase DDG-51 buys, their expense will probably prohibit that option, as will the expense of any destroyer variant. The only alternative is a frigate. Yet starting from ground zero, even a lower-level ship has often proven expensive. Therefore, both combined and dual-use programs should be revisited.

The most obvious solution would be a new U.S.-led NFR-2000, using the NFR-90 design with the latest "off the shelf" equipment. As noted in Chapter 4, with the changes in Europe and the possible emergence of SACLANT as the senior NATO military leader, more attention should be

Table 11-2. Surface Combatant Modified Mix Proposals

Level	Class	Concept/Comments
High	BB (East)	Combined/NATO flagship
	BB (West)	In reserve/reserve
	CSGN	Dreadnought
	CG-51	Transition-up/DDG-51 Flight III
	CL-963	8″ gun cruiser on 963 hull
Mid	DDG-51 (TH)	Transition-up/DDG-51 II telescopic hangar
	DDG-51	Hop a generation/build few
	CMC	Prototype/study
	DDG	Combined/study/non-Aegis
	DD-963 (Variants)	Dual use/study/APD/V/STOL
Low	FFG	Combined/NATO frigate
	FF	Dual use/combined
	FF (Knox)	Modernize/in reserve
	Corvette (Sa'ar)	Combined/dual use/export
	Patrol	Dual use/export

given to the role and needs of NATO navies. It will not be easy, but then NATO navies themselves will also be looking for assistance. While the United States should take the lead, there seems room for considerable compromise to overcome NIH problems. Some of the Europeans already are building interesting smaller frigates. The latest British type-23 *Norfolk* class, only 3,500 tons, has a VLS. The Germans have their Meko "modular" frigate specifically designed for many different weapon suites. There are recent reports of a possible Royal Navy–French joint frigate project the United States could join.[8] Most European propulsion systems are combined diesel–gas turbine (CODOG). The French have made advances in large diesel propulsion. Diesel or even combined systems are easier to operate than manpower-intensive, boiler-driven steam ships. There is currently a consortium of six countries looking at NAWS, a naval antiair system for smaller ships. And the list goes on. There are, in short, no lack of NATO navy options, either on the shelf or already under development.

Besides NATO, there are many countries that are likely candidates for purchasing such a frigate. Australia has in the past bought American ships, the *Adams* DDG and more recently the FFG-7. It is currently looking at the German Meko design. Taiwan may buy as many as sixteen French light frigates,[9] and Korea has a KDX destroyer replacement program;[10] both are longtime friends and allies of the United States. Some twenty-odd World War II American-built destroyers in the service of foreign navies will soon need replacing. Many Latin American Rio Pact allies are similarly looking for affordable replacements.

The United States should also consider dual-use ships for the reserves and possibility even the Coast Guard. The Coast Guard has nine *Hamilton*-class, frigate-size cutters, built in the late 1960s and early 1970s, that will probably need replacing in the next two decades. At one point, thirty-six *Hamiltons* were planned to meet further needs—and this was even before the Coast Guard took the lead in the antidrug war. The best place for a U.S. dual-use frigate might be in a rejuvenated Naval Reserves force. Current plans are for the *Knox* class to be placed in the reserves. They are all steam driven and difficult to maintain, especially for part-time sailors. A diesel-driven frigate, or even combined diesel–gas turbine systems, would be considerably easier to maintain and far less expensive in manpower or material than those with steam boilers. A few of these new diesel or CODOG frigates could even be built as training ships.

Thus, between NATO, other potential foreign buyers, and U.S. dual-use, Coast Guard, reserve, and training needs, there should be sufficient volume to initiate a new program. An NFR-2000 would not necessarily have to be a completely new design. There are many existing hulls, propulsion systems, and even weapon systems on the shelf or in development to make a Frigate 2000 a quite capable ship.

* * *

There are two other low-level options that should be considered: building corvettes and patrol boats. The U.S. Navy has always eschewed building smaller ships like corvettes. While corvettes have some limited open-ocean capabilities, they are usually considered coastal craft. Since the U.S. Navy has to operate overseas, corvettes were generally deemed unsuitable. However, corvettes have many export, combined, and even dual-use capabilities that make them a viable option. In fact, the United States is currently building a very capable corvette class, the Sa'ar V, for Israel. The Sa'ar is an extremely versatile ship, chockablock with weapons including helicopter, ASW, ASuW, and even AAW capabilities all contained in an 86-meter (284-foot), 1,170-ton ship capable of making over thirty knots while carrying a crew of only sixty or so. It even has state-of-the-art technology to minimize radar cross section and infrared contrast as well as acoustic signature automated controls for machinery.[11]

The Sa'ar already has satisfied one extremely important criterion for the future—start-up costs. It *is* being built (for export). For the first time, the United States finally has a design to compete in the lucrative smaller-ship export market. It is also, incidentally, being built with American foreign military sale (FMS) funds, which could undoubtedly be offered to other countries as well. The Sa'ar should also be considered for some U.S. dual-use missions. While it has limited open-ocean capabilities, these corvettes could certainly be deployed in the Persian Gulf permanently out of Bahrain, since the United States will undoubtedly need some presence in that part of the world for many years to come. They could also operate in the Caribbean, the Mediterranean, and perhaps even in some ASEAN areas.

A Sa'ar variant might also be used in a dual-use mode by the Coast Guard. In 1990 the Coast Guard commissioned the last of the somewhat similarly sized *Bear*-class cutter, which has been severely criticized as undergunned and underpowered. The thirty-three-knot, well-armed Sa'ar certainly answers those criticisms. Some Sa'ars could also be placed in the reserves, and with only sixty-man crews they would be perfect for new state Navy National Guards with perhaps another dual use as Coast Guard reserve ships. And they would also give more junior officers, probably lieutenant commanders, some command opportunities again. Since the retirement of the old DEs, LCDRs have generally been frozen out of surface combatant commands.

The United States should also look at new patrol boat options. There were once plans to build a follow-on to the hydrofoil *Pegasus*-class PHMs built in the 1970s, but that was dropped. Once again, there could be some export, combined, and possibly even dual-use possibilities. One author long ago suggested that the Navy and Coast Guard look at building a common minesweeper/patrol boat. If a small ship is built, there should be some commonality so that these craft can be easily converted to mine-sweepers. The National Oceanic and Atmospheric Administration (NOAA) is building oceanographic research ships that might be perfect as backup oceangoing minesweepers since they would already have some sophisticated equipment. The Navy has a program called "Craft of Op-portunity" (COOP) that provides for the conversion of smaller craft for minesweeping. Building some initial commonalities into Coast Guard and NOAA boats would certainly facilitate any conversion.

Perhaps most important, building some patrol boats would maintain a so-called "brown-water navy" island riverine capability. The U.S. Navy developed a vast armada of various brown-water boats during Vietnam, but that capability is almost gone. With Third World operations once more foremost, that capability should be rebuilt in some manner. Patrol boats could also be used for Navy National Guards and the reserves as well as for training ships.

* * *

What about the DDG-51? Although something must be done, and soon, to ensure that adequate numbers of surface combatants are built, the DDG-51 should not be abandoned at this point. The *Burke* is a definite improvement over previous DDG classes and should be continued. It does appear, however, to be a good candidate for "hopping a generation." The DDG-51 was once needed to fill two gaps: the numbers gap from the thirty-three retiring DDGs of the *Coontz* and *Adams* classes and the mis-sions gap between carriers and CG-47s to meet the Soviet threat. While the current thirty-three DDGs will still be retired, the changes in the world situation have made the mission gap less apparent. The twenty-seven GC-47s should more than satisfy most current AAW screen re-quirements. Today, more important than meeting CIS threats is the need for versatility for Third World operations, meaning that the DDG-51 should have full helicopter capabilities. Therefore, it seems appropriate that only a minimum number of flight I and II DDG-51s be built (one or two per carrier battle group), "hopping" to a helicopter-capable mode as soon as possible.

Under current plans, the DDG-51 was not scheduled to receive full helicopter capabilities until flight III, which also adds magazine space that will lengthen the ship. Hopping to flight III immediately would probably be too expensive, but there might be a compromise. A consortium of European companies has submitted a proposal to equip *Burkes* with a telescopic hangar and appropriate equipment for only $2 million.[12] Incorporating telescopic hangars into the flight II DDG-51s would make them, once again, truly multimission destroyers capable of some independent Third World operations. In sum, the DDG-51 seems a good candidate for a generation hop—build a few to start the series production, and then make the transition up to a limited helicopter capable flight II when ready and finally to a fully helicopter capable flight III, larger, cruiser-size "CG-51," after the turn of the century.

There are other surface ship options that should be considered. At the high end, two of the four recommissioned battleships could have been kept in commission, with a little imagination. As mentioned in Chapter 4, consideration should be given to maintaining one battlewagon on the East Coast as a NATO flagship complete with multinational crew. Another could be maintained "in reserve" on the West Coast with a one-third active, two-thirds reserve crew. A primary reason for the BB retirements was the intense manpower requirements, but that could be solved in the one case by multinational crews, and the other with reserves. These BB could also make good training ships for both recruits and midshipmen. Another high-level option might be the building of a nuclear-powered "strike" cruiser (CSGN) prototype "dreadnought." During the 1970s there were proposals for a strike cruiser that could operate independent of air cover with only a few escorts as a surface action group (SAG). With long-range Tomahawks and Aegis, that becomes even more of a possibility.

*   *   *

There are other destroyer and even lower-cost cruiser options that might be considered, especially since the versatile DD-963 hull is still being built (for the CG-47s). One would be a non-Aegis DDG for combined and possibly even American use. There are AAW electronic suite alternatives to the Aegis such as the New Threat Upgrade that would be quite adequate for Third World threats. The DD-963 hull might also be adapted for a new amphibious escort, APD-variant. These large ships could easily carry some Marines or Navy Seals while still providing some ASW escort duties. The two-helicopter capability of an APD-963 would be perfect for special operations.

Also, the lightweight eight-inch gun proposal might be revisited for these new APDs, or a CL-963 gun cruiser might be built. There were proposals for a lightweight eight-inch gun in the 1970s to give Marines additional gunfire support.[13] And with the retirement of the BBs, some CL-963s with 8 inch guns might be needed. APD or CL-963 variants with two eight-inch guns and LAMPS ASW helicopters will make perfect escorts for amphibious ready groups. Even better might be an APDG with limited AAW capabilities. As mentioned in Chapter 9, the DD-963 hull should also be reconsidered for a small V/STOL variant, complete with Skyhook. To test the cruise missile carrier (CMC) concept, the DD-963 hull might again be used, but chockablock with VLS and with no guns or helos. The new DDV variant proposals should not necessarily be abandoned, but rather reevaluated in light of these other options. Finally, to maintain a viable surface combatant force through the 1990s, the *Knox* class should be modernized somewhat, even if sent to reserve status or laid up in ordinary. It has been estimated that all forty-seven could be modernized for only $500 million, half the price of a DDG-51.[14]

In short, and as shown in Table 11-2, there are a host of proposals to revitalize the surface combatant force ranging from high to low, from battleships and strike cruisers to patrol boats; many meet the cost criteria imposed by an era of decreasing budgets. With the exception of a CSGN, none of the proposed modified mix alternatives would actually involve the considerable expense of starting from the drawing boards. Many are simply adaptations of existing designs. The "new" frigate would be a combined NATO and dual-use FFG, something that has been under study for years. A non-Aegis DDG, CL, APD, CMC, or even V/STOL-capable ship should only be constructed if readily adaptable from the current DD-963/CG-47 hull.

RECONSTITUTION/INDUSTRIAL BASE

The only work that has kept American shipyards busy has been Navy repairs and upkeep and new construction. With the fleet shrinking from 600 to 450 (or fewer) ships, yard availability requirements will similarly decrease. Also, since only newer ships are being maintained, they should require less upkeep. New construction is similarly slowing down. There were once plans to build the DDG-51 in three shipyards, but now only two can sustain the levels. As will be noted in the next chapter, auxiliary and amphibious shipbuilding rates are also declining drastically. In short, American shipbuilding capacity will probably decline even further during the 1990s.

Returning to a modified mix of surface combatants could help ease that decline. Moving to dual-use and combined programs could also help, especially for lower-level ships. For example, if the United States built a corvette or a cheaper frigate, it might be able to compete for "light frigate" contracts in the Third World markets. Ships like the DDG-51 are simply too expensive, even for most Western European countries.

To maintain the American shipyards, something like an industrial policy might be followed by the United States and the Navy, with certain yards designated to build smaller vessels such as patrol boats and mine craft, others for corvettes and frigates, and a third level for major surface combatants such as destroyers and cruisers. Others could be designated to build the less sophisticated auxiliary and amphibious ships. While industrial policy is anathema to most Americans, considering that virtually all foreign shipyards are subsidized in some manner there seems little alternative pending some formal trade agreements. The United States, a maritime power, must maintain this reconstitution/industrial base in some new, imaginative manner.

RESERVE/DEPLOYMENT OPTIONS

There are several deployment and reserve options for the surface forces, many of which have already been mentioned—maintaining the two battleships in commission, one as a NATO flagship and the other in reserve with a combined active-reserve crew, for example, or forward-deploying corvettes in appropriate places such as the Persian Gulf. As mentioned in Chapters 5 and 6, new frigate STANAVFORs in NATO and certain Third World areas could also be considered. If built around new standard frigates, they could be more easily maintained in forward areas.

New reserve options should be explored. Traditionally, surface combatants have moved into the reserves as they got older; this appears to be the current plan for the older frigates now slated for the reserves. The exception has been that some of the early but still relatively young FFG-7s were moved into the reserves in the mid-1980s to upgrade reserve capabilities. With the importance of the reserves increasing, two new notions should be considered. First, reorganize them into truly battle-ready squadrons. In the past, older destroyers or frigates were simply placed near larger cities and generally operated independently. Squadrons or at least smaller divisions might be appropriate especially if made part of the "flying squadrons" built around the reserve carriers and LPHs, as suggested in Chapter 9. It might be most appropriate to have specific assignments or perhaps two *Knox* FFs and FFG-7s for each flying squadron as a permanent screen. They should be co-located in order to train and operate with the reserve carriers and LPHs.

Second, build ships specifically for the reserves. As noted, diesel ships are considerably easier to maintain. If, as some predict, the reserves will become a greater part of the total force, serious consideration must be given to designing ships for part-time sailors. This includes not only propulsion systems that are easier to maintain and operate, but electronic suites as well. An Aegis ship, for example, would probably require too much constant upkeep and maintenance for a reserve crew to handle. Corvettes would make good reserve ships, as would patrol boats—with the latter maintaining some brown-water capabilities in the U.S. Navy.

COMMENTS AND CONCLUSIONS

Surface combatants, which have always formed the backbone of the Navy, may be outnumbered by the submarine force when the *Spruance* DD and *Perry* FFG-7 classes reach block obsolescence in the first decade of the twenty-first century. The force might end up consisting of only the CG-47 and DDG-51 classes, which, while sophisticated, will not be nearly numerous enough considering the multitude of surface combatant mission requirements envisioned for the future. And they may not be the right ships for many Third World situations, especially for closed waters. Considerably more useful for Third World situations would be an all-gun CL or APD variants built on the DD-963/CG-47 hull.

The major problem is numbers. CG-47s and DDG-51s are too expensive to be built in any numbers. The only alternative is the return to a more traditional surface combatant mix, requiring a frigate to offset the expensive cruisers and destroyers. While building corvettes or even patrol boats might help in some limited areas, the top priority should be to build a new ship in the old destroyer escort (now frigate) range. Numbers will always be important.

12 / Balance of the Fleet

Maintaining the "Blue"

THIS BOOK, LIKE most books on navies, invariably looks at the "warships"—the carriers, submarines, and surface combatants. But they are only part of the fleet, and, some could argue, not even the most crucial part. There are three other important forces: the auxiliaries, the amphibious fleet, and the mine craft. Also not to be forgotten is the Marine Corps. This chapter will look briefly at these four forces.

AUXILIARY FLEET

Most naval analysts, when defining "blue-water" navies, usually refer to battleships, aircraft carriers, cruisers, and large destroyers—that is, those ships capable of operating far from coastal waters. While these large ships usually do have a greater capacity for fuel and supplies, for any sustained operations (especially in wartime) they must still be constantly supplied with "beans, bullets and black oil"[1]—and that requires auxiliary and support ships. As Adm. Carlisle Trost stated while chief of naval operations, "It is the ability to resupply our forces at sea that separates a coastal Navy from a truly 'blue water' force that can remain at sea without dependence on forward bases."[2] Without adequate support, no fleet can last long. One reason why many naval analysts never considered the Soviet Navy a true blue-water fleet despite its large ships (including aircraft carriers, cruisers, and even "battle-cruisers") was "the short reach of Soviet naval logistics."[3]

Historically, the most limiting factor for a ship has always been supplies. While armies could "live off the land," navies had no such luxury.

The major modern problem developed when ships started to switch from sail to steam. Alfred Thayer Mahan in his lectures at the Naval War College noted, "It would be amusing, were it not painful, to see our eagerness to have fast ships, and our indifference to supplying them with coal."[4] At another time he stressed the importance of logistics in strategic matters: "For fuel is the life of modern naval war; it is the food of the ship: without it the modern monsters of the deep die of inanition. Around it, therefore, cluster some of the most important considerations of naval strategy."[5] It should be recalled that part of the "race" in the latter part of the nineteenth century during the so-called Age of Imperialism was for support bases, then called "coaling stations." Great Britain had her magnificent system—from Gibraltar and Malta in the Mediterranean to Aden, to ports in India and Ceylon, and then Singapore and Hong Kong in the Far East. In addition to this depot system, the Royal Navy in 1911 established the Royal Fleet Auxiliary of civilian supply ships for the fleet.

The U.S. Navy also has a long and proud history. When the United States entered World War I, two destroyer tenders were sent to Queenstown and, to the surprise of some, were able to adequately support the destroyer force[6]—a forerunner of events in the Pacific in World War II. While there were some interwar innovations, the greatest developments and growth came during World War II. The U.S. Navy developed many new tactics; alongside "abeam" replenishment was one of the most innovative. The Royal and German navies used the "astern" method of refueling, which, while simpler, was considerably slower. Also, only fueling could be accomplished. The U.S. Navy developed the now standard abeam "underway replenishment" (UNREP) method, which was faster and allowed the transfer of stores and ammunition as well as fuel. The U.S. auxiliary and support force was crucial for victory in the Pacific. Its importance can be seen from its numbers, which grew from just seventy-seven ships in 1940 to over two thousand in 1945.[7]

The generic terms "auxiliary" and "support" do not do justice to the complexity of these categories. As shown in Table 12-1, there are some thirty different types. These are often broken down into two broad categories, which themselves have subgroups.[8] The two broad categories are Mobile Logistics Ships, capable of providing underway replenishment to fleets, and Material Support Ships, which are repair ships or tenders. Then there are Support Ships designed to provide general support to either the fleet or shore establishments. The ships in these categories are:

- *Mobile Logistics Ships*
    Underway Replenishment—AE, AF, AFS, AO, AOE, AOR
    Material Support (Tenders)—AD, AR, AS

Table 12-1. U.S. Navy Auxiliary and Support Ship Types

Designation	Definition
AD	Destroyer tender
AE	Ammunition ship
AF	Store ship
AFS	Combat store ship
AG	Miscellaneous auxiliary
AGF	Miscellaneous flag
AGDS	Deep submergence support ship
AGM	Missile range instrumentation ship
AGOR	Oceanographic research ship
AGOS	Ocean surveillance ship
AGS	Survey ship
AH	Hospital ship
AK	Cargo ship
	Maritime prepositioning ship
AKR	Vehicle cargo ship
AO	Fleet oiler
AOE	Fast combat support ship
AOG	Gasoline tanker
AOR	Replenishment oiler
AOT	Transport oiler
AP	Transport
AR	Repair ship
ARC	Cable repair ship
ARL	Small repair ship
ARS	Salvage ship
AS	Submarine tender
ASR	Submarine rescue ship
ATA	Auxiliary tug
ATF	Fleet tug
ATS	Salvage and rescue ship
AVB	Aviation logistic ship

Source: Norman Polmar, *Ships and Aircraft of the U.S. Fleet,* 14th ed. (Annapolis, Md.: Naval Institute Press, 1987).

- *Support Ships*
  Fleet Support—ARS, ASR, ATA, ATF, ATS
  Other—AG, AGDS, AGF, AGM, AGOR, AGOS, AGS, AH, AK, AKR, AOG, AOT, AP, ARC, ARL, AVB

The underway replenishment types, often simply referred to as UN-REP ships, are now called the Combat Logistics Force (CLF). The Navy has developed a sophisticated three-step wartime replenishment process. Step one consists of merchant ships transporting supplies from the United States to civilian ports or naval forward bases close to the fleets. In the second stage, supplies are transferred to single-product oilers and ammunition, dry good, and food store ships referred to as shuttle ships. The shuttle ships in turn transfer their goods to multiproduct ships referred to as station ships, which are fast combat support ships (AOEs) or fleet replenishment oilers (AORs). In the third stage, the station ships transfer supplies to the combatants, acting as either a "gas station" with the combatant steaming to a rendezvous point or as a "delivery truck" with the station ship steaming to the fleet. The multiproduct station ships can transfer supplies to two combatants at one time, while also using helicopters for "vertical replenishment" (VERTREP).

Current Forces

As shown in Table 12-2, the United States has approximately 180 ships in the auxiliary fleet, about eighty with Navy crews and the rest in the

Table 12-2. U.S. Navy Auxiliary Force

Type		Total	USN	MSC
AD	Destroyer tender	9	9	
AE	Ammunition ship	13	12	1
AF	Store ship	1		1
AFS	Combat store ship	10	7	3
AGM	Missile range ship	3		3
AGOR	Oceanographic research	4		4
AGOS	Ocean surveillance	10		10
AGS	Survey ship	9		9
AH	Hospital ship	2		2
AK	Cargo ship	3		3
	Maritime preposition	8		8
AKR	Vehicle cargo ship	1		1
AO	Fleet oiler	22	7	15
AOE	Fast combat support	4	4	
AOR	Replenishment oiler	7	7	
AOT	Transport oiler	24		24
AR	Repair ship	2	2	
ARC	Cable repair	3		3
ARL	Small repair ship	1	1	
ARS	Salvage ship	10	10	
AS	Submarine tender	12	12	
ASR	Submarine rescue ship	6	6	
ATF	Fleet tug	9	2	7
ATS	Salvage & rescue ship	3	3	
AVB	Aviation logistics	2		2
	Totals	178	82	96

Source: Normal Polmar, *Ships and Aircraft of the U.S. Fleet,* 14th ed. (Annapolis, Md.: Naval Institute Press, 1987); *Jane's Fighting Ships,* 1989–90 edition.

civilian-manned Military Sealift Command (MSC). MSC ships, which have the prefix designation "T," are an important part of the auxiliary structure and could well become even more crucial in the future.

While all the ships are important in their own way from a fleet perspective, the most critical are the fast combat support ships. Until the early 1960s, replenishment fleets and tactics varied little from those developed in World War II. Replenishment ships were single-product ships— AOs, AEs, and store ships. That changed in the early 1960s with the deployment of the *Sacramento* (AOE)-class fast combat support ships. These large ships were multiproduct and had the speed (twenty-six knots) to keep up with the fleet. At 54,000 tons, the *Sacramentos* are still the world's largest support ships (with the exception of the single Russian *Berezina*). They can carry 194,000 barrels of fuel, 2,100 tons of munitions, 250 tons of dry stores, and 250 tons of refrigerated stores. They were soon followed by the *Wichita*-class AORs, which although a little smaller and slower were still capable of fleet support.

The U.S. Navy currently has four *Sacramento*-class AOEs built from 1964 to 1970, and seven *Wichita*-class AORs built from 1969 to 1976. Work has begun on a new AOE-6 *Supply* class, with at least four planned. This would give the fleet a combination of fifteen fast combat support ships, one per carrier group. The Navy is also building some nineteen MSC *Henry J. Kaiser* T-AO fleet oilers, which have a limited UNREP capacity for dry stores. Service life for auxiliaries has usually been at least forty years, so most of these ships should remain in the fleet well into the twenty-first century.

A few other ship types deserve special mention. The Material Support Ships, or "tenders," are also important. While tenders cannot perform extensive upkeep and maintenance, they can normally provide for those minor, constant repairs that are needed during prolonged deployments. The tenders in the Sixth and Seventh Fleets have helped maintain forward combatants on station for years. During the Iran-Iraq War, the U.S. Navy acquired three former Royal Navy auxiliary replenishment ships and, after some minor modifications, they were transferred as MSC-controlled T-AFS. With the current glut of merchant shipping, the Navy has been purchasing excess commercial ships, including eight former high-speed merchant ships of the SL-7 class built by Sealand Corporation. These thirty-three-knot ships proved uneconomical for commercial fleets but useful for the Navy as fast sealift ships (FSS) with easy-to-handle roll-on/roll-off (RO/RO) capabilities.

The Maritime Administration has 328 vessels under its custody, of which 239 comprise the National Defense Reserve Fleet (NDRF). Within the NDFR are 96 Ready Reserve Force (RRF) ships maintained in a state of readiness so that they can be activated within five, ten, or twenty days, as well as another 121 vessels considered militarily useful for activation within 30 to 120 days. Unfortunately, 92 ships of the NDFR, or about 40 percent, are of pre-1946 design.

Future Plans

Current plans are to continue building AOE-6-class fast combat support ships and T-AOs. The *Supply* AOE-6 was launched in 1990, with commissioning set for 1992. To date, two other AOEs have been authorized, and at least one more is anticipated. At one point, a fifteen-AOE force was planned, one per CVBG; but that program has been postponed, with AORs replacing further AOEs. Besides the AOE-6, some nineteen *Kaiser*-class T-AOs are commissioned or under construction.

These plans might have once been quite adequate, but conditions are changing drastically. With the closing of overseas bases, especially Subic Bay with its major shipbuilding and supply facilities, the Navy's already long repair and supply chain in the Pacific will get longer. While countries such as Singapore have offered some facilities, they will be limited. This could mean that instead of upkeep and maintenance in Philippine shipyards, tenders might have to suffice; and instead of relying on forward bases for resupply, the Navy might have to rely on even more shuttle AOs and then fleet AOEs.

The changing conditions and troop withdrawals in Europe mean that resupply, sealift, becomes even more important. Congress has on several occasions given the Navy funds for new sealift vessels, which the Navy has always sought to reprogram for warships. There are many good reasons for this, such as the lack of an appropriate design, but the real reason might be that the Navy simply does not want to get into the "merchant" sealift business. Even though Congress would appropriate initial shipbuilding funds, the upkeep and maintenance might continually come out of the Navy's decreasing budget.

After much prodding by Congress, the Navy finally submitted a plan for two classes: a 950-foot conventional sealift ship for carrying prepositioning equipment, and a 700-foot ship for commercial use.[9] The commercial ships would be built by the government and then leased to shipping firms. Both types will have twenty-four-knot speed capabilities, which designate them as strategic sealift. Both will also have RO/RO capabilities. Considering the rapidly fading U.S. Merchant Marine, both should be started as soon as possible.

Alternatives

Although the Navy has announced that it will look at an AOE follow-on, there are currently no definite alternative plans on the drawing board. Until world conditions are sorted out, it would probably be best to continue building the large, high-level AOEs and T-AOs. Some consideration might be given to increasing the dry-good capabilities of the *Kaiser*-class T-AOs, making them T-AORs. Or they could be "jumboized" (i.e., enlarged) to add some dry-good and even ammunition facilities, especially when they come in for normal yard upkeep. Since there still exists a slight glut of merchant shipping on the world market, continuing to purchase appropriate commercial ships for the fast-breakout RRF remains a viable option. The recent Iraq crisis once again illustrated the need for sealift. Despite a few initial problems, the rapid breakout did work well.

However, to really solve the support ship problem the nation (not just the Navy) must eventually bite the bullet on the future of the U.S. Merchant Marine, which has been sliding precipitously downward for years. The first American-built merchant ship contract *in almost ten years* was let in 1991, and that was only because current law required it: the ship will ply between American ports, necessitating construction in the United States. The American merchant marine has been the most studied (and probably overstudied) industry in the United States, the subject of lengthy reports from congressional, industry, foundation, and private sources. The problems are well known—major declines caused by increasing shipbuilding and operating costs. The United States simply cannot compete against subsidized foreign yards, especially those in the Far East, nor with foreign-flag ships paying nonunion crews. While shipbuilding cost differences have in fact narrowed, the real answer is to bite the budget bullet and once again build a subsidized merchant ship that also has some military applications. The two new classes of proposed sealift ships, if built, should improve the situation.

There is a mid-level alternative that might also be pursued. The David Taylor Center "carrier of large objects" (CLO) design (to be described in more detail below) might also be an alternative, if it is ever developed. And some combined low-level alternatives might even be studied. While the one-stop multiproduct AOR has become standard with most navies, they do not necessarily need larger ships. The Italian Navy, for example, is building the 9,000-ton *Stromboli*-class AOR, adequate for closed waters. It has also been built for export. The United States might consider building smaller AOEs and AORs for export and for its own fleet. Smaller auxiliaries could be useful in closed waters, in the reserves, or with decreased optempos.

Reserve/Deployment Options

The current Navy auxiliary force structure is probably the most flexible within the fleet. Less than half of its ships are in the active force. The majority are already civilian manned, with others in the reserves and even some merchant ships held "in reserve," the RRF, for rapid breakout. All of these programs could be expanded. That is, place even more ships in the civilian-manned MSC, and more merchant ships on fast-breakout RRF status or in the less ready NDFR reserves.

Comments and Conclusions

Between a combination of prudent building plans, the long life span of auxiliaries, and the purchase of former merchant ships kept in readiness status, the Navy has a fairly balanced, adequate auxiliary force for current requirements. The question is whether it will fit future world conditions. On the one hand, with the closing of overseas bases and the withdrawing of troops from Europe and Korea, more auxiliary and support ships seem required. On the other hand, with probable decreased optempos and increased warning time, more may not be needed; or more could be placed under civilian control and even placed in reserve for rapid break-out. For now, the most prudent program would be to continue building the AOE-6 class, buying excess merchant ships, and placing more in the Military Sealift Command. The major problem, which lies well beyond the scope of this book, is the rapidly declining state of the U.S. Merchant Marine. The United States can no longer fall back on a strong merchant marine for support.

AMPHIBIOUS FORCE

I predict that large-scale amphibious operations will never occur again.

—General of the Army Omar Bradley, 1949

Less than a year after General Bradley made that prediction before the U.S. Congress, the First Marine Division made one of the most spectacular and certainly most daring amphibious assaults in all of history at Inchon, Korea. As shown in Table 2-1, there have been many more since 1951. While most were relatively small in scale, they were all politically and militarily important, requiring the special forces, skills, and techniques that can only be provided by a very well trained Navy–Marine Corps team.

There was a similar "assault" against amphibious warfare in the post-Vietnam interwar period. In the mid-1970s, the Brookings Institution issued a provocative book entitled *Where Does the Marine Corps Go from Here?* The argument was that "the need for its principal mission—amphibious warfare—is less apparent."[10] Since that time, however, there has been little criticism of this Marine Corps role. Of course, subsequent events such as Grenada and the Falklands did disprove that Brookings study. As was noted in Part I on missions, the Marine amphibious force "projection ashore" requirements will probably grow in this new interwar period. These could vary from rapid reinforcement in Europe after Army troops are withdrawn to, more likely, responding to those constant crises in the Third World. Today, General Bradley's Army is now trying to "lighten up" in order to more readily participate in what many consider traditional Marine Corps missions.

* * *

Today, the Navy–Marine Corps team appears to be on the threshold of the fourth, and perhaps final, stage of amphibious warfare. Those stages are:

On-Hand Stage—The first stage might be called the "on-hand" stage; that is, the task of getting troops ashore was accomplished with available equipment. Warships or merchantmen were loaded up, the ships anchored offshore, and the troops and equipment transported to the beach with whatever small boats these ships happened to carry. Amphibious operations were extremely vulnerable. Ships usually anchored within cannon range, with troops and equipment moving ashore in slow, long boats.

Specialized Stage—The second stage, developed during the 1920s and 1930s, came to fruition in World War II with specifically designed amphibious ships and landing craft such as LSTs and LCM "mike" boats. Ships still operated fairly close to shore, often within range of shore batteries, and although a mike boat was faster than a long boat, it was still a relatively slow and very vulnerable process.

Vertical Envelopment or Limited OTH Stage—In the 1950s, amphibious warfare underwent a true revolution with the introduction of the helicopter and the development of what was then called "vertical envelopment." This gave the amphibious forces at least some "over the horizon" (OTH) capabilities. However, since helos had only limited lifting capabilities, all heavy equipment including armor still moved ashore by slow landing craft.

Complete OTH Stage—With the introduction of the landing craft air cushion (LCAC), the Navy–Marine Corps team is on the brink of what might be considered the final stage of amphibious warfare. The LCAC not only has the range, two hundred miles, but also the speed, about forty knots, to quickly approach the beach before opposing forces can be mobilized. Equally important, the air cushion capabilities expose about 70 percent of the world's beaches, versus the current 17 percent available to conventional amphibious landing craft.[11] The LCAC, in combination with helicopter-transportable light armored vehicles (LAV), Harrier AV-8B V/STOL aircraft, and possibly the tilt-rotor V-22 troop carriers, now give the projection ashore forces complete OTH capabilities.

Current "Gator" Force

As shown in Table 12-3, there are sixty-two ships in the amphibious or "gator" (short for alligator) force, as it is usually known, with some thirty others that should also be considered. The fleet is not large by past standards. During the Korean War the gator navy stood at over 200; at

Table 12-3. U.S. Navy Amphibious Force

Ship class	Current inventory	Under construction
Amphibious assault ships		
LHD-1 Wasp	1	3+1
LHA-1 Tawara	5	0
LPH-2 Iwo Jima	7	0
Dock landing ships and transport docks		
LSD-41 Whidbey Island	5	3
LSD-41 (CV) Whidbey Island, Cargo Variant	0	1+4
LSD-36 Anchorage	5	0
LSD-28 Thomaston	1	0
LPD-1 Raleigh	2	0
LPD-4 Austin	11	0
Other		
LST-1179 Newport	18	0
LKA-113 Charleston	5	0
LCC-19 Blue Ridge	2	0
Total amphibious	62	7+5
Other ships		
Active reserve LST	2	
Former LPD command ship	2	
Maritime prepositioning ships	13	
TAVB aviation support	2	
Hospital ship	2	
Battleship	2	
Inactive reserve LST	9	
Total all	94	

the height of Vietnam, around 160; and in World War II, over 3,000. On the other hand, while it is small it is a relatively modern force, with all of its ships capable of making at least twenty knots—no more ten-knot "Large Slow Target" LSTs. Most of the ships (or at least their "types") have been in the fleet for years: the LST landing ships, LSD dock ships, and LKA cargo ships all date to World War II designs. The LPD platform with some helicopter capabilities is a post–World War II design, as are all the large assault classes, the LPH, LHA, and now LHD. As noted in Chapter 9, the LPHs are about 19,000 tons, but the LHDs and LHAs are some 40,000 tons—the size of World War II carriers. These large ships can carry about 1,900 troops, a full Marine Expeditionary Unit (MEU). While the current gator force might be adequate, it faces major block obsolescence after the turn of the century, as shown in Figure 12-1. The seven LPHs, thirteen LPDs, and the large twenty-ship *Newport* LST class, a total of forty of the sixty-two amphibious ships, will be retiring within the next ten years or so.

Besides the sixty-two amphibious ships, there are others that deserve mention. The most numerous are the thirteen Maritime Prepositioning Ships (MPS), now deployed in three squadrons in the Atlantic, western Pacific, and Indian oceans. The MPS squadrons are commercial ships loaded with enough equipment and supplies to support a Marine Expeditionary Brigade (MEB) for thirty days. Although they are not true amphibious ships since they must be off-loaded in benign ports, they still provide backup to Marines. Two of the MPS squadrons were used during Desert Shield. There are also two T-AVB Marine "aviation support" ships for marine air units, and two hospital ships. These four ships are all kept in a semi-active "in reserve" status for rapid deployment and were also used during the Iraq crisis. Although these ships are not considered part of the active amphibious force, they are really only used for projection ashore missions. These amphibious-related ships could become more important for the future. For example, the Army, which once rejected the MPS concept, is now reportedly interested in having its own ships to support troops that would deploy by air to the scene of crisis or action.

Future Plans

The amphibious force currently has three different ship types under construction. Two large LHD assault ships have been built, with three more under construction or authorized. As noted in Chapter 9, the final number for LHAs has been listed at anywhere from five to eleven, but apparently construction will stop at six. The eight *Widbey Island*-class LSD-41s are almost finished, with six already commissioned. These are

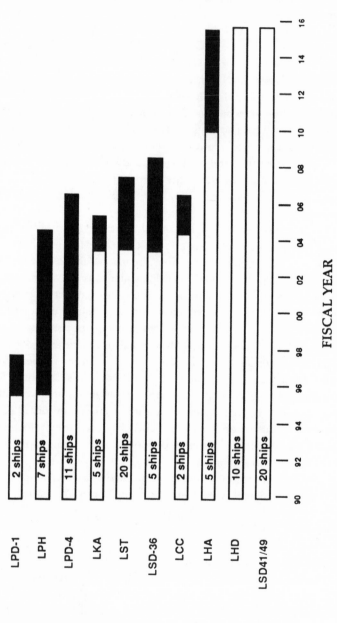

Figure 12-1. Amphibious Ships Retirement Schedule

now being followed by the LSD-41(CV) for "cargo variant," also some-times known as the LSD-49 *Harper's Ferry* class. They are very similar to the LSD-41 class but have greater cargo capabilities at the expense of well deck space. The LSD-41 can carry four LCACs, while the cargo variants will carry only two. Nine LSD-41 (CV)s were once planned, making a total of seventeen LSD-41s and LSD-41(CV)s, but the latest 1992 budget has dropped an LSD-41(CV).

In some respects, the long-term plans for the amphibious force are the best known. Plans for amphibious follow-ons might use the Taylor Center CLO multimission variant concept, which for amphibious force has been designated LX. The LX is planned as a functional replacement for the thirty-six ships of the LPD, LSD, and LST classes.[12] She will have an LPD-type well deck that can carry two LCACs and will be capable of supporting two helicopters. At about 30,000–40,000 tons according to one report,[13] the LX will be considerably larger than the ships it replaces. Construction of the LX is scheduled to begin in the late 1990s, which might be too late to avoid major block obsolescence in the amphibious force. The LHAs will be succeeded around 2011 by an LVX, which will have a secondary mission of sea control.

Alternatives

Unlike most of the other forces, there are in fact some long-range plans and alternatives for the amphibious force—first to build an LX, to be followed by an LVX. Both are based on the Taylor Center CLO common design for not just amphibious but also auxiliary ships and even warships. Presumably, this common design could be "punched out," saving money. However, one can only wonder if replacing 10,000-ton LSTs, 14,000-ton LSDs, and 17,000-ton LPDs with 30,000-ton LXs, no matter how they are built, will be cheaper. There will be some economies of scale. Still, a 30,000-ton ship would definitely fall into the higher end of a modified mix spectrum.

There are also some mission questions. LSTs, for example, are the only ships with any kind of beaching capability. That is an extremely useful and flexible function. LSTs also carry pontoons forming temporary "docks"—another extremely useful capability, especially for any kind of sustained operations. Finally, LSTs are relatively inexpensive. Of the three thousand–odd World War II amphibious ships, over one thousand were LSTs. These old LSTs proved invaluable during Vietnam as every-thing from amphibious ships to jury-rigged repair and depot ships. Even today, the twenty *Newport*-class LSTs constitute one-third of the amphib-ious force. They are still considered to be at the low end of the spectrum.

Unless very large economies of scale can be proven from the CLO-LX modes, a lower-cost LST follow-on might be considered. It might also have some combined and export possibilities. There are many old U.S.-built LSTs still in use in foreign navies that need replacing. A common NATO design for an LST might also be considered.

For a true mid-level option, still another LSD-41 variant might be considered. That is an L"P"D-41 variant to replace the two *Raleigh*-class and especially the eleven *Austin*-class LPDs built in the 1960s. Both these classes will reach block obsolescence around the turn of the century. The LSD-41 has now been produced in two variants; why not three? With an LPD design very similar to that of an LSD, an LPD-41 variant might be the more appropriate hull for LPD follow-ons. Since the LSD-41s are larger than the *Austin*-class LPDs, there seems no reason why telescopic hangars cannot be added in some manner.

In short, a future amphibious modified mix would consist of the LHDs and LHAs at the high end of the spectrum, LSD-41s, LSD-41(CV)s, and LPD-41s in the middle, and a new LST follow-on for the lower end. The CLO-LX-LVX options should not be ruled out, but unless major savings can be proven they should probably be delayed. The LHAs and LHDs will last well into the twenty-first century. Since the basic LSD-41 hulls are still being built, an LPD variant should not entail massive start-up costs. The only new ship would be a low-end LST follow-on, which need not be terribly expensive, especially if built on a NATO-wide common design.

Reserve/Deployment Options

With over half the amphibious force facing block obsolescence, there are quite a few reserve deployment options. The most obvious is simply placing the older ships into the reserves for a few years as they reach retirement age. There are some other options. For example, as was once done after the Cuban missile crisis when it was discovered that insufficient amphibious ships existed for both Marine and Army requirements, a small squadron of older LSTs could be kept on active duty, "in reserve," about one-third manned. As the *Newport*-class LSTs start to age, some of them could be placed in this status.

However, considering the probable new importance of the reserves, the best solution would be the creation of Reserve Amphibious Ready Groups (RARGs)—at least one for each coast. RARGs could be built around the two latest LPHs, the two *Raleigh*-class LPDs built in the early 1960s, and the two *Newport*-class LSTs already in the reserves. A three-ship RARG consisting of an LPH, LPD, and LST would be quite a formidable force—almost the equivalent of an active group, which normally has four ships. RARGs would give reserve Marines their own training ships, with Marine pilots having the LPH for training. RARGs would also create a stand-alone "vertical" amphibious reserve Navy unit that would fit well with the vertical integrity concepts of the Marine Corps reserves. Finally, as mentioned in Chapter 9, active-duty ARGs could substitute for carrier battle groups in certain situations. ARGs built around ski jump–equipped LHAs and LHDs with APD-963 escorts would be more than adequate for most Third World crisis situations.

Comments and Conclusions

The USN has tended to build amphibious ships in groups and usually (as with surface combatants) has followed a modified mix scheme. In the 1950s, the mid-level *Thomaston*-class LSD was balanced with two less expensive LST classes, the LST-1156 *Terrebone Parish* followed by the LST-1173 *Suffolk County* class. During the 1960s, there was a true modified mix: the high level, *Iwo Jima*-class LPHs were balanced with one LSD and two LPD mid-level classes, and twenty *Newport*-class LSTs also were constructed. This building mix changed in the 1970s interwar period, when only the high-level LHAs were built. During the 1980s, only the mid-level LSD-41s were built, followed by high-level LHDs and mid-level LSD-41(CV)s. There has not been a low-level, modified mix LST since the 1960s. With the amphibious force facing major block obsolescence after the turn of the century, a return to a modified mix seems warranted and necessary.

THE MARINES

One of the most interesting interwar, interservice fights might be the anticipated Army–Marine Corps squabble over future roles and missions. With the drawdown from Europe and Korea, the Army is looking for new roles. Stories under such titles as "Friendly Fire: Army and Marine Corps Fight over Combat Role"[14] and "Go Marines! Beat Army"[15] are appearing more frequently. There is, of course, a certain sense of déjà vu over this anticipated interwar fight. It was during the interwar period between the two world wars that the Marines, alone, developed the amphibious tactics that served so well during World War II, yet it was the Army that conducted the major landings, including the largest in history on D-Day. However, the Army gave up this capability fairly quickly. General Bradley felt the era of amphibious warfare had ended with World War II, and the Army finally closed its Fort Story amphibious training facility in the early 1960s. Since the end of World War II, the Army's main role has been to counter the Soviet threat on the central front. This required "heavy" armored units. The "light" crisis response missions were generally left to the Marine Corps.

During the 1980s, however, even before the recent events in Eastern Europe, the Army apparently saw the handwriting on the wall and started to revamp its forces for a quick reaction role. While the Army did not return to amphibious training, it did create several new "light" divisions for rapid deployment, and it has long had airborne divisions. The problem with these light and airborne divisions is their limited staying power and muscle. The light divisions carry only forty-eight to seventy-two hours worth of supplies and have limited (light) armor—and no air support. An article in *Time* entitled "Who Needs the Marines? From the Halls of Montezuma to the Shores of Redundancy," offered the Marine-Army unit comparison shown in Table 12-4.[16] This actually represents only part of the "imbalance," since the Marines would be backed up by the Navy.

The Marine Corps is uniquely configured for crisis response. They have developed MAGTFs (Marine Air-Ground Task Forces) that are prepared and trained to be deployed to any part of the world on short notice. A MAGTF has four major components: Command Element, Ground Combat Element, Aviation Combat Element, and Combat Service Support Element. There are three MAGTF organizations: the Marine Expeditionary Force (MEF), with 30,000 to 60,000 Marines and sailors; Marine Expeditionary Brigade (MEB), with 4,000 to 18,000; and the Marine Expeditionary Unit (MEU), with 1,000 to 4,000. MEFs are configured for sixty days of support, MEBs for thirty, and MEUs for about fifteen. MEUs are constantly forward-deployed in the Pacific and the Mediterranean.[17] The Army has no such comparable organization.

And this is really only part of the picture. The Marines are carried and backed up by USN Amphibious Ready Groups, and during crises by Navy air and surface combatant gunfire support as well. MPS ships also

Table 12-4. Comparison of Marine and Army Units

	Marine Division	Army Light Division
Personnel	18,000	14,000
Tanks	17 (heavy)	58 (light)
Armored vehicles	74	0
Artillery	33	62
Attack helicopters	12	29
Attack aircraft	74	0

provide additional supplies and equipment sufficient to support a flown-in MEB for thirty days. Neither the Army nor Air Force has such capabilities. The Marine Corps Reserve also uses the "vertical" approach, meaning that complete unit integrity is maintained through battalion level. That will be a useful concept for the new world conditions if reserves are to play a larger role. This vertical approach would enable a reserve battalion to move quickly and deploy in new RARGs.

In short, while the new interwar Army–Marine Corps fight might be a great spectator sport, there should really be no contest. Without a top-to-bottom reorganization including major changes in its massive reserve component, the Army simply is not configured for the normal Third World crisis response situations. In fact, the Marines are now looking at becoming slightly heavier and assuming a "medium" role for some of the new Third World conditions.[18] The Army should stick with what it does best—preparing for major, "heavy" wars. As the recent Iraq crisis has shown, there is still a need for armored and mechanized divisions.

MINE CRAFT

Mines have been appropriately described as "weapons that wait";[19] the same description could also be applied to U.S. mine craft programs. The USN has been "waiting" for a new mine countermeasure ship for over thirty years. Few questioned the importance of the ships, yet for one reason or another (usually budgetary restraints) none were built. It looked like the self-imposed minesweeper "holiday" was about to end in the Reagan-Lehman administration. But once again programs were delayed another decade, although it appears the problems have finally been resolved.

Mines are extremely cost effective. Kill ratios in World War II for the Allies were one ship per thirty-seven mines.[20] Operation Starvation against the Japanese in 1945 virtually cut off all shipping. There are numerous post–World War II examples as well. Mines were used very effectively by the North Koreans at Wonsan, resulting in an eight-day delay for 250 allied ships carrying 50,000 troops and causing the U.S. commander to say, "The U.S. Navy has lost control of the seas." Quite a statement about an enemy with no fleet! Mines were used in the various Arab-Israeli wars to close the Suez Canal and in Vietnam, where most commentators felt it was the U.S. mining of Haiphong harbor that finally brought the North Vietnamese around to serious negotiations. Mines planted by terrorists in the Red Sea damaged several ships and took a six-nation, twenty-six-ship armada to neutralize. And of course it was the mining during the Iran-Iraq War that caused so much trouble, including the near-loss of the U.S. frigate *Samuel P. Robert*. During the Iraq war, an LPH involved with minesweeping was hit, as was the *Princeton* CG-59. Soviet inventories were estimated at about a quarter-million mines; the fleet contains some 300 mine craft.

There are also the psychological aspects of mining, which may be even more important.[21] Two examples often cited both involve Haiphong. During World War II, U.S. forces dropped just six mines and sank only one ship, yet Haiphong harbor was closed. In 1972 only thirty-six mines were initially dropped, but that closed the harbor for 300 days. Just a few mines—only one was ever recovered—in the Red Sea caused a massive concern. It might be one thing to "damn the torpedoes," as mines were called during the Civil War era, but most captains and merchant marine masters also remember that "all ships are minesweepers—once!" In short, mine warfare is far from ancient history.

Current Forces

The backbone of the current U.S. mine force still consists of twenty-one old MSO ocean minesweepers built in the mid-1950s. All but three are in the reserves, although they are manned with approximately 60 percent active duty personnel. The MSOs are out of date and have been for years. There have been plans to update the force for many years, but usually when something had to be cut the mine craft were the first to go. Finally, after two decades of neglect, the Reagan administration decided to build two classes: a high-low mix of oceangoing MCM mine countermeasure ships and coastal MSH air-cushion harbor craft. Both programs ran into serious problems.

The MCM-1 *Avenger* class consists of large, 224-foot, wooden-hulled, 1,300-ton ships with the latest minehunting gear, the AN/SQQ-32 mine-hunting sonar system. However, it has been plagued with serious and at times embarrassing engine problems that apparently persist. The most embarrassing was the discovery that drive motors and reduction gears were mismatched, but there are also continuing problems with potential fire hazards. Although the first of the fourteen planned *Avengers* are finally starting to join the fleet, according to one report the engineering difficulties persist, and some thought has been given to replacing the engines and drive trains.

The original harbor MSH *Cardinal* class became so troubled that the air-cushion design was finally scrapped altogether. The Navy turned to a lengthened and modified version of the Italian *Lerici* mine craft with a reinforced fiberglass hull designated the MHC-51 *Osprey* class. Apparently this new program is on track, although the first ship has yet to be deployed. Like the MCM-1, the MHC-51 class will also have the sophisticated AN/SQQ-32 minehunting sonar. Seventeen coastal mine hunters were planned, although the program might end at twelve. Overall, it has been a sad commentary on the ability of both the Navy and American shipbuilders to build smaller ships.

Future Plans

Future plans are to complete the two original programs. This is certainly not meant as a criticism: these twenty-six mine craft will be the first commissioned in over forty years. While twenty-six are obviously not adequate for a major confrontation, they are probably sufficient for the conditions of the immediate future missions such as the Persian Gulf escort or Desert Storm.

Alternatives

The 1989 Surface Warfare plan does mention that a follow-on MCM may be required sometime in the future and that any new class will investigate a common hull design to satisfy "both an overseas deployer and for U.S. coastal requirements."[22] The latest long-range plan calls for an MHC(V)-class ship described as a "deployable" version of the *Osprey.* Considering the problems with both the *Cardinal* and the original *Osprey,* it might be better to simply continue those designs, assuming all problems are resolved. The 1989 plan also mentions that air-cushion landing craft testing will continue, with several LCACs configured specifically for mine clearance.

Other alternatives that might be explored include building some minesweeping capabilities into both hydrographic and smaller Coast Guard ships. There was a program called COOP (for "Craft of Opportunity") that utilizes older, smaller boats such as former Naval Academy training ships and converts them to jury-rigged mine craft; building in some initial commonality might help. Both the National Oceanic and Atmospheric Administration (NOAA) and the Coast Guard have dozens of boats in the 100- to 200-foot range, perfect for both ocean and coastal minesweeping capabilities. NOAA recently announced requirements for twenty new boats. Many NOAA ships already have sophisticated sounding gear, while all Coast Guard ships are designed to military specifications.

Reserve/Deployment Options

Plans were to place some of the MCM-1 and MHC-51 classes in the reserves. Two other options should be explored. As mentioned in Chapter 5, consideration might be given to having an MCM or an MHC join a NATO standing channel mine force, and then using another MCM or MHC in the Mediterranean for a new standing Med mine force. This would serve two purposes: first, to maintain NATO navy solidarity, which should become more important throughout the 1990s; and second, to always have two to four USN mine craft forward-deployed, avoiding the embarrassment of towing them across the ocean as was done with the MSOs. Besides, this could be great overseas duty. A few mine craft could also operate unobtrusively out of Singapore, or South Korea, placing some forward in the Pacific.

Some new mine craft might also be kept in active service in the United States for training. Three MSOs were always kept on active duty. The MCM and MHC designs might also have some dual-use capabilities—for example, as SAR vessels for both a new Navy National Guard and the Coast Guard. They could be built without all the sophisticated electronics.

Comments and Conclusions

While the Reagan administration must be congratulated for finally starting to build mine craft after a thirty-year naval holiday, both mine craft programs have, unfortunately, experienced serious problems. Once they are resolved, however, the USN should have a modern if still somewhat small mine force. This means that converting or being able to convert smaller craft to this role will continue to be important. Between the Coast Guard and NOAA, there are in fact many boats available, but some commonality should be planned. Finally, the USN should consider keeping more of these new craft in the active fleet, with a few forward-deployed in allied roles.

COMMENTS AND CONCLUSION: MAINTAINING THE "BLUE"

Although in the past the four forces described in this chapter have been crucial to the future of the Navy, they were often treated as stepchildren. As funds decrease, that could well happen again. Both the auxiliary and the amphibious forces have already been cut. Yet without the large auxiliary force, the Navy simply cannot operate. It is the auxiliary force that

Table 12-5. Auxiliary, Amphibious, and Mine Craft Modified Mix Alternatives

	Auxiliary	Amphibious	Mine Craft
High	AOE continue	LVX study LHD continue	MCM continue
Mid	T-AOR modernize T-AO continue 2 sealift classes	LX study LPD-41 transition-up APD	MHC continue
Low	AORs combined	LST-21 initiate	Coast Guard dual use NOAA dual use

makes a "blue-water navy" really "blue." The Navy–Marine Corps "power projection" amphibious capabilities are unique, and crucial; yet it is that force that faces major block obsolescence after the turn of the century. And despite the fact that even a few unsophisticated mines laid by virtually any vessel can stop the world's mightiest navies, mine warfare has traditionally been lowest on the Navy shipbuilding pecking order (although that might be changing). The Navy, however, should not make the "army mistake" of placing all of its minesweeping capabilities in the reserves.

These forces must be maintained, and, as summarized in Table 12-5, there are reasonable alternatives. The amphibious force should probably return to its traditional modified mix, adding new-generation, lower-cost LSTs to its future plans. The auxiliary force has many different deployment and reserve options, most already in place, requiring only minor expansions and adjustments. Most important, the United States must start rebuilding the merchant marine. Starting the two sealift proposals would be a good start. And the minesweeping capabilities of the United States could probably be tripled during emergencies by building some initial commonality into NOAA and Coast Guard boats. Recent lessons in the Red Sea and Persian Gulf should also have taught us that even a few forward-deployed mine craft are extremely useful. They could serve a dual purpose by being attached to permanent allied mine groups. In short, maintaining the "blue" can probably be done at a relatively small cost with a little imagination. It would also go a long way in maintaining the U.S. shipbuilding reconstitution and industrial base.

Part III

Comments and Conclusions

13 / Lessons of Desert Shield/Desert Storm

Forerunner or Fluke?

JUST WHEN MANY were starting to spend the end of the Cold War "peace dividend" Iraq invaded Kuwait, bringing about the largest and fastest movement of American and allied forces since World War II. Perhaps the only thing larger and faster has been the plethora of instant books on the war. If they are anything like the armchair analyses preceding the invasion, most will turn out to be wrong.

From a service standpoint, the winner appears to be the Air Force, followed by the Army mostly in the person of General "Stormin'" Norman Schwarzkopf; the Navy, according to some commentators, is the big loser. Perhaps in this instance the real winner was jointness. Also, according to the instant analysis, "If it wasn't used in Desert Storm, it won't be funded"—and there is some indication that Congress is now following this advice. For example, there was a move to reprogram some Air Force airplane funding in order to purchase more of the F-117 stealth fighter-bombers that proved so useful. This could mean that traditional Navy priorities such as ASW could face tough sledding for funds.

The intent of this chapter is to look briefly at some of the broader strategic and tactical considerations raised by Desert Shield/Storm, especially those relating to the Navy, ending with the most important question for the future—whether this was a forerunner of events for the new interwar period or simply a one-shot operation, a one-time fluke.

A Brief History

Although Iraq invaded Kuwait on 2 August 1990, the true roots of the conflict are lost in the shifting desert sands of both geography and time, dating back centuries. In modern times, boundaries were more or less artifically drawn for these seminomadic peoples: first by the Ottoman Turks, then by the French and the British when they carved up the Middle East in the late nineteenth and early twentieth centuries, and finally by the British in creating Kuwait. Baghdad has never accepted that partition. This was not, therefore, the first such border conflict. When the British left the gulf in the early 1960s, Iraq made similar threats against Kuwait. An Iraqi invasion of Kuwait was thwarted in 1961 when British troops were quickly sent back, but Baghdad had never given up its claims on that small piece of oil-rich land.

Knowledge of this long history and the British response in 1961 seems to have been the first casualty of the conflict. It would not be the last. Also forgotten were the history and lessons of the three Middle East wars between modern, Western-oriented states and Arabs. These are the three Arab-Israeli wars. The 1956 Suez crisis and subsequent Israeli attack on the Sinai and British-French attack on the Suez Canal started 29 October and was over eleven days later on 8 November, although actual combat lasted only some 100 hours. Casualties for the Israelis, British, and French were about 200 personnel. The June 1967 Six-Day War cost Israel 700 lives; the 1973 Yom Kippur War, which surprised Israel, still took only sixteen days, causing 2,700 deaths. Therefore, the previous three wars had lasted a total of just thirty-three days and had cost approximately 3,600 lives. Of course, the more recent Iran-Iraq War between similar Third World countries lasted some eight years with casualties listed in the hundreds of thousands—but that was (or should have been) obviously the wrong precedent.

On 2 August 1990, Iraqi forces invaded Kuwait and within forty-eight hours had conquered the country. Although there had been a few diplomatic and intelligence warning signs, generally the action came as a complete surprise. (As noted earlier, on that same date the president delivered a major address on a new defense policy that has since become somewhat overlooked because of the invasion.) American Ambassador to Iraq April Glaspie has been severely criticized for a meeting she had with Saddam Hussein in June in which she reportedly implied that the United States had "no opinion" on "your border disagreement with Kuwait," but any criticism of her must be shared by Washington. The fact that she went on vacation just before the invasion with State Department approval indicates that the department did not take the dispute seriously. Intelligence warnings of Iraqi troop movements were ignored, but such movements were not totally out of the ordinary. Although hindsight might now dictate otherwise, the invasion was a surprise.

As is usual with any Third World situation, the only American forces in the area were naval. These included six ships from the Middle East Force, which has had a continuous presence since 1949. The *Independence* carrier battle group in the Indian Ocean was immediately alerted and sent to the North Arabian Sea. The *Eisenhower* carrier battle group was similarly alerted and began transit of the Suez Canal on 7 August. Only the Navy had ready forces in the area when the president ordered U.S. forces into the area on 8 August. The Army's 82nd Airborne Division arrived that same day. Thus began the massive buildup.[1]

All services responded quickly. On 10 August Air Force F-16s from Shaw Air Force Base flew into Saudi Arabia, and 12 August F-15E fighter-bombers also started to arrive. Advance elements of the First Marine Expeditionary Force and the Seventh Marine Expeditionary Brigade began arriving on 14 August, and the next day ships from the Maritime Prepositioned Squadron 2 from Diego Garcia began unloading in Saudi Arabia.

Almost forgotten today is the fear that Saddam intended to continue his invasion into Saudi Arabia. This would have given Saddam control of over 50 percent of the world's oil supply as well as removing a close ally of the United States. According to some analysts, it was really this fear for Saudi Arabia rather than a concern for Kuwait that prompted the American response. Thus, the relatively "heavy" Marines with at least some armor from the MPS squadron became crucial for an immediate Saudi defense. It was almost two weeks later on 27 August that elements of the Army's 24th Mechanized Division would start to arrive in Saudi Arabia—and late fall, with the arrival of other Army armored units, before General Schwarzkopf would feel comfortable about countering Iraqi tanks. This mid-August deployment by the Marines was probably one of the few times in history when they were considered the heavy forces. While the symbolism of the 82nd Airborne should not be overlooked, even that elite Army force could not stand up to Iraq's armor.

The purpose of this brief history is not to chronicle every force buildup, but several maritime actions deserve special mention. First was the theater coalition fleet, which quickly formed and reportedly operated smoothly. Table 13-1 shows this buildup from eighteen different countries from Argentina to the Soviet Union over the Desert Shield time period.[2] From all reports coordination and cooperation were excellent, and all went relatively smoothly since most participants were NATO allies—an indication that more STANAVFORs around the world could be both symbolically and militarily important. Second was the fact that, as usual,

Table 13-1. Theater Coalition Ships

Country	22 Aug.	18 Sept.	21 Oct.	12 Nov.	21 Jan.
Argentina				2	2
Australia					3
Belgium	3	3	3	3	6
Canada	3	3	3	3	3
Denmark		1	1	1	1
France	7	14	14	15	14
Germany	6	—	—	7	5
Greece		1	1	1	1
Italy	2	3	4	3	10
Netherlands	2	2	3	3	3
Norway		1	1	—	1
Poland			1	—	1
Portugal			1	1	1
Spain	3	3	3	3	4
Turkey					2
U.S.	45	45	55	65	100
U.K.	7	—	12	16	18
USSR		2	2	4	4
Total	78	78	104	127	179

Total ships in theater on the date specified.

Source: Time 27 Aug. 1990, 28 Jan. 1991; *New York Times,* 18 Sept., 21 Oct., 12 Nov. 1990; *Washington Post National Weekly Edition,* 21–27 Jan. 1991. Taken from *The United States Navy in "Desert Shield" and "Desert Storm"* (Department of the Navy, Office of the Chief of Naval Operations, 15 May 1991).

over 90 percent of all supplies and equipment came by sealift. The first response was from MPS Squadron Two out of Diego Garcia, followed by ships from the other MPS squadrons. The MSC's eight sealift ships, the fastest such ships in the world at thirty-three knots, were used to transport the crucial 24th Mechanized to Saudi Arabia quickly. MSC was also able to call on forty other Ready Reserve Force (RRF) ships.

Sealift Phase I, supporting the initial deployment through mid-December, had more than 180 ships assigned to or chartered by MSC. Sealift Phase II, which supported the additional reinforcement of Desert Shield forces, saw 220 ships under MSC control. With the exception of the Normandy landing, which took two years to prepare, this represented the largest and fastest sealift to a single theater in history. There were, of course, many problems with sealift, such as breakouts that took longer than expected and some embarrassing breakdowns, but all told it was considered successful.

Another Navy success story was the breakout of the two 1,000-bed floating hospitals that are normally kept in a reduced readiness status. They were quickly activated and sent to the area. It has since been revealed that one of General Schwarzkopf's major concerns was lack of hospital capacity, a problem that would have been exacerbated without these fine ships.

On 16 January 1991 the Desert Shield buildup changed to Operation Desert Storm to carry out the liberation of Kuwait. Desert Storm began with the firing of 100 Tomahawk cruise missiles, some from submarines. They were the first weapons to hit Baghdad. Overall, Tomahawk effectiveness was an amazing 80 percent. Thus began an air offensive that lasted some six weeks. Contrary to some fears, the Iraqi air force was quickly overcome, with many airplanes taking refuge in Iran. Iraqi ground fire was heavy at times, causing some loss of coalition aircraft; but generally the skies belonged to the allies. The hero of the air war became the Air Force's new stealth F-117 fighter, which was used to bomb critical targets in Baghdad. The only other weapon used against heavily guarded Baghdad was the Tomahawk. The Navy flew about one-third of the combat missions.

Although there was some hope that Saddam might succumb to this air war, he stubbornly refused. Thus, on 22 February the ground offensive began—and within 100 hours, the war was over. Due to the earlier bombing and the good tactics and leadership of General Schwarzkopf, the whole operation took an amazingly short time.

LESSONS

Ignoring the Past

According to an old saw, the first casualty of war is truth. But in this case the first casualty seemed to be knowledge or understanding of the past. First to be overlooked were the lessons from the British response under somewhat similar circumstances. Had the Americans responded immediately upon any intelligence warnings as the British did in 1961, the whole crisis might have been averted.

Perhaps more appalling was the general ignorance of the pre–Desert Storm armchair analysts. This author, like most Americans, was riveted to the television set during the crisis, watching every show from CNN to the network specials to the almost nightly analysis on public television's McNeil-Lehrer show. Although there might have been some exceptions that this author missed, in general the analysis was dead wrong. This simply points out once again the desperate need for more study on both old and new Third World military conditions. The American national security community, which has concentrated on the East-West conflict for so long, displayed an almost total lack of understanding of these new conditions—or took an extremely myopic viewpoint, concentrating on the Iran-Iraq War.

The predictions ran from 50,000 to 100,000 casualties to "another Vietnam"—or more likely, "another Beirut." A few even predicted a stalemate, which would have meant a strategic victory for Iraq. No wonder Saddam hung on. General Schwarzkopf has made sarcastic reference to these "fairies," but some were not amateurs. For example, the first reference this author heard to an allied attack on Iraqi positions becoming another "Bull Run" was from a senior retired general with advanced degrees and an intelligence background. (Talk about fighting the last war!) Another so-called expert explained how the much simpler Soviet-made Iraqi tanks would easily defeat the more sophisticated American M-1 in desert warfare. Virtually all of these "experts" cited the eight-year Iran-Iraq War, claiming that Iraq now had a "battle-hardened" army. It was, of course, utter nonsense!

The right analogy was not Bull Run or the Iran-Iraq War but the three Arab-Israeli wars, which lasted a total of only thirty-three days and caused fewer than 4,000 casualties to Israel. That last figure would have qualified as a skirmish in Civil War terms. Fortunately, despite its eight-year war with Iran, the Iraqi army was still a typical Third World force. One of these days Third World nations are going to realize that a noncorrupt, well-trained army is worth more than the latest-mode MIG or Soviet tank. When that day comes, the West might be in for some rude shocks, but until that time there is little to fear—which leads into the next lesson.

Stormin' or Stallin' Norman

Despite their oft-expressed bravado, and the lack of training in most Third World armies, the days of "sending in a few Marines" are over. On the other hand, the six-month buildup of Desert Shield must also be questioned. Obviously, the more forces and training the better. But, there is some question as to whether it was necessary, and perhaps more important, whether it establishes an extremely bad precedent for what was a very unique situation.

Considering the precedents of the three Arab-Israeli wars, this author is under the impression (admittedly unprovable) that the war could have begun considerably sooner yet ended with similar results. The delay allowed Saddam to build up his defenses, reinforcing what many armchair analysts felt were already impregnable positions. This delay also allowed for the laying of mines, which was a major consideration in preventing an amphibious operation. Whether the ground offensive could have begun sooner might be open to question, but there seems little question that the air war could have begun earlier. Thus, after the bulk of troops (including some armored units) had arrived by late fall, this author began to wonder whether Stormin' Norman should have been called Stallin' Norman— whether he was a George McClellan rather than a George Patton. It looked like that old Army penchant for building up massive forces. To be fair, according to reports General Schwarzkopf was not even allowed to plan for an invasion by the Pentagon for some time.

On the other hand, as operational commander he certainly had the authority to plan, and one can only wonder what that CENTCOM staff in Florida has been doing for the last ten years. After all, a war in the gulf was not, or should not, have been a surprise. Once again, however, the Persian Gulf war scenario always envisioned a Soviet thrust—another example of old, Cold War thinking. This author has also been told that Marine Corps generals were greatly disturbed at the situation they found in Riyadh. The generals were reportedly called back to Quantico by Commandant General Gray for consultations, where they conducted some war-game scenarios. One can only wonder whether the timing (not the outcome) would have been different if the CENTCOM command rotation had placed a Marine in charge.

The real problem may be the precedents established. Desert Storm was an extremely unique situation. For example, not only was there a friendly (and very frightened) country, Saudi Arabia, from which to stage forces, there were also magnificent and empty piers, warehouses, etc., for that buildup. Thus, General Schwarzkopf was able to build up his forces and his staff, which numbered in the hundreds, to plan his truly brilliant victory. Once unfettered by Washington, Norman did indeed storm. The question is whether this six-month, 500,000-force buildup will now become the main lesson. If so, it ignores the history of crisis response and sets another extremely bad precedent.

The Navy and Jointness

The real victor in Desert Shield/Storm was jointness, and all those supporters of the Goldwater-Nichols reforms are probably cheering. All three services as well as the Coast Guard did a magnificent job, and all were truly needed. It was not, as has often been the case in recent crises (e.g., Grenada and the Libyan air raids), jointness for the sake of jointness. Despite the fact that this author thinks the Navy should remain in charge of a new Atlantic Command and be placed in rotation for any new Contingency Command, it was proper for an Army or Marine general to be placed in command of Desert Shield/Storm. Admirals make poor generals—as witness the few times in the Pacific during World War II when an admiral tried to maintain operational control over troops in amphibious operations once they were ashore. (Of course, generals also make poor admirals.)

But the Navy still has not learned to play the jointness game. It made a bad operational and perhaps public relations mistake by not placing a senior admiral, preferably a three-star, ashore in Riyadh. The senior operational admiral ashore was a one-star who did a superb job but was simply "out-starred," according to many reports. Surprisingly, there was a three-star change of command during the operation. On 19 August, Vice Adm. Henry Mauz, Commander U.S. Seventh Fleet, also became Commander U.S. Naval Forces Central Command (COMUSNAVCENT) and assumed command of all naval forces including the maritime intercept force. On 1 December, Admiral Mauz was relieved by Vice Adm. Stanley Arthur. Rather than this switch, one of them should have stayed as COMUSNAVCENT and moved ashore. Such a move might have been supported by the allied fleet commanders as well. This would have solved the seniority and communications problems (according to reports, at-sea communications were also inadequate).

Incidentally, while jointness might have been the big winner in Desert Shield/Storm, one can only wonder what would have happened if a Marine Corps general had been in charge of the CENTCOM command at the time. Would the Army have lined up under him? If the history of Army-Marine command relations is any guide, the answer is: probably not.

The Continuing Mining Stepchild

The Navy had many successes: early sealift, blockade control, the first use of Tomahawks in battle, the exploits of Navy pilots during Desert Storm. However, one major fault remains. The Navy's attitude toward mine warfare continues. It cost not only casualties but two ships, and might have prevented the Marines from launching an amphibious assault. Yet the lessons go unheeded.

On 18 February 1991 the *Tripoli* (LPH-10) and the *Princeton* (CG-59) both struck mines. Somewhat ironically, the *Tripoli* was acting as flagship for minesweeping operations. It sustained a sixteen-by-twenty-foot hole that might have sunk the ship without quick action. The *Princeton* was also hit by a mine and similarly took quick action. Both captains and crew acted well and must be commended, but the larger questions remain: Why were they hit? And how did the mines get there in the first place?

Although reports are still coming in, it appears that the mines were laid in November, four months into Desert Shield, and were placed farther from the beach than expected. In fact, according to some reports, it was the fear of more mines closer to shore that was a major factor in the decision not to try an amphibious assault. Of more concern is why the mining was not detected; at this point, one can only speculate. However, a few smaller, expendable corvettes patrolling those waters might have prevented the laying in the first place. It would seem that this incident would be enough to keep a few mine craft in the active forces. But once again, the stepchild might move into the reserves.

Forerunner or Fluke

The real question for the future is whether Desert Shield/Storm is a forerunner of future conflicts or a one-time fluke. History suggests the latter. While the history of the Middle East is replete with conflicts and crises, with few exceptions the United States has remained aloof. There are some similarities to the United Nations action in Korea forty years earlier, but even that was a quite different affair.

Today, Saddam seems to be a unique case. This was not true just a few years ago: then, the area was full of somewhat irrational characters, which, besides Saddam, included Libya's Qaddafi, Syria's Assad, and Iran's Ayatollah Khomeini. The Ayatollah is now dead, and his successors are somewhat more rational. Qaddafi has been noticeably quiet since the air attacks and reportedly is moving toward the West slightly. And Assad has also apparently mellowed somewhat and is now part of the Middle East peace process. This leaves only Saddam, and his days are probably numbered.

There are other important factors to indicate that this was a fluke. The fact is, Kuwait was a major oil producer, and threats to it and to Saudi Arabia were simply intolerable for Western economies. If a similar invasion had occurred elsewhere, the United States probably would not have responded.

Looking into a crystal ball can be dangerous, but it seems hard to believe that an Iraq-type situation will occur any time in the future. More likely will be those routine crisis situations that seem to occur at least semiannually.

COMMENTS

The intent of this short chapter was not to give an in-depth analysis of Desert Shield/Storm, but rather to point out some of the broader strategic and tactical lessons. There are many more. The whole situation was an obvious intelligence failure—first in the early detection of the crisis, and later on the battlefield. The old joint communications bugaboos apparently still exist, with the Army, Navy, and Air Force unable to talk to each other. After all these years, it is a wonder that the Secretary of Defense does not lock the chiefs in a room until this problem is solved. And, although this is perhaps unfair, considering what Admiral Stockdale and many other Vietnam prisoners of war went through for years, this author was a little uncomfortable with the performance of some downed pilots after only a few days. Better POW training might be required.

Of course, the biggest failure might have been the outcome, which is another indication of the lack of policy for these situations. Although "100 hours" has a nice ring to it, stopping the war without eliminating Saddam Hussein was a major strategy blunder and yet another example of old thinking. While going into Baghdad could have been bloody, there were probably alternatives. This is perhaps another intelligence failure. Is our human intelligence now so bad that we do not have contacts with at least some Iraqi generals to pass the word?

But these failures, even the failure to eliminate Saddam, should not distract from the many successes. The Air Force has a right to be proud of its performance. It was an air war—perhaps the first one in history; and with more time the Air Force alone might have subdued Saddam. Expensive systems like the stealth F-117 did prove their worth. The Army also has a right to be proud of its performance. After training for forty years to fight the Soviet Union in Europe, it adapted quickly. General Schwarzkopf also deserved all the accolades he received. He apparently was that right combination of a Dwight Eisenhower and a George Patton. An admiral on the staff was amazed by how General Schwarzkopf handled the "assortment of characters" that comprised the allies, which was Eisenhower's great strength during World War II. But, as Desert Storm indicated, he was also a Patton.

What about the Navy? Perhaps the best summation came from General Schwarzkopf himself, speaking at the Naval Academy:

> The Navy was the first military force to respond to the invasion of Kuwait, establishing immediate sea superiority. And the Navy was also the first air power on the scene. Both of these firsts deterred, indeed—I believe—stopped, Iraq from marching into Saudi Arabia.

The general then went on to list a series of "firsts":

> It was the first time that we had six carriers at war at one time under one operational commander since World War II, and the first time since 1974 that we had a carrier in the Arabian Gulf.

It was the first combat launch of the Tomahawk cruise missile . . . from battleships and Aegis cruisers, and the first shots fired in anger from a submarine since World War II. It was the first combat launch of the new standoff land attack missile from carrier-based aircraft; the first combat deployment of the AV-8 Harrier, our Aegis cruisers, our air-cushion landing craft, and our remotely piloted vehicles, which were used to adjust the gunfire from our powerful battleships. It was the first combat use of F/A-18s, in both fighter and bomber roles on one mission. It was the first tandem deployment of battleships since the Korean War.

Regarding sealift, the general noted:

It was the quickest and largest military sealift buildup since World War II, an 8,000-mile, 250-ship haze-gray bridge, one ship every fifty miles from the shores of the United States to the shores of Saudi Arabia. And they off-loaded some nine million tons of equipment and petroleum products for our forces. It was the first-ever employment of maritime prepositioning ships

Regarding the Marines, Schwarzkopf added that they

were sensational. . . . U.S. Marines easily punched through what the world's media and Saddam Hussein had called an impenetrable tank-proof barrier, Iraq's Maginot Line.[3]

This is a fitting tribute and summation of the Navy–Marine Corps team's accomplishments in Desert Shield and Desert Storm.

14 / Naval Arms Control

An Unknown Factor

THERE ARE MANY unknowns in the new interwar period, one of the most important of which is the resurgence of naval arms control (NAC) and its possible effect on future forces and operations. Naval arms control has always played a major role in modern interwar periods. During the 1920s and 1930s, the Washington and London Naval Arms Control Agreements limited the shipbuilding programs of the major powers. Many observers felt that their true effect was contributing to the disillusionment of that famous interwar period: countries simply built ship types that were not restrained, while the agreements generated a false sense of security. During the post-Vietnam era, there were also NAC-related proposals including the Indian Ocean Zone of Peace (IOZP) talks and the Conventional Arms Talks (CAT), negotiations that might have placed limits on navies. Fortunately, both failed. Depending on the final language, an IOZP accord might have prevented a response to the Iraqi aggression, and a CAT agreement would have been a verification nightmare.

Currently, there are literally dozens of NAC proposals—traditional Washington Naval Conference–type limitations on forces, operational restraints, what are popularly called confidence building measures (CBMs), and calls for unilateral reductions and restraints. Rationales vary from the changing world conditions to "capturing the inevitable" to frankly, a general dislike by some for navies. These many NAC proposals are often broken down into four general categories: quantitative or structural, qualitative, operational restraints, and finally CBMs, the latter two often grouped together under the broader term "confidence and security building measures" (CSBMs). This chapter will look briefly at each category, listing the important pros and cons of each proposal.[1] It will end with a section on the politics of negotiations, a subject often overlooked by the services—usually to their eventual chagrin.

QUANTITATIVE OR STRUCTURAL MEASURES

The first category covers those measures that actually limit naval forces. There are currently three different approaches:

(1) Restraints on U.S.–Russian Advantages—One suggestion has been to limit those forces most important for the respective fleets. For the USN, this would be aircraft carriers; for the Russian Navy, submarines. The Soviet Union, for example, once offered to eliminate seventy-five submarines if the United States scrapped six carriers. There are several problems with this approach. The most obvious is the classic dilemma of trying to balance dissimilar apples with oranges. (Even worse, there have been proposals to offset Soviet ground forces with carriers. Just how do you really balance army divisions with carriers?) While it might be nice to restrict the Russian submarine advantage, the fact remains that the United States needs carriers more than the CIS needs submarines.

(2) Ways to Capture Current Defense Cuts—Another very popular notion is to capture the downward trend in defense spending. Since the fleet will be reduced over the next few years from nearly 600 to 450 (or fewer) ships with budgets similarly decreasing, why not negotiate that somehow into a formal agreement? While this does have a certain initial appeal, there are problems: for one thing, the Russians read the newspapers too. And again, it would be hard to balance often dissimilar types and missions. Besides, Congress would surely get into the act, making budget cuts just for arms control reasons. This author remembers being involved with chemical weapons negotiations in Geneva where the Soviet team knew before the Americans—and so informed us with a smirk—about a congressional cut in binary weapons, which was doubly embarrassing since that was our main "stick and carrot." The Soviet Navy also has many rusting "hangar queens" to throw into that pot.

(3) Equal SS(N) Limits—A more specific approach, and one that might merit a second glance, is the call for equal U.S.–Russian SSN limits. Since the Soviet Navy's main, and perhaps only, advantage was always its three-to-one superiority in submarines, equal strengths might be advantageous to the West. Of course, many of those submarines are nonnuclear

and (presumably) would not be restricted. This would be another reason for the USN to start building nonnuclear submarines. One author has suggested adding NATO submarines to the equation to balance Soviet nonnuclear types.[2] Counting British and French SSNs would give the ex-Soviet Navy a slight numerical advantage over the USN in that category, but overall, equal submarine limits might be to the West's advantage.

There have also been calls for other limits such as equal fleet strength in the Mediterranean, traditional 1920-era equal ship-type limits, overall equal tonnage, etc. Equal tonnage is a problem considering the large size of U.S. carriers. With the possible exception of equal submarine strengths, most of the structural limits seem to be detrimental to USN interests.

QUALITATIVE LIMITS

Another approach involves some type of "qualitative" limits like the old 1930 arguments between light and heavy cruisers. The most popular qualitative proposal prior to the president's unilateral decision was for a negotiated agreement with Moscow to eliminate tactical nuclear weapons (tacnucs)—that is, all but SLBMs—from naval ships. Since the Russian navies have yet to reciprocate, this might merit a second glance for several reasons. First, most analysts agree that the main loser in a "nuclear war at sea" would be the U.S. and Western fleets with their large carrier battle groups and convoys. Also, the Russian navies have considerably more tacnucs at sea than the USN, which had actually been unilaterally disarming itself of nuclear ASW and SAMs for years.[3] The only USN tacnucs left were the TLAM-N SLCMs and presumably some old nuclear gravity bombs on carriers.[4]

Proponents of a no-tacnucs policy also pointed out that the Navy's "neither confirm nor deny" (NCND) policy was coming under increased attack, and pressure was mounting for more safety controls such as permissive action links (PAL) on nuclear weapons.[5] The Navy itself was split on the tacnuc issue.[6] With all the safety requirements, few captains or crew welcomed nuclear weapons on board. Finally, the Navy had little to lose since there were no future plans for new nuclear weapons. At one time there were proposals for nuclear Harpoons, new nuclear ASW weapons, SAMs, and a nuclear Sea Lance, but all have been canceled.

On the other hand, as noted in Chapter 4, when the dust finally settles from START the TLAM-N might be the only remaining single-warhead weapon left in the inventory, crucial for any option; and after INF II and CFE II, the only remaining theater nuclear deterrent. Removing

TLAM-N might have been a mistake. A possible compromise might have been taking tacnucs off surface ships (where their use was always questionable) and perhaps most submarines. Even with the longer range of the Tomahawks, a surface ship would probably have to come within enemy aircraft envelopes to launch them. And, as noted, few surface ship captains or crews would shed a tear over losing the stringent safety requirements and restrictions placed on any ship with nuclear weapons.

Submarines were always much better platforms for the nuclear Tomahawk; but even here, restrictions were possible. Only three or four *Los Angeles*-class VLS SS"G"Ns were needed on each coast as TLAM-N shooters. That would have been enough for deterrence and limited options, but not enough for major and devastating first strikes. To use nuclear strategy jargon, that would be perceived as a "stabilizing" approach. Similar restraints on Russian SSGNs would remove the oft-expressed fear of a devastating cruise missile "leading edge" attack that would take out all U.S. bombers and submarines in port. These few nuclear SSGNs could have been appropriately marked for verification and operated like SSBNs with sixty-day patrols and only a few port visits, eliminating the NCND problem. In short, the whole question of a negotiated No Nukes at Sea Treaty should be reexamined, especially in light of the recent Soviet breakup. New republic navies with nuclear weapons on board could be dangerous and should be formally eliminated.

Another, more traditional qualitative NAC measure might also be considered; that is, some type of restrictions on mines. One of the oldest NAC measures, dating back to the original turn-of-the-century Hague international arms control conferences, was to outlaw mines. While an outright ban might be unrealistic considering their usefulness during wars, restrictions during peacetime might be considered. As noted in Chapter 12, just a few rogue mines in the Red Sea disrupted shipping. They also caused considerable problems in the Persian Gulf during both the Iran-Iraq War and Kuwait operations and were a contributory factor in canceling an amphibious operation during Desert Storm. Mine use could be outlawed during times of peace. For limited wars, mine laying would be restricted to home waters. In other words, Iran and Iraq could have mined each other's harbors but not international waterways. Also, countries could be required to report sales, with all mines having internationally identifiable markings. Violators would be considered outlaw nations subject to United Nations sanctions.

Such a ban on mines should cause few problems for the United States. It would not have prohibited the mining of Haiphong, although it might have stopped the ill-advised mining of Nicaragua; and U.S. sales are limited to responsible allies. The purpose would be to stop the rogue and terrorist mine operations and especially sales by the Russian Republic, looking for hard cash.

There have been other qualitative proposals such as permitting only defensive weapons or tactics or setting range limits, but these are often hard to define and would be even harder to negotiate. Just what is a "defensive" weapon? How do you verify range limitations? While these broad qualitative proposals should be avoided, a few specific suggestions such as banning most tacnucs and rogue mine operations might be worth a second glance.

OPERATIONAL RESTRAINTS

There are a whole slew of plans for operational restraints, varying from advance notifications to actual exclusion zones. One of the most often-mentioned operational restraint proposals is advance notification of sailings and exercises and limits on their size. These come closer to the CBM category and will be discussed in the following section. Actual operational restraint proposals consist of everything from exclusion zones to expansions of the Incident at Sea (IncSea) agreements. Exclusion zone proposals include such notions as extended territorial buffer zones, limitations on amphibious or attack (carrier) operations near countries, and forbidding any large formations. One of the favorite exclusion proposals is for "ASW Free Zones" (ASWFZ). The basic idea, or fear, is that SSBNs should be given ASWFZ so that the superpowers would not be presented with the classic "use 'em or lose 'em" dilemma during any prolonged conventional war.

"Nuclear Weapon Free Zones" (NWFZ), where countries promise not to introduce nuclear weapons, have been proposed. The United States does, in fact, support the NWFZ concept with the proviso of innocent passage of warships and respect for the NCND policy. There are proposals for NWFZ in virtually every area of the world. Three multilateral NWFZ treaties have been signed—the Antarctic in 1959, Latin America (Treaty of Tlatelolco) in 1967, and the Southwest Pacific (Treaty of Rarotonga) in 1986. The United States is a signatory to the first two and was ready to sign the Treaty of Rarotonga when New Zealand challenged the NCND policy. With the president's decision on tacnucs, the United States might be able to sign the treaty. Others have suggested expanding the IncSea accord with new restrictions, or making it multilateral. Similarly, there have been suggestions to expand the Sea Beds Treaty, which outlaws placing nuclear weapons on the sea beds.

There are many pros and cons to these operational restraint proposals, but in general they all restrict traditional naval freedom of the seas in some manner or have other problems. For example, building on the generally successful U.S.–Soviet IncSea agreement by making it multilateral might have an initial appeal; but would we want Libya and Cuba as signatories, forcing us to sit down with them? Since the Russian Navy seldom strays far from home, the major burden of all these operational restraints invariably falls on the West—and particularly the USN.

CONFIDENCE BUILDING MEASURES (CBM)

Probably the most popular NAC proposals today fall into the CBM category. These, often called static CBMs, include such items as exchange of information on force size, budgets, future building plans, major exercises and sailings, and strategy; officer exchanges; and even naval production "impact" statements. Since most of this data currently exists in Defense Posture statements, congressional reports, or other open literature, many support this approach. At the United Nations there was a proposal called Reporting/Reduction of Military Budgets (ROMB), with the United States usually supporting the "reporting" part as a "first step." Since the Soviet Union was a generally closed society, many felt this exchange of data favored the West.

Other CBM proposals include advance notices and restrictions on (usually large) sailings and exercises. The proposals vary from requiring advance notification of large sailings to restricting the number, size and location of sailings and exercises. Those that support these proposals often see them as simply extensions of the current CSCE requirements for troop movements and notifications. Once again, however, they all seem to restrict traditional freedom of the seas.

There is some overlap between operational restraints and CBM. Many use the broader term "confidence and security building measures" (CSBM), and the term is now used at the European negotiations. Moscow has put forward the following CSBM ideas:

- limiting major naval exercises to once every three years
- precluding amphibious exercises within an agreed distance from signatory country shores
- inviting military observers to exercises
- notifying other nations of major naval exercises
- establishing minimum distances from naval ships and aircraft approaches
- expanding IncSea talks from bilateral to multilateral

- disclosing periodically the numerical strength, structure, numbering, and location of all naval forces
- publishing major military activities, including ship visits
- notifying other nations of the transfer of forces by sea into adjacent territory
- extending provisions of Stockholm CSBMs to naval activities

Since many of these CSBM proposals are minor or already accomplished in some other manner, there is some inclination to support them. (The U.S. government has in fact offered to supply some of this information over the years, especially that currently available in posture statements.) On the other hand, some, while minor, may not be worth the effort and could lead to major restrictions, especially considering the politics of multilateral forums.

NEGOTIATING NAVAL ARMS CONTROL

One of the interesting yet often overlooked aspects of NAC involves the negotiating forums and their politics, which are usually not favorable to the United States. NAC is usually presented in a U.S.–Soviet bilateral context, yet the major calls for NAC have come from multilateral forums such as the United Nations or the CSCE. There are four U.N. arms control–related bodies. The first is the United Nations Disarmament Committee (UNDC), which dates back to the 1950s. Sweden has been pushing for NAC in the UNDC for years. One of the seminal NAC documents is a Swedish-initiated UNDC study from 1985.[7] The United States has usually boycotted sessions of the UNDC relating to NAC. The second major forum is the First Committee of the U.N., which debates arms control. In the past few years, the United States has often found itself completely isolated on NAC during debates in the First Committee. There is also the forty-nation Committee on Disarmament (CD), loosely connected to the U.N. Currently the CD is negotiating a multilateral chemical weapons treaty. Finally, there have been so-called Special Sessions on Disarmament (SSOD). These are quite elaborate affairs, lasting about three weeks. Although barely covered by the U.S. press, they are considered very important throughout the world.

The CSCE forums consist of the Conventional Force in Europe (CFE) and the Confidence and Security Building Measures (CSBM) negotiations. The CFE is often considered a follow-on to the old MBFR talks since the East-West context remains. The CSBM talks have fifty-three members, including neutrals, from the CSCE. To date, naval arms control has been kept off the mandate of both the CFE and CSBM talks, but that could change. Since both are now considered "ongoing" talks, many observers consider NAC inevitable.

As usual, in these bodies the politics are often more interesting, and more important, than the actual substance. Virtually all these multilateral forums have three groups or caucuses: the "neutral nonaligned" (NNA), the West, and the East. The largest is usually the NNA. At the U.N., the NNA number over one hundred, with most, unfortunately, supporting just about any arms control proposal, no matter what the subject or merit. The Western group likes to stick together, although most of our allies usually want to negotiate (and compromise) with the NNA, many of which are their former colonies. The Eastern group usually follows Moscow's lead (even today), especially on arms control measures. Thus, at the U.N. the United States often finds itself quite isolated on arms control matters as it has on NAC proposals.

There are similar caucuses in the CSCE. The CFE negotiations are currently East-West. The CSBM talks, however, have neutrals including Sweden, a strong proponent of NAC. While Western caucus solidarity on NAC has been good to date, that could change. The allies are not as opposed to NAC as the United States is. Also, within the Western caucus there is now an "EC" (virtually all of Western Europe) caucus, which excludes the United States (and Canada). With Margaret Thatcher now retired, many expect NAC to appear as an agenda item in some future round. Adding to the pressure is the fact that the CSBM forum is now looking for something to do. In short, regardless of the merits some American diplomats fear that politics will eventually place NAC on the CSCE agenda.[8]

COMMENTS AND CONCLUSIONS

Although conventional wisdom is that arms control is OBE in this new post–Cold War period, if history is any guide it will continue to be a recurring subject during this new interwar period as it was during the 1920s and 1930s and even the 1970s. As briefly noted in this chapter, there are a host of issues from actual naval reductions to operations limits and exchanges of information. The Navy could undoubtedly live with some of the proposals, and a few might even be advantageous. A much larger group seems to fall into that grey area of "arms control for arms control's sake" and are perhaps not worth the effort. Many, however, do restrict traditional naval freedom of the seas—which the United States, as a maritime nation, needs considerably more than does the land power Russia.

The politics of NAC do not favor the United States. While some of the proposals could be negotiated in a U.S.–Russian bilateral forum, most would fall into the multilateral arenas—probably the CSCE, where the United States is losing control. When the CSCE arms control forums were being constructed in the early 1980s, many considered them as simply "another MBFR," where negotiations dragged on for some sixteen years to no avail (which, incidentally, was their intent). But these new CSCE forums are quite different. The first CDE talks produced a new package of land-related CSBMs in less than two years, a remarkably short time for that sort of agreement. CFE I was decided in only three years. The United States tightly controlled MBFR, but now it is only the first amongst equals in CFE; and if current trends such as the establishment of a new EC caucus for Western Europe continue, it might find itself completely isolated. In short, if a proposal has merit, then it should be considered; but if not, it should be resisted fully. Trying to negotiate and correct detrimental naval arms control proposals in today's multilateral forums could well be a fool's game.

15 / Other "New World Paradigms"

Do They Really Matter?

BESIDES NAVAL ARMS control, there are many more "unknowns" in this new interwar period, one of the most important being the future political-military landscape of the world itself. One of Washington's favorite op-ed and think-tank guessing games these days seems to be either deducing or designing "new worlds" or "paradigms" for the future.[1] Some attempt to decipher the future of the Russian Commonwealth of Independent States—will it disintegrate or become a resurgent superpower?—while others predict a return to a more traditional balance-of-power world; still others suggest idealistic "condominium" models, and a few even speculate on the "end of history" itself. This chapter will briefly examine some of these paradigms, and more specifically the question, "Does any of it really matter to the future of the U.S. Navy?" As noted throughout Part I on mission analysis, the "known" changes will have quite an effect on the Army and the Air Force, with probable increases in naval responsibilities. But what about the "unknowns"?

FUTURE OF THE (RUSSIAN) COMMONWEALTH OF INDEPENDENT STATES

This author is not a Sovietologist, which means he has about the same fifty-fifty chance of being right about the future of the Russian commonwealth as anyone. That is not meant to be *entirely* sarcastic; however, experts had been predicting the demise of the communist Soviet Union since the 1917 revolution, yet those same experts missed the radical changes that took place within the last five years or so. Rather than focusing on Kremlin tea leaves for predicting the future, as Sovietologists were wont to do, they should examine more traditional and historical factors. There are two fundamental points to consider when pondering the future of what was the Soviet Union. First are what used to be called in the study of international relations "the elements of power" such as size, natural resources, and demographics. Second is the up-and-down history of that often-turbulent nation.

The Elements of Power

Although it is often overlooked because of his focus on sea power, Alfred T. Mahan was also one of the first to analyze the basic underlying elements of national power. They have since been refined over the years. These elements, in general order of strength for the Russian commonwealth, are:

Strengths
- geographic
  size, strategic location
  raw materials, degree of autarky
- military strength
- scientific-technological base

Questionable Elements
- demographics
- historical-psychological-sociological

Weaknesses
- economic
- organizational-administrative

At the top of the list must come the Russian commonwealth's geographic strength—it is the largest country in the world, spread through eleven different time zones. It is also strategically situated in what geopoliticians have long considered the "heartland" of the Euro-Asian landmass.[2] While Soviet propagandists usually liked to emphasize the fact that its geography led to many invasions of Russia over the centuries, they somehow neglected the reverse—that its strategic location also made it easy to invade and intimidate weaker neighbors, many of which ended up as part of the Soviet Empire. Equally important, the Russian commonwealth is virtually self-sufficient, an autarky, in all raw materials from food stuffs to minerals. Autarky used to be considered the ultimate goal of national power.

Militarily, the Russian commonwealth is still a "superpower" by any measure, with one of the world's largest armies and air forces equipped with generally top-of-the-line weaponry. Its nuclear arsenal is by far the largest in the world. Only its navy is rated second-class, although not in all areas. The commonwealth's final strength is its underlying scientific-technological base. Any nation that can place satellites (and missiles) in orbit at will has a sound scientific-technological base. Soviet military equipment, to which most resources have been funneled over the years, is generally considered first-rate.[3] Soviet universities also turn out literally thousands of scientists and engineers each year.

The commonwealth's questionable elements of power are demographics and those intangible yet often very important historical-psychological-sociological factors. Although the commonwealth has generally well educated peoples, a strength, its demographics are weakened by old ethnic and nationalistic strife. It was the problems of ethnicity and nationalism as much as the fall of communism that tore apart the old Soviet Union, and many predict the same fate for the new commonwealth. This is why some observers, including Russian writer and historian Alexander Solzhenitsyn, feel that a return to the historic "Russia" (with perhaps Ukraine and Byelarus) would actually be a stronger country than the old Soviet Union. The rural, less well educated Republics, many Moslem and oriental, are considered by many as much a liability as a strength. In short, shedding those non-Russian republics could actually strengthen the country. On the other hand, there are also many Russian experts such as Richard Pipes who note a certain fatalistic spirit to the Russian soul that brings even that conclusion into question. These demographic and psychological-sociological problems are certainly challenges for the future of the commonwealth.

The real problems for the commonwealth are economic and administrative. Today, the CIS is considered almost a Third World "economic basket case"—not because of any underlying elements since, as noted, it is autarkic, but rather due to the still top-heavy, stifling organizational-administrative bureaucracy inherited from the old Soviet Union. For example, even though people might be starving, the problem is not lack of food, which is apparently literally rotting in the fields or at the train stations, but rather the poor distribution system. Of all the elements, however, distribution can, or at least should, be the easiest to fix—if the commonwealth would abandon the stifling communist bureaucratic system for the free market.

In other words, looking at the traditional basic elements of national power, rather than at who stands next to whom on Lenin's tomb, as Sovietologists have done for years, presents quite a different picture about the future of the commonwealth (or even of Russia). The commonwealth will remain quite strong in the three most crucial elements of national power—geographic, military, and scientific-technological. There are questions about the current demographics and the psychology and sociology of the various peoples, but a still quite large and powerful Russia might actually be strengthened by a breakup. The real weaknesses are economic, caused not so much by underlying problems but by the organizational-administrative element—perhaps the easiest to correct. While the difficulty of moving from a communist to a free-market economy should certainly not be underestimated, neither should it be overestimated. For example, after a few painful years, most analysts predict that formerly communist East Germany will be absorbed into the robust West German economy, making the united Germany stronger, not weaker. While there are obvious differences between absorbing a small country and changing a large one, those differences are not insurmountable considering the underlying strength of what was the Soviet Union.

Finally, it is interesting to look back at Alexis de Tocqueville's prediction from *Democracy in America*, written in 1835—many years before Lenin, or even Marx:

> There are now two great nations in the world which, starting from different points, seem to be advancing toward the same goal: the Russians and the Anglo-Americans. Both have grown in obscurity, and while the world's attention was occupied elsewhere, they have suddenly taken their place among the leading nations, making the world take note of their birth and of their greatness almost at the same instant. All other peoples seem to have nearly reached their natural limits and to need nothing but to preserve them; but these two are growing. . . . The American fights against natural obstacles; the Russian is at grips with men. The former combats the wilderness and barbarism; the latter, civilization with all its arms. America's conquests are made with the plowshare, Russia's with the sword. To attain their aims, the former relies on personal interest and gives free scope to the unguided strength and common sense of individuals. The latter in a sense concentrates the whole power of society in one man. One has freedom as the principal means of action; the other has servitude. Their point of departure is different and their paths diverse; nevertheless, each seems called by some secret desire of Providence one day to hold in its hands the destinies of half the world.

Historical Leadership Changes

The other point that should never be forgotten is the often rapid swings in Russian and Soviet leadership. All countries have major leadership changes. This country has had good and bad presidents, England powerful and weak kings; but perhaps nowhere have there been such radical swings in leadership as in Russia and the Soviet Union. An Ivan the Terrible was followed (much later) by a Peter the Great. Many historians blame the weak Czar Nicholas II for the Russian Revolution. The Soviet Union has seen similar swings. The communist revolutionary and Machiavellian Lenin changed (according to some historians) to the pragmatic Lenin by initiating the NEP "new economic policy," which borrowed from or even bordered on capitalism. After a brief interim, Lenin was followed by Stalin, undoubtedly one of the most cruel and ruthless men in all history, who was then succeeded (after another brief interim) by the moderate Nikita Khrushchev. Khrushchev was followed by the corrupt Brezhnev, who was in turn succeeded by the supposedly enlightened Andropov, who was followed by the Brezhnev clone Chernenko and finally by Gorbachev. Russian President Boris Yeltsin has emerged as first among equals in the new commonwealth, but many see him as an interim leader. According to historical precedent, Yeltsin could well be followed by another dictator. There has already been one reactionary coup attempt. It should also be kept in mind that many of these "left-right-moderate" terms, when applied to Soviet (or even Russian) leadership, are simply relative. Lenin could be quite ruthless, Khrushchev once threatened to "bury the West," Andropov was head of the KGB, Gorbachev never forsook communism (and may be waiting for a comeback), and virtually all of the current republic leaders, including Yeltsin, were once communists. There is absolutely no democratic tradition in Russia.

Regardless of the future of the commonwealth, or Russia, it will remain a major power—and due to its large nuclear arsenal alone, always at least a semi-superpower. There is simply no country, not even a reunited Germany, that could come close to the level of Russian military power in the near or even midterm future. As a major power, it will continue to influence events. And from a military standpoint, its only instrument for direct influence will probably be the Russian Navy. The old Soviet Army and Air Force units will undoubtedly be out of East Europe soon, with returns, short of war, unlikely. After the Afghanistan experience, "the Soviet Union's Vietnam," similar overt military interventions also seem unlikely. That leaves little choice for asserting direct power save for using its navy.

It will be interesting, therefore, to see future Russian shipbuilding trends. While the Soviet Navy was still building at old Cold War rates—six to nine submarines a year, along with aircraft carriers, cruisers, and destroyers—according to some reports submarine construction has slowed to two to four a year, with similar cuts in the other types. Of course, this is still well over double U.S. rates. The commonwealth, and its navy, could be a quite formidable, unpredictable force for many years to come.

TOWARD A NEW BALANCE-OF-POWER WORLD?

One favorite future paradigm foresees a return to traditional multi-polarity, balance-of-power politics. Those most mentioned as moving up to major-power status are a reunited Germany or an "EC Europe," a rearmed Japan, and China. Former powers such as France and the United Kingdom will continue to play some roles. Other analysts see a variation of this theme with major regional powers, such as India in South Asia, China in Asia, Brazil in South America, Iraq in the Persian Gulf, Egypt in the Middle East and North Africa, Nigeria in Africa, and the like. Also, if the Russian-dominated CIS does break up, several of the larger republics such as Ukraine, as well as any with nuclear weapons, would have to be added to any balance-of-power list. While balance-of-power politics have never completely disappeared, even in the post–World War II, bipolar Cold War period, a return to traditional nineteenth-century politics seems unlikely under closer examination.

The country most often mentioned as moving up (actually returning) to great-power status is Germany. Some of the predictions are rather alarming, perhaps even shameful. During late 1989, with the Berlin Wall coming down and providing great television shots and the reunification of East and West Germany in the works, those television shots would invari-ably be followed by movie clips from 1939 showing Hitler addressing and haranguing a large crowd—implying that goose-stepping Nazis would be the first group marching through the reopened Brandenberg Gate. Others like to point out that Germany has the largest army in Western Europe. Germany is, and has been for some time, an *economic* superpower; but military power is quite different. The German Army might be the largest in Western Europe with over 300,000 soldiers and a dozen divisions, but that is a far cry from Hitler's army of millions with dozens of divisions. Germany does not even have an indigenous airplane fighter- or bomber-building capability. Imagine going to war without that! The German Navy started World War II with sixty-two submarines and *almost* won, but *did* lose. Today the German Navy has some twenty submarines, none nuclear powered.

There are two factors that will prevent Germany from becoming a major military power in the near to even mid-future. These are lack of nuclear weapons and that intangible yet important psychological-sociological element of national power. First and foremost is the lack of any nuclear weapons, even a few for "deterrence." Not only does Germany have no plans for such weapons due to the current antinuclear sentiment, but it would probably be prevented from initiating any such program by world public opinion, France, the United Kingdom, *and* the Russian CIS, all with American backing. This could be one of those "condominium" world decisions where the United States and the Russian commonwealth would be in agreement. It might simply be a "wink and a nod" by the United States to a Russian threat against Germany if it built nuclear weapons, but there would probably still be common agreement. It is also hard to see France and Britain standing idly by as they did in the late 1930s interwar period while Germany rearmed.

More important are the psychology and sociology of the German people themselves. Public opinion would not even support Chancellor Kohl when he contemplated sending German troops under multilateral U.N. authority in the Iraq crisis, although some airplanes were finally sent to NATO ally Turkey. The German people are also strongly opposed to nuclear weapons. Before the tearing down of the Berlin Wall, many German political observers thought Kohl's conservative alliance would lose out to the liberal, antinuclear coalition of the socialists and far-left "Greens." There are small right-wing groups and a few nascent signs of anti-Semitism in Germany, causing many to remember how small Hitler's own party was at the outset. However, a resurgent, militaristic Germany is one interwar analogy that does not seem to pertain. The politics and economics of Germany, and Europe, in the 1990s are not that of the 1920s Weimar Republic.

Some observers predict that the combination of new world politics, American troop withdrawals, arms control proposals, changes in the former Soviet Union, and especially "EC '92" (the economic and limited political union of Europe in 1992) will see a "United Europe" emerge as an important world player, on a par with Russia and the United States. There has been considerable talk of rejuvenating the generally moribund Western Europe Union (WEU) defense agreements that still exist, if only on paper. The EC now meets as a group in the CSCE. Certainly, a truly united Europe would be a strong power, even a superpower, by any calculation. It could even have a significant nuclear capacity with France's and Britain's arsenals at its disposal.

But, can the EC really become a major power? Probably not. For one thing, England and certainly France would never surrender control of their nuclear capabilities to a joint EC command. A rejuvenated WEU might be a "defensive" organization, but not the offensive force necessary to exert any true influence. Also, most Europeans (especially the smaller nations) still want to keep NATO and American military involvement intact in some manner. This is often expressed as the desire to "keep the Russians out, the Americans in, and the (reunited) Germans down." Finally, historic nationalism even within a common market would probably prevent common military action. While there has been considerable discussion of multilateral military units, these are mostly symbolic.

* * *

A rearmed Japan has also been mentioned as a potential major actor, with some even predicting a *"coming war with Japan."*[4] Although the fact is barely covered by the American press, the Asian countries have certainly not forgotten about World War II and truly fear a resurgent Japan. A few, such as Singapore, have been honest enough to mention this aloud, which is one reason it has offered the United States base rights to keep American forces in the area. However, Japan has to face the same psychological and sociological problems as Germany before becoming a major actor on the international political-military stage. It does not have, or desire, nuclear weapons. As an island nation, Japan would also require a blue-water navy complete with aircraft carriers and a large amphibious force. While Japan certainly has the industrial shipbuilding capabilities to build such a fleet, if started tomorrow it would take at least a decade, probably two. You simply do not build and deploy aircraft carriers overnight. Besides, building amphibious forces would *surely* incite world opinion. Poll after poll has shown that the Japanese people have no desire to rearm; and like the Germans, they even balked at sending forces to the multilateral efforts under U.N. authority against Iraq. A change in Japanese law to permit U.N. peacekeeping precipitated a riot in the Diet. Once again, some analysts have confused economic with military power.

For years, China was considered a major player on the threshold of superpower status. The "China card" was played by several presidents hoping to offset the influence of the Soviet Union. As a large country in both size and population, with the world's largest army and third largest nuclear arsenal, China cannot be ignored. However, the "opening" of China has also exposed its considerable vulnerabilities, both economical and political. With the geriatric leadership still in charge and clinging to the old ways, few expect major changes in China's favor in the near term. It has extremely limited military capabilities beyond its borders. Once the "long march" veteran, octogenarian leadership passes, China could, considering the vitality of the people, become a major regional power in the twenty-first century; but it will undoubtedly take many years of first placing its own house in order.

* * *

More likely than the development of new superpowers will be the emergence of regional powers and the continuation of intraregional conflicts. Regional powers include India in South Asia, China in Asia, Egypt in the Middle East and North Africa, perhaps a militant black South Africa or Nigeria in Africa, Brazil in South America, and the like. There might also be considerable intraregional conflicts or grabs for power, such as that between Iraq, Iran, and Syria in the Persian Gulf area; the continuing India-Pakistan and India-China tensions; tribal rivalries in Africa; ongoing Central American crises; and perhaps the reemergence of the old ABC (Argentine-Brazil-Chile) tensions in South America, although that seems unlikely. The old Balkan states have once more become a tinderbox that reminds many of the roots of World War I. And, as noted, Ukraine and any former Soviet republic with nuclear weapons would automatically become a major player in regional politics. This might even involve several new navies, some with tactical nuclear weapons.

In short, there are no lack of areas, or reasons, for potential conflicts. And the U.S. Navy could well be the favorite instrument for American power in any traditional balance-of-power scenario. What most scholars consider the golden age of balance-of-power politics, the post–Napoleonic Wars nineteenth century, was after all the zenith of British seapower. It was through skillful use of seapower that Britain emerged as the world's greatest power, and it was seapower that brought about the hundred-odd years of Pax Britannia.

"Condominium" Worlds

Another popular paradigm for the future has been a so-called condominium world, with two variants—one of U.S.–Soviet (Russian) arrangement, and the other multilateral under a rejuvenated United Nations. Both of these models emerge from the recent crisis in the Persian Gulf and the Iraqi invasion of Kuwait. Many analysts felt that it was only the explicit support of the Soviet Union that allowed the American-led buildup against Saddam Hussein, once an ally of the Kremlin. Without that support, their argument goes, the United States would not have dared to challenge Iraq, fearing Soviet intervention. They note the U.S.–Soviet tensions during the 1973 Arab-Israeli war, during which both sides made threats and the United States went to a worldwide DEFCON Three.

Whether the superpower cooperation in the Persian Gulf will lead to an actual U.S.–Russian "condominium" remains to be seen. Until recently, both countries were still supporting opposite sides in several conflicts, including those in Afghanistan, Central America, and Africa. Soviet Foreign Minister Eduard Shevardnadze's resignation was in part a result of criticism by the Soviet military and hard-liners of his cooperation with the United States. The Soviet Union was also careful not to send forces to the Middle East. Boris Yeltsin actually asked about joining NATO—although even NATO allies often quarrel. Post–Cold War detente, after all, is still not entente.

Others have speculated on a new, rejuvenated United Nations, with countries "uniting for peace" against aggressor nations as they did for the Korean conflict in 1950 and again against Iraq in 1990. Many thought that the old precedent the United Nations used against North Korea was long dead; but the U.N. played an important, perhaps crucial role in the recent Iraq crisis. Whether this becomes the norm or simply another unique event remains to be seen. Most countries did seem shocked by the open, naked aggression of Saddam Hussein. Instead of looking the other way as generally has been the case over the past forty years, the U.N.—even the neutral nonaligned nations, for a change—seemed genuinely affected. The U.N. has also played major roles in the Middle East, Yugoslavia, and even El Salvador recently. People such as Paul Nitze have suggested that the U.N. might become a potent force in settling disputes, as was originally envisioned.

Of course, both these condominium models would still require military forces to deter and, if necessary, to fight aggression. For a U.S.–Russian condominium, the most obvious arrangement would be for the maritime nation, the United States, to supply the naval forces, with land forces coming from the land power, Russia. There are actually provisions for a U.N. military "condominium" force in the U.N. Charter. Again, it would probably be appropriate for the United States to supply the naval elements to any U.N. force. In fact, while all countries have land forces, only the United States has the large, blue-water Navy necessary for such a deployment.

THE END OF HISTORY?

One of the most intriguing notions in years was set forth by a State Department employee in a provocative article entitled "The End of History."[5] The author argued that the recent admission by the Soviet Union and Eastern Europe of the failure of the communist model and its abandonment for the Western liberal-democracy paradigm constituted the "end of history" since there would no longer be societal struggles. Furthermore, democracies seldom initiate wars against each other.

This provocative article has come under the expected criticism. First, not all communist countries, including all the commonwealth republics, have clearly adopted the liberal-democratic model, which also includes free-market capitalism. Many of the republics and countries in Eastern Europe are struggling with the political conversion—with the old leadership still in place in some cases. Second, even democracies have different interests and have fought wars. Third, history is unfortunately replete with examples of liberal democracies falling to dictatorships, which in turn often become militaristic. It is this "Weimar Republic" precedent that still bothers people. Fourth, many countries in the Third World (where all of the post–World War II conflicts have taken place) still have not accepted the liberal-democratic, free market model, or are under constant threats from "men on horseback" the minute economic conditions deteriorate. Fifth, there are enough other potential problems stemming from nationalism, religious differences, border disputes, and the like to ignite tensions.

Still, as a paradigm the "end of history" model is interesting, particularly for the long term. While it is certainly not impossible, it *is* hard to imagine Western-oriented liberal democracies going to war against each other in today's environment. What does a reunited, democratic Germany really have to gain by going to war? It is by far the wealthiest country in Europe. Japan has more wealth and economic power under today's informal economic "co-prosperity sphere of influence," and without the cost of maintaining a large military, than it ever had under the formal arrangements of the 1930s. Why would a liberal-democratic, capitalistic Russia that freed not just Eastern Europe but the "Soviet republics" now go to war? And most Third World nations are also accepting the liberal-democratic, capitalistic approach. For at least the next few years, however, the "end of history" paradigm must simply be that: a model and a goal.

INTERWAR OR INTERWORLD PERIOD?

The world does seem to be changing. As an editor of a new world order forum stated, "Whatever direction events take in the next decade, the world will never return to the status quo *ante bellum frigidum.* And while the emerging world order will no doubt contain elements of its predecessors, its departure from cold war strictures and consequent potential for dynamic change will certainly be new."[6] Whether it is an "interwar" or new-paradigm "interworld" transition will probably not be known for some time. Also, all these new "paradigms" do not necessarily make for a better, safer world. A balance-of-power world with a resurgent, nuclear-armed Germany and Japan (or even several nuclear-armed ex-Soviet republics) would certainly not be welcomed. However, it is more likely that Germany and Japan will emerge as economic superpowers, which also, of course, has a downside. Economic strength is, after all, one of the major underlying elements of power. While this author does not subscribe fully to Paul Kennedy's thesis of the automatic decline of powers that stress military over economic power,[7] as with all broad theses there are elements of truth. As the Russian commonwealth is undoubtedly learning to its chagrin, military power alone can only last so long.

However, only one of these paradigms, the "end of history" model, would eventually affect U.S. naval forces. The others would have little effect or, like the "known" factors from Part I, probably lead to an increase in naval forces. As noted earlier, the classical balance-of-power world of the nineteenth century was also the heyday of the Royal Navy. The more likely scenario, regional balances of powers and regional conflicts, would still see U.S. involvement—as witness the need for American leadership to counter Iraq's aggression. Even the more idealistic "condominium" models would see continued American naval involvements. Finally, a resurgent Russian commonwealth, or even Russia alone, would similarly require U.S. maritime power to balance the old Russian bear. In short, regardless of the new world paradigm, flexible navy forces will still be needed for many, many years.

16 / Conclusions

The Perils of "Less of the Same"

FEW WOULD ARGUE with Secretary Garrett's assessment that "we are at an historic threshold . . . a point in history that happens once every century." Whether it will be, as history seems to dictate, another interwar period or, as we all hope, an interworld transition to a better paradigm, remains to be seen. Because of the uncertainty, there is understandable confusion on the future direction of the Navy, and the somewhat natural inclination to simply continue with "less of the same" or some very ad hoc solution. That could be a mistake, especially considering the already well known, discernible trends. Moreover, alternatives that can maintain both the quantity and the quality of the Navy, as well as satisfy new mission requirements, do exist.

THE PERILS OF "LESS OF THE SAME"

There are serious problems with today's "less of the same" course. These include:

Decreasing Numbers

Since the Navy is currently building only high-level, sophisticated, and very expensive ships and aircraft, the major problem is that decreasing budgets will drastically lower procurement rates, eventually leading to a much smaller fleet. Warship-building rates have already fallen to fewer than ten per year, enough to sustain only an approximate 300-ship Navy. There are no frigates to balance the Aegis cruisers and destroyers, no LSTs to balance the LHDs, and no A-6s or even A-7s to offset the very expensive AX (if ever built). Lower mix alternatives might have also eased the necessity to rush current high-tech programs. For example, had the A-6 line remained open perhaps the A-12 problems could have been resolved smoothly, with less pressure on program managers to rush to production. Since only high-level and expensive units are being purchased, the numbers will invariably decrease. Some shortages are already occurring.

Erosion of Industrial/Reconstitution Base

Another problem is that building only high-level equipment could actually end up eroding the industrial and reconstitution base in several ways. First, as noted above, with unit costs high only a few can be built. There were once plans for building the DDG-51 in three yards, but now only two may be used. The second problem is that in order to save and fund these high-cost programs, lower-cost programs and modernizations are being sacrificed. One reason the Navy did not want to modernize the *Knox* class was that it would take away from *Burke* funds.[1] All submarine modernization programs were being sacrificed for SSN-21 *Seawolf* funding. Yet, ironically, a main rationale for those new programs was to "save" the industrial base.[2]

Although an extensive and comprehensive look at the American shipbuilding industry is beyond the scope of this book, it would seem to this author that refueling and modernizing thirty-seven *Sturgeon*-class SSNs, developing and building SSns, and building under license a new NATO AIP SS and an old SS for export would help the submarine industrial base considerably more than building just one SSN-21 per year. Or that building many LSTs, frigates, and corvettes would help those shipyards considerably more than building just one LHD every few years and a few DDGs per year. These types of ships would also give American shipyards some export possibilities. The struggling American shipbuilding industry has been barely kept alive through the 1980s on Navy shipbuilding, modernization, and repairs. It will decrease further if funds are channeled to just a few expensive ships, none with export potential.

Yesterday's Mission Requirements

There are also many questions about *today's* mission requirements for these high-level ships, generally built for yesterday's conditions. The period when the SSN-21, the DDG-51, stealth aircraft, etc., were originally designed, the late 1970s and early 1980s, was probably the zenith of Soviet military strength. The foray into Afghanistan, fears of Euro-communism—whatever happened to Euro-communism?—and the decline of Western strength and resolve had many worried in the late 1970s. Even President Carter reversed his assessment on Soviet intentions. This author once wrote two very strongly pro-DDG-51 articles in the mid-1980s. But times have changed. The DDG-51—designed to meet the Soviet threat *within* a large, layered, carrier battle group structure, without helicopter facilities—is not the right ship for flexible and often *independent* Third World operations. Better would be an APD-963 with an eight-inch gun that could also act as an escort for Amphibious Ready Groups. Stealth aircraft designed to penetrate the sophisticated Soviet air defenses may simply not be needed today. Rather, the top priority might be an advanced STOVL airplane capable of taking off and landing on amphibious assault ships equipped with ski ramps, and to save the industrial base both the Air Force and the Navy should look at light aircraft for both indigenous use and export.

The Squeeze on Future Programs

However, the greatest problem with "less of the same" building programs of these expensive ships is that they might actually squeeze out those future programs truly needed for the twenty-first-century environment. There are already signs of this. The fully capable flight III DDG-51 with a larger magazine capacity and helicopter capabilities might be permanently on hold. Part of the "Revolution at Sea" plans for switching to all-electric drive has quietly been dropped. An all-electric drive has many advantages including eliminating the need for long shafts in ships, thus allowing for more design flexibility and increased magazine space. Admiral Trost once called electric drive the wave of the future, but *current* priorities have apparently pushed Revolution at Sea aside. Many felt that the main problem with the SSN-21 was not cost but capabilities; yet current funding precludes looking at a follow-on. Trying to build all high-level aircraft based on yesterday's mission requirements may result in none being built for tomorrow's environment. Building some mid- and lower-level systems would have freed funds for future systems.

Sow's Ear Syndrome

Perhaps even worse are current proposals that attempt to make silk purses out of some sow's ears. The most obvious example is the proposal to stretch, twist, and pull the F/A-18 into areas and missions never imagined, but the same sow's ear syndrome has apparently struck the other two Navy communities. The surface community is looking at an only slightly lower-cost destroyer alternative, but without some frigate capabilities, while the submariners want a new, low-cost mode to be capable for all missions. In other words, instead of balancing today's *more* capable ships and aircraft with some lower-cost systems in order to afford truly futuristic weapons for the twenty-first century, the Navy will be building a series of jury-rigged, *less* capable, but still too expensive modes. Historically, this would be the first time since the post–Civil War era that the Navy has deliberately built less capable ships. That long, sad interwar period became known as the "dark ages" in U.S. naval history.

Deployment Requirements

Another problem with "less of the same" building and thinking is that deployments will ultimately suffer. This could become particularly acute if, as noted in Part I on missions, naval deployment requirements actually increase. The JCS now wants a carrier in the Persian Gulf area at all times. In short, trying to maintain (much less increase) deployments with less of the same simply cannot work, and will contribute to the final and perhaps ultimate problem—reduced morale.

Morale Problems

There are several morale problems facing the Navy in the new interwar period. The causes range from longer deployments in trying to maintain traditional commitments to decreased command opportunities for all, especially more junior officers. This author is not talking about crises like the one in the gulf, which required long times on station for much of the Navy. These are quite understandable, and morale did not seem to suffer. However, if JCS and national requirements demand maintaining Sixth Fleet, Seventh Fleet, and Indian Ocean commitments with decreasing forces, morale will ultimately suffer as more time is spent away from home ports. Alternatives must be found.

Building simply a few large ships will drastically limit officer command and promotion opportunities. Many junior officers, the future of the Navy, are already seeing the handwriting on the bulkhead regarding their future command opportunities. If current trends continue, it could well be that only captains will end up with commands. We are already seeing this with the forty-one Polaris and Poseidon SSBNs skippered by commanders being replaced by only eighteen Tridents with captains in command. Once again, alternatives should be sought. Building SSs, corvettes, mine craft, etc., would once more give lieutenant commanders command opportunities. Building frigates, LSTs, and SSBns would maintain commander commands for the surface and submarine communities. Enlisted personnel often like these smaller ships as well, with regulations often relaxed but morale increased. There is nothing wrong with bringing some fun back into the Navy.

The (Goldwater-Nichols) Proportional Problem

Finally, less of the same falls into the one-third, one-third, one-third service proportional reduction trap exacerbated by the relatively new mid-1980s, Goldwater-Nichols Cold War "jointness" requirements. That is, each of the services will take approximately proportional cuts regardless of their mission requirements for the new post–Cold War period. While it does appear that the Army and the Air Force will be taking slightly larger budget cuts, the new Base Force still comes close to one-third proportional reductions even though the Navy's responsibilities should grow. This could be even further exacerbated by proportionally "divvying up" the major CINC commands, again regardless of the merits. It needs emphasizing that this author is not concerned with the all too frequent Navy parochialism, but rather with the sound organizational principle that he who has the majority, especially the preponderance, of forces should be in charge. The whole Goldwater-Nichols Act may be another relic of the Cold War and should be seriously reexamined.

OTHER PROBLEMS

There are a host of other problems facing the Navy. These include:

Parochialism

One of the major internal problems with trying to change direction within the Navy has been traditional community parochialism. The Navy has three communities, air, surface, and submarine, each with its own designator, insignias, informal promotion systems, and priorities. They are headed by senior three-star vice admirals known within the Navy staff as "the Barons." To overcome this turf problem, the Navy has what might be called an overlapping matrix system of "warfare" areas with their own three-star "chiefs"; but they often find it tough to take on the Barons. While there have been a few mavericks such as Vice Admiral Metcalf, who suggested surface warfare alternatives, generally the Barons promote building high-level ships. Then there is a great reluctance to change course, especially once fully committed to Congress.

While some of the events are fairly recent, such as the creation of the CIS, the trends have now been discernible for over five years. After all, Gorbachev took over in 1985 and almost immediately announced glasnost (openness) and perestroika (restructuring), formally initiating a period of change. It has been three years since the Berlin Wall came tumbling down. The last three national security statements have noted the shift from the old Cold War anti-Soviet posture to the new Third World crisis response role. In short, it is time for change, and for the weapons appropriate for these new conditions.

Shooting or Silencing the Messenger

Another problem is the frequent service tendency to "shoot the messenger" who brings the bad news—or, more recently, to simply "stifle the messenger." During the post-Vietnam era the messenger was Adm. Elmo Zumwalt, whose name can still generate a spark or two among Navy Officer Club patrons. With today's shipbuilding rates falling to single digits, more may soon sympathize with Admiral Zumwalt's double-digit high-low mix procurement rates. And in this new interwar period, just when some *glasnost* might be most needed, there are attempts to require all naval authors to submit papers for both security and "policy" clearance. While security clearances are certainly understandable, policy censorship is not. If the services truly want "to air creative ideas, no matter how controversial," as Secretary Garrett stated, changes must be made in current policy.

Emphasis on Operations Research, Not "Ideas"

Another disturbing element is the emphasis by most governmental research organizations, whether they are civilian "beltway" bandits or organizations like RAND, on number-crunching "operations research" (OR) solutions to all problems. In certain cases, such as conducting specific weapons research, OR is certainly needed. On the other hand, the uses, needs, and requirements for any weapon are based on NCA declaratory policies, which are political-military statements. However, the real problem is that the OR requirement for "justifying" new ideas usually means using old data and ideas, and all too often form becomes more important than substance.

There are many examples. One of the clearest is the old concern of strategists over the declining numbers of SSBNs. Strategists focus on such unquantifiable notions as "deterrence" or "stability," not the targeteers' concern about "number of warheads on target." Naval strategists, for example, worry about day-to-day naval presence, that somewhat nebulous "misunderstood mission," while the community Barons worry about the seldom-seen "worst possible case" vulnerabilities. Operations research has its place, as do unquantifiable ideas. There is room, and need, for both.

Congressional Interference

Congressionally mandated programs, studies, and general interference are bound to increase in this new interwar period. In Congress's defense, part of the problem must be attributed to the administration, which has yet to articulate a fully coherent defense policy. Since the start of the administration there have been rumors of forthcoming new policies, yet little has emerged. The president did announce the new defense policy in August 1990, but details are very slow in appearing. Since Congress, like nature, abhors a vacuum, it may soon pick up the mantle, especially with strong leadership from the likes of Senator Sam Nunn and Congressman Les Aspin, chairmen of the Senate and House Armed Services Committees, respectively. Senator Nunn has already called for new strategies and debates including missions competition, while Chairman Aspin has established his own committee think tank and commenced issuing "white papers."

Arms Control

Although many feel that arms control might be OBE in this emerging interwar era, the current agenda certainly seems full, with new START, INF, and conventional CFE agreements recently signed and their follow-ons already under way or planned. And for the first time, all these agreements will bring real cuts, not just the traditional freezes. Many observers anticipate eventual naval arms control negotiations. Therefore, designers of weapons systems and the military as a whole must now take into account these new "rules of the game." For the Navy this includes building a smaller SSBN or perhaps SSBns with fewer launch tubes. Historically, interwar periods have always been times of intense arms control.

Personnel Problems

Finally, there are a whole host of personnel problems facing the military in this new post–Cold War period. For probably the first time in history, good personnel are actually being forced out of the services. Many see this as a major breaking of faith for the all-volunteer force. Others remember the hollow force from the post-Vietnam era, and the terrible morale problems that ensued. To their credit, both the civilian and the military leaderships are fully aware of this problem, but further budget cuts, congressional interference, and the inevitable lowering of the guard during any interwar period could spell trouble. One year Congress increases the requirements for military academy graduates to six years, and the next it denies them regular commissions. In their desire to save guard and reserve units in local districts, Congress forces cuts in ready, active duty forces. The Army is under pressure to maintain recruiting while losing strength, meaning that the whole lower infantry ranks could see a complete turnover in three to four years. And the list goes on. The true strength of today's U.S. forces is, after all, not the latest weaponry, but the best-trained personnel.

THE NEED FOR A NAVY STRATEGY THINK TANK (NSTT)

The Navy, indeed all the services, are faced with a real "advice dilemma" today, with at least a five-way struggle. At the top are the services, with their strong parochial interests and their tendency to shoot anyone with a different message. On two sides facing each other are the Brookings Institution–type think tanks, with their more philosophical yet often very provocative and *widely read* political-military studies, countered by generally tepid, often unnecessarily classified government-related think tanks with their OR studies, invariably based on old data. At the bottom is Capitol Hill with 535 Congressmen and their large staffs, all with their own solutions. Added to this four-way pull is a fifth actor, OMB, trying to cut the budget. It is not an easy dilemma to resolve.

There are two often-suggested solutions to this problem. One is the resurrection of the old Navy Board in the form of a council of retired senior officers, perhaps sprinkled with a few elderly civilian "wise men" such as a Paul Nitze. These relatively young retired officers with all their experience are often underutilized. Fears have sometimes been expressed that they would constantly second-guess their active duty brothers, but this need not happen. For one thing, the active duty flag officers are usually so wrapped up in day-to-day matters that they have little time for long-range planning or thought. Besides, the advice could be given in confidence.

The best solution might be the creation of a new Navy Strategy Think Tank (NSTT). The Navy has a history of creating think tank–type organizations both within and outside the formal Navy organization, using them for a few years, and then discarding them. This seems somewhat ironic considering their proud history. During the 1950s, Admiral Burke had OP-93, which at various times was headed by Charles D. Griffin, Roy L. Johnson, Horacio Rivero, and Thomas P. Moorer—all of whom went on to four-star rank. In the 1970s, OP-96 gathered in the cream of the crop, including Admiral Trost. Now, just when it might be needed the most, there is no such organization.

Better would be a semiautonomous, civilian-military organization. Civilians are needed for continuity and their own particular expertise, but some senior officers in the commander and captain ranks should also be assigned, with perhaps a one-star codirector allowing direct access to the senior Navy leadership: in short, a mix of "scholarship with salt." The civilians should also have some salt in their veins. All too often civilians with no naval (but invariably with operational research) experience are hired for these positions, with predictable results.

In this new post–Cold War era there might also be an annual, public naval conference of record. In the early 1980s the Center for Naval Analyses came up with the good idea of an annual "Sea Power Forum" rotating among four maritime topics: the U.S. Navy, communist navies, the Marine Corps, and allied navies. Some were held and subsequently published, with the one on the U.S. Navy currently on the CNO's reading list. The forum process has since become quite sporadic.

Perhaps a new NSTT and the Naval Institute could pick up the baton with annual, published conferences. This would give the NSTT an opportunity to display some of its studies along with other scholars and, yes, even some critics. The Naval Institute could then publish the proceedings. A conference every year on rotating maritime topics would eventually create an interesting record and progression of naval thought and history like the old Brassey's Annual. It could also be a good way for the Navy to present their case, yet in a semidetached fashion.

Another suggestion that might be most appropriate in this uncertain era is the "blue team–gold team" approach, with two different groups looking at the same problem with the same budget restrictions. A 500-ship Navy could easily be built and maintained within current budget and manpower limits with some frigates, corvettes, LSTs, and SSs to complement and supplement the more sophisticated ships. This team approach would foster some competition and might produce what is really needed—alternatives.

ALTERNATIVES

As described throughout Part II, there is in fact a wide spectrum of different alternatives—some old, some new, others modifications—that could maintain both the quantity and the quality of the fleet. Many would not cost much yet have potentially high payoffs. For example, adding ski ramps to the amphibious assault ships would literally *double* naval air "presence" overnight. A ski-ramped LHD with Harriers or perhaps a few F-18s would never be equivalent to a CVN, but it would provide "presence" and adequate air support for the vast majority of crisis response situations. ARGs with these ski-ramped LHDs and LHAs and a few escorts could also substitute for CVNs on occasion, thus greatly increasing deployment options.

Another low-cost option would be initiating nonnuclear submarine programs, especially considering the recent advances. The Navy's arguments against building old diesel boats were somewhat valid. However, with the new AIP options, including even the small nuclear reactor proposal, most of those arguments no longer pertain. The surface community should also look at some alternatives, such as designing a combined/dual-capable frigate model and using corvettes where appropriate. A lower-cost amphibious LST should also be a top priority.

All of the alternatives listed in Part II may not be practical. For example, a "low-cost" SSN, an APD using the DD-963 hull, or VSS program might be too expensive no matter what the intent. However, they should all be explored. All combined and dual-capable possibilities should also be investigated. If the A-12 medium attack bomber had been a committed joint Navy–Air Force venture it might still be in production. With all countries slashing defense funds, some allied navies might now wish they had signed up and committed themselves to a NATO frigate.

New U.S. fleets, deployment patterns, and combined STANAVFORs might also be considered to maintain some forward and surge capabilities. New reserve First and Second Fleets built around RBGs, with a carrier RCVBG and amphibious RARG plus some nonnuclear reserve SSs, would give the Navy considerable reserve and surge options. These RBGs could easily be formed around retiring CVs, LPHs, and older frigates. This would make the new Third and Fourth Fleets ready "home fleets," with the Seventh and Sixth the traditional forward fleets. The new fleet organization could facilitate transitions to readiness during emergencies. For example, during a crisis the combat-ready Fourth Fleet could immediately surge forward, with the reserve Second taking its place as it increases training operations for possible deployment.

There are also many combined STANAVFORs that could be either expanded or created. The current STANAVFORLANT could be strengthened with the addition of a multinational-manned battleship as the new NATO SACLANT flagship. The United States could easily contribute a mine craft to a channel command. A new Med mine force could be established and the on-call STANAVFORMED group made permanent. In the Pacific an ANZUS force could be created, and perhaps even an on-call SEATO/ASEAN force. The Rio Pact UNITAS exercises could be strengthened with an on-call STANAVFORRIO. Depending on situations in the Persian Gulf, multinational naval forces might be created either by NATO allies or under the U.N. "blue" flag, using frigates, corvettes, or mine craft.

While the primary purpose of the combined STANAVFORs might be as much symbolic as military, the military capabilities should not be underestimated. The combined patrols during both the Iran-Iraq War and the Iraqi invasion of Kuwait helped considerably. The STANAVFORs might even relieve some of the pressure for USN deployments. Or, after an initial crisis response by a USN task force, the combined naval force (perhaps operating under a U.N. flag) could continue the naval presence. As illustrated in Figure 16-1, the creation of these new U.S. reserve fleets and multinational STANAVFORs would place ready forces around the world.

While maintaining that forces and deployments are important, the best defense and deterrent policy might be a sound R and D program. Full series production may not be needed in all cases, although some production is necessary to maintain an industrial base. In fact, the best deterrent might simply be the constant building of prototype "dreadnoughts"—that which makes all else obsolete. Some of the current programs fit into that scheme. The SSN-21, the DDG-51, new stealth aircraft, and weapon systems such as AMRAAM are all major advances, undoubtedly the envy of friend and foe alike, none of which can probably afford to build or counter these systems—the ultimate purpose of deterrence. Many Sovietologists felt that just starting SDI research convinced Soviet military leaders that they could no longer compete unless they changed their ways. Whether these items all have to be built in series for today's environment is doubtful. Rather, they should be used as stepping-stones for the next generations. After all, HMS *Dreadnought* itself was obsolete by World War I.

THE NEED FOR DECLARATORY POLICY

The greatest need in the new interwar period may not be for forces, or mission analysis, or even R and D, but for declaratory policy. On two of the three political-military levels, the recent Iraq crisis was a complete failure due to lack of a clear-cut policy. First was the initial response and confusion perhaps caused in part by Ambassador April Glaspie's meeting with Saddam Hussein in the summer. As the *Washington Post* commented:

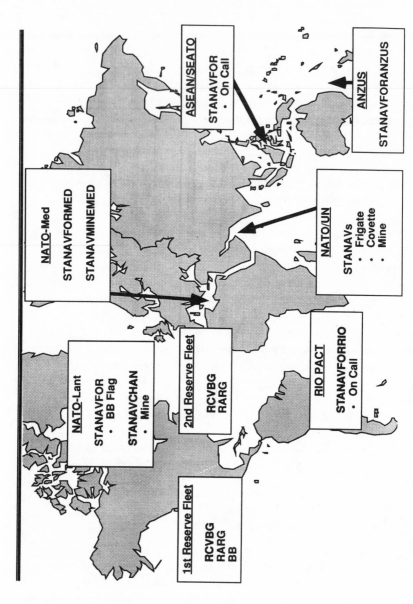

Figure 16-1. New U.S. Fleets and STANAVFORs

The crucial moment was U.S. Ambassador April Glaspie's July 25 meeting with Saddam, at which time she told him, according to the Iraqi transcript: "We have no opinion on the Arab-Arab conflicts, like your border disagreement with Kuwait." Some analysts say that was enough of a yellow light for Saddam to invade.[3]

No former U.S. ambassador to Eastern or Western Europe with forty years of clear-cut NATO strategy behind them would have made this same blunder.[4]

That blunder, however, was compounded by the lack of any further resolve from Washington, which must share in any blame. The response to this first post–Cold War crisis should be compared to what many scholars felt was the first Cold War crisis—the Soviet Union's threats on Turkey after World War II. As the Brookings study noted in its introductory chapter:

> On November 11, 1944, the Turkish ambassador to the United States, . . . died in Washington; not a very important event. . . . Sixteen months later, however, the ambassador's remains were the focus of world attention as the curtain went up on a *classic* act in the use of armed forces as a political instrument. On March 6, 1946, the U.S. Department of State announced the late Ambassador Ertegun's remains would be sent home to Turkey aboard the USS *Missouri*, visibly the most powerful warship in the U.S. Navy. . . .
>
> Between the ambassador's death and this announcement, not only had World War II ended, the cold war—as yet untitled—had begun.

As the Brookings study concluded:

> *The meaning of this event was missed by no one; Washington had not so subtly reminded the Soviet Union and others that the United States was a great military power and that it could project this power abroad, even to shores far distant.* Whether the visit of the *Missouri*, or it together with other U.S. actions that followed, deterred the Soviet Union from implementing any further planned or potential hostile acts toward Turkey will probably never be known. *What is clear is that no forceful Soviet actions followed the visit.*[5] (emphasis added)

While immediately sending a battleship to Kuwait for a "visit" would have been considerably more symbolic, simply sending the Persian Gulf–based COMIDEASTFOR flagship flying the admiral's flag with the large holiday Ensign constantly lit up with a spotlight might have sufficed.

* * *

All the same, time, thought, study, and debate that went into strategic nuclear and NATO strategies must now be given to the conditions of the new interwar period. But another change is required—the Navy should no longer sail on the sidelines of these national declaratory debates as it did during the Cold War. The development of "Massive Retaliation" was understandably led by the Air Force with the Army more or less taking the lead on "Flexible Response," although obviously all services were concerned with both. While the Navy has usually taken the lead by quoting the Brookings and other crisis response studies, it has never developed an adequate policy. This was somewhat understandable during the Cold War, when defense of Central Europe and nuclear strategy were foremost in strategists' minds. Even the Maritime Strategy was essentially (or at least originally) a Cold War response. While Third World crisis response was important, it was still considered a sideshow to the Soviet threat. Those priorities have now changed.

While all the services face major problems with the end of their old Cold War missions and declining defense budgets, to many observers the Navy appears in particular crisis. Indeed, the word "disarray" seems to be the favorite description of current Navy programs. But, contrary to much of this commentary, the real problem is not in shipbuilding or personnel—or even naval air programs, to which the word is more often applied. In fact, the Navy is currently retiring perfectly good ships and personnel, and even potential airplane problems will not show up until the turn of the century. Nor, contrary to some other opinions, is the problem a maritime view of the lessons of Desert Shield/Storm. The problem is considerably more fundamental: What is the Navy's role in the new post–Cold War world? The real dilemma is, therefore, naval long-range plans.

In the new interwar period, considering the forthcoming roles and missions requirements, the Navy should now lead the debate on national defense strategy—first by reexamining and refining traditional maritime missions such as naval presence, sea control, and projection ashore, but then by placing them in national terms. These are the missions that will become increasingly more important in the future. In short, "maritime missions" could well be "national missions" in this new interwar period.

Notes

CHAPTER 2.
Background: Will the Past Be Prologue?

1. John J. Mearsheimer, "A Strategic Misstep: Maritime Strategy and Deterrence in Europe," in Miller and Van Evera, eds., *Naval Strategy and National Security*, 76.
2. Gray and Barnett, eds., *Seapower and Strategy*, x.
3. Demetrious Caraley, *The Politics of Military Unification: A Study of Conflict and the Policy Process* (New York: Columbia University Press, 1966).
4. See, for example, Jeffrey G. Barlow, *The "Revolt of the Admirals": The Postwar Fight for Naval Aviation* (Washington, D.C.: U.S. Government Printing Office, forthcoming).
5. See, for example, the different interpretations from the Air Force and Navy in, respectively, Herman S. Wolk, "Revolt of the Admirals," *Air Force Magazine*, May 1988, 62–69, and Barlow, *The "Revolt of the Admirals."*
6. For a good overview of naval operations in Korea, see Cagle and Manson, *Sea War in Korea.*
7. For a good overview of naval actions in Vietnam, see Frank Uhlig, Jr., ed., *Vietnam: The Naval Story* (Annapolis, Md.: Naval Institute Press, 1986).
8. Blechman and Kaplan, *Force Without War*, 38–39.
9. David A. Rosenberg, "The Origins of Overkill: Nuclear Weapons and American Strategy, 1945–1960," *International Security*, Spring 1983.
10. For a survey of all these proposals, see Robert E. Osgood, *NATO: The Entangling Alliance* (Chicago: University of Chicago Press, 1962), 283–95.
11. Leon V. Sigal, *Nuclear Forces in Europe: Enduring Dilemmas, Present Prospects* (Washington, D.C.: The Brookings Institution, 1984), 24–53.

12. Adm. Elmo R. Zumwalt, Jr., USN (Ret.), *On Watch: A Memoir* (New York: New York Times Book Co., 1976), 439–44.

13. Norman Friedman, "Soviet Aegis-like Radar Unveiled," U.S. Naval Institute *Proceedings*, Oct. 1988, 197.

14. Rear Adm. C.A.H. Trost, USN, "The Size of the Fleet," in George, ed., *Problems of Sea Power as We Approach the Twenty-First Century,* 325–26.

15. Norman Polmar, *The Ships and Aircraft of the U.S. Fleet,* 12th ed. (Annapolis, Md.: Naval Institute Press, 1981), 1.

16. Adm. William Crowe, USN (Ret.), remarks at 1990 Sea Power Forum, 25 Sept. 1990.

17. The reader is forewarned that there is a slight mixture of different constant-dollar years in this section due to different sources and available data. The historical paragraphs use 1990 constant dollars. The more recent numbers are a mix of 1991 and 1992 (and projection) dollars. With inflation low, the differences are slight; the purpose is to look at trends, not necessarily specifics.

18. Budget data from William W. Kaufmann, *Glasnost, Perestroika and U.S. Defense Spending* (Washington, D.C.: The Brookings Institution, 1990), table 1, p. 55.

19. Data for this section taken from *National Defense Budget Estimates for FY 1991* (Washington, D.C.: Office of the Comptroller of the Department of Defense, March 1990), tables 6–10, pp. 98–100.

CHAPTER 3.
The Changing Missions of the 1990s

1. Senator Sam Nunn, "Implementing a New Military Strategy: The Budget Decisions," remarks prepared for delivery, 20 Apr. 1990, 1.

2. "Unsurprisingly, Navy Skeptical of Nunn Proposals on Mission Competitions," *Inside the Navy,* 7 May 1990, 5.

3. Stan Zimmerman, "Talk of Mission Consolidation Grows in the Senate," *Navy News and Undersea Technology,* 14 May 1990, 1–3.

4. Adm. Carlisle A. H. Trost, USN, "Maritime Strategy for the 1990s," U.S. Naval Institute *Proceedings* (Naval Review 1990), May 1990, 92–100.

5. H. Lawrence Garrett III, Secretary of the Navy, Adm. Frank B. Kelso II, Chief of Naval Operations, and Gen. A. M. Gray, Commandant of the Marine Corps, "The Way Ahead," U.S. Naval Institute *Proceedings,* Apr. 1991, 36–47.

6. Maj. Francis G. Hoffman, "Comment and Discussion on 'The Way Ahead'," U.S. Naval Institute *Proceedings,* June 1991, 14.

7. *National Strategy of the United States,* Jan. 1988, iv.

8. *National Strategy of the United States,* Mar. 1990, v.

9. John D. Morrocco, "New Pentagon Strategy Shifts Focus from Europe to Regional Conflicts," *Aviation Week and Space Technology,* 13 Aug. 1990, 25.

10. "Remarks by the President to the Aspen Institute Symposium," Office of the Press Secretary, The White House, 2 Aug. 1990.

11. James J. Tritten, *America Promises to Come Back: A New National Strategy* (Monterey, Calif.: Naval Postgraduate School, 13 May 1991).

12. Paul H. Nitze, "Arms, Strategy and Policy," *Foreign Affairs*, Jan. 1956, 187–98.

13. David A. Rosenberg, "Reality and Responsibility: Power and Process in the Making of the United States Nuclear Strategy, 1945–1968," *Journal of Strategic Studies*, Mar. 1986, 36–37.

14. Robert P. Haffa, Jr., *Planning U.S. Forces* (Washington, D.C.: Government Printing Office, 1988), 4–5.

CHAPTER 4.
Nuclear Deterrence: All at Sea?

1. For a brief history and text of SALT I and II, see Arms Control and Disarmament Agency, *Arms Control and Disarmament Agreements: Texts and Histories of the Negotiations*, 1990 ed. (Washington, D.C.: Arms Control and Disarmament Agency, 1990), 150–76 for SALT I and 261–300 for SALT II.

2. U.S. Arms Control and Disarmament Agency, "Nuclear and Space Talks: U.S. and Soviet Proposals," *Issues Brief*, 8 Feb. 1988.

3. R. Jeffrey Smith, "Treaty Would Cut Few U.S. Warheads: START Will Not Eliminate Modernization of Superpower Arsenals," *Washington Post*, 3 Apr. 1990, 1.

4. Ibid.

5. Harold Brown and Brent Scowcroft, *Deterring Through the Turn of the Century* (Washington, D.C.: The Foreign Policy Institute and the Center for Strategic Studies, 1989).

6. Barbara Amouyal, "ICBM Freeze Would Save $30 Billion," *Defense News*, 11 June 1990, 1.

7. Tony Capaccio, "Air Force Admits to New B-1 Problems," *Defense Week*, 1 Oct. 1990, 1.

8. David F. Bond, "USAF Uncertain About B-2 Costs; Congress Lacks Budget Details," *Aviation Week and Space Technology*, 11 June 1990, 24.

9. For an elaboration of this down-loading problem, see James L. George, "START and U.S. Strategic Force Vulnerabilities: Can 'Downloading' Provide the Answer?" *Strategic Review*, Fall 1988, 21–27.

10. James L. George, "INNF: Intermediate Navy Nuclear Forces," U.S. Naval Institute *Proceedings*, June 1987, 35–47.

11. Capt. Linton F. Brooks, USN, "Dropping the Baton," U.S. Naval Institute *Proceedings*, June 1989, 32–37. This same point was also made ten years earlier; see James L. George, "SALT and the Navy," U.S. Naval Institute *Proceedings*, June 1979, 28–37.

12. Ibid. See also Capt. William C. Green, USN, "The Navy's Strategic Role: Orphan or Legitimate?" U.S. Naval Institute *Proceedings*, July 1982, 103–5.

13. Andy Pasztor, "Strategic Air Command to Be Eliminated in Sweeping Reorganization of Air Force," *Wall Street Journal*, 18 Sept. 1991, 2.

CHAPTER 5.
NATO: The Emergence of SACLANT

1. For example, Peter Corterier, "Quo Vadis NATO?" *Survival*, Mar./Apr. 1990, 141–56.
2. Nick Cook, "JMSDF May Become First Operator of UK's Skyhook," *Jane's Defence Weekly,* 10 Oct. 1987, 784.
3. Len Famiglietti, "V-22 Team Looking for More Partners," *Jane's Defence Weekly,* 3 Oct. 1987, 769.
4. Norman Friedman, "Western European and NATO Navies," U.S. Naval Institute *Proceedings,* Mar. 1987, 40.
5. Jan Breemer, "Royal Netherlands Navy: Status Report," *Navy International,* Oct. 1987, 492.
6. Patrick Oster, "European Shelving Rivalries over Big Weapons Contracts: Possible Trend Concerns U.S. Defense Firms," *Washington Post,* 11 Sept. 1991, C1.
7. See, for example, "Interview with Vice Admiral Daniel Cooper," *Sea Power,* July 1990, 11.
8. As this book was going to press, there was a NATO reorganization proposal to eliminate the Channel Command. But a U.S. mine craft could still be deployed and stationed in Britain for combined NATO exercises.
9. If this is deemed inappropriate, one of the new oceangoing MCMs could be considered.
10. See note 9.
11. For an elaboration of this point, see George, "INNF," 35–39.
12. Douglas Bland, "Time for SACEUR to Come Home?" *Strategic Review,* Spring 1991, 44–53.

CHAPTER 6.
Third World Operations: The Past Is Prologue

1. Philip D. Zelikow, "Force Without War, 1975–1982," *Journal of Strategic Studies,* Mar. 1984, 29–54.
2. Adam B. Seigel, *U.S. Navy Crisis Response Activity, 1946–1989: Preliminary Report* (Washington, D.C.: Center for Naval Analyses, 1989).
3. Walt W. Rostow, *The Economics of Take-Off into Sustained Growth* (New York: St. Martin's Press, 1965).
4. Sources for this section and Table 6-1 are Robert D. Shuey et al., *Missile Proliferation: Survey of Emerging Missile Forces* (Washington, D.C.: Congressional Research Service, 1989), 38–42; Robert S. Spector, *The Undeclared Bomb* (Cambridge, Mass.: Ballinger Publishing Company, 1988), 23–66.
5. William W. Webster, Director of the CIA, testimony before the Senate Committee on Government Affairs, 18 May 1989.
6. Shuey, *Missile Proliferation,* 34.
7. Sources for this section and Table 6-2 are Shuey et al., *Missile Proliferation,* 30–37; Jill Smolowe, "The Search for a Poison Antidote," *Time,* 16 Jan. 1989, 22.

8. Sources for this section and Table 6-3 are Spector, *The Undeclared Bomb*; Robert L. Beckman and Warren H. Donnelly, *The Treaty on the Non-Proliferation of Nuclear Weapons* (Washington, D.C.: Congressional Research Service, 1985), passim.

9. As this book was going to press, North and South Korea were having a rapprochement, with North Korea promising to open its nuclear facilities to inspection. However, many feel that North Korea might continue to hide some facilities; the fact that it is a signatory to the Nuclear Nonproliferation Treaty did not prevent it from doing so in the past.

10. James R. Blaker, *United States Overseas Basing: An Anatomy of the Dilemma* (New York: Praeger Publishers, 1990), 1.

11. As this book was going to press, the United States was preparing to evacuate in 1992, although some expect there to be a reprieve and an extension of the lease for a few years. Nonetheless, the long-term future of Subic Bay looks dim.

12. Quoted in Uhlig, ed., *Vietnam: The Naval Story*, 68.

13. Vice Adm. Joseph Metcalf III, USN (Ret.), "Revolution at Sea," U.S. Naval Institute *Proceedings*, Jan. 1988, 34–39.

14. George H. Quester, *The Falklands and the Malvinas: Strategy and Arms Control* (Los Angeles: UCLA, 1984).

CHAPTER 7.
Maritime or National Missions?

1. For an excellent history of the Maritime Strategy's development, see John B. Hattendorf, "The Evolution of the Maritime Strategy: 1977 to 1987," *Naval War College Review*.

2. Adm. Thomas B. Hayward, "The Future of U.S. Sea Power," U.S. Naval Institute *Proceedings*, May 1979, 66–71.

3. Vice Adm. Stansfield Turner, USN, "Missions of the U.S. Navy," *Naval War College Review*, Mar.–Apr. 1974, 2–17.

4. Comdr. James F. McNulty, USN, "Naval Presence—The Misunderstood Mission," *Naval War College Review*, Sept.–Oct. 1974, 21–31.

5. For an elaboration of this point, see James L. George, "Maritime Missions or Strategy?" *Naval War College Review*, Winter 1989, 47–55.

6. Hattendorf, "Evolution of the Maritime Strategy," 18.

7. "EIC Predicts Pentagon Will Reduce Command Structure from Ten to Four," *Inside the Pentagon*, 18 Oct. 1990, 1, 4.

CHAPTER 9.
Naval Air Forces: "Where Are the Planes?"

1. "Persian Gulf Crisis Could Reignite Carrier Debate Between Navy and OSD," *Inside the Pentagon*, 4 Oct. 1990, 1, 12.

2. See, for example, Maj. Art Nalls, USMC, "Why Don't We Have Any Ski Jumps?" U.S. Naval Institute *Proceedings*, Nov. 1990, 79–81.

3. Naval Studies Board, *Future Aircraft Carrier Technology* (National Academy Press, 1991).

4. James L. George, "Maintaining a Western Carrier Capability," U.S. Naval Institute *Proceedings*, Oct. 1977, 30–41.

5. Nalls, "Why Don't We Have Any Ski Jumps?"

6. Ronald F. Crook, "The Carrier of the Future," *Navy International*, July/Aug. 1990, 252–56.

7. Philip Gold, "No Jets of Future on Deck," *Washington Time*, 6 Oct. 1991, 7.

8. Ibid.

9. Bert H. Cooper, Jr., "AX Aircraft Program: Issues and Options," *Congressional Research Service Issue Brief*, 12 Aug. 1991, 3.

10. Ibid.

11. John D. Morrocco, "Senior Navy Officials Doubt AX Adaptable to Multirole Capability," *Aviation Week and Space Technology*, 13 May 1991, 25.

12. David S. Steigman, "Navy Expands Role Planned for AX," *Navy Times*, 16 Sept. 1991, 28.

13. Stanley W. Kandebo, "Versatile and Flexible F-14 Offered as Best Choice When Pitted Against F/A-18," *Aviation Week and Space Technology*, 29 Apr. 1991, 65.

14. "F/A-18E/F 'Clear Choice' Over F-14—Cheney," *Defense Daily*, 9 Sept. 1991, 374.

15. David S. Steigman, "Shortfall Will Push P-3 Back into Production," *Navy Times*, 30 Sept. 1991, 29.

16. Stanley W. Kandebo, "Grumman Makes 11th-Hour Offer to Get F-14 into Fiscal '92 Budget," *Aviation Week and Space Technology*, 6 May 1991, 24.

17. Kandebo, "F-14 Offered as Best Choice," 65.

18. Peter Grier, "Technology of 'Stealth' Warplanes Keeps on Developing," *Christian Science Monitor*, 2 Dec. 1991, 9.

19. Michael Berger, "Testimony on Naval Aircraft," Congressional Budget Office, 8 May 1991, 7.

20. Barbara Opall, "F-22 Can Be Modified to Meet Navy Needs, ATF Team Officials Say," *Defense News*, 27 May 1991, 32.

21. Patricia A. Gilmartin, "Britain Asks U.S. Navy to Assess Common Needs for STOVL Aircraft," *Aviation Week and Space Technology*, 23 Apr. 1990, 31.

22. Patricia A. Gilmartin, "Navy Issues Tentative Requirement for STOVL Fighter Sought by 2010," *Aviation Week and Space Technology*, 23 Apr. 1990, 31.

23. "Japan Eyes the AV-8B," *Aviation Week and Space Technology*, 2 July 1990.

24. Le Bourget, "Yakovlev Bureau Develops New V/STOL Fighter Aircraft," *Aviation Week and Space Technology*, 24 June 1991, 25.

25. Naval Studies Board, *Future Aircraft Carrier Technology*, 106.

26. Thomas G. Donlan, "Riding for a Fall? Long-Term Prospects for McDonnell Douglas Are Cloudy," *Barron's*, 21 Oct. 1991, 1.

27. *Washington Post*.

28. "Persian Gulf Crisis Could Ignite Carrier Debate," *Inside the Pentagon*, 13.

29. One was actually an admiral-selectee who was finally forced to retire over the incident.

30. Vice Adm. Richard M. Dunleavy, Assistant Chief of Naval Operations for Air Warfare, testimony before the Conventional Forces and Alliance Defense Subcommittee of the Senate Armed Services Committee on "Naval Aviation Modernization Requirements and Acquisition Plans," 7 May 1991.

CHAPTER 10.
Submarine Forces: Transition Time?

1. Vice Adm. Roger F. Bacon, USN, "Force Commander's Forum: Commander Submarine Force, U.S. Atlantic Fleet," *Submarine Review*, Oct. 1990, 84.
2. Rear Adm. James Fitzgerald, USN, and John Benedict, "There Is a Sub Threat," U.S. Naval Institute *Proceedings*, Aug. 1990, 57–63.
3. David S. Steigman, "Seawolf's Combat System Missing Deadlines," *Navy Times*, 9 Apr. 1990, 25.
4. Ibid.
5. "Total Costs for First SSN-21 Seawolf Exceed $5 Billion," *Navy News and Undersea Technology*, 18 June 1990, 1.
6. "BSY-2 Delays, SSN-21 Cost Overruns Plague Sub Review," *Navy News and Undersea Technology*, 25 June 1990, 1.
7. William Flannery, "Destroyer, Submarine Under Fire," *St. Louis Post-Dispatch*, 15 April 1990, B4.
8. Norman Polmar, "The Design of Superiority: The Soviet Submarine Fleet of the Future," *Sea Power*, Sept. 1990, 24.
9. Ibid., 25.
10. Flannery, "Destroyer, Submarine Under Fire."
11. "A Voice for the Silent Service: Interview with Vice Admiral Roger F. Bacon," *Sea Power*, July 1991, 9.
12. Robert Holzer, "U.S. Navy Starts New Sub Effort: Project May Replace Seawolf Program," *Defense News*, 30 Apr. 1990, 1.
13. "Navy Flatly Denies Existence of SSN-21 Successor Design," *Navy News and Undersea Technology*, 21 May 1990, 4.
14. Christopher Drew, "Navy Pushing Proposal for Streamlined Attack Subs," *Chicago Tribune*, 23 June 1991, 3.
15. "Interview with Vice Admiral Daniel L. Cooper," *Sea Power*, July 1990, 12.
16. S. R. Menno, "Needed: Submarine Design Competition," U.S. Naval Institute *Proceedings*, Oct. 1988, 115–16.
17. Lt. Comdr. Paul E. Simon, "Comment on 'Needed: Submarine Design Competition'," U.S. Naval Institute *Proceedings*, Feb. 1989, 88.
18. Rear Adm. James Fitzgerald, USN, and John Benedict, "Air Independent Propulsion," U.S. Naval Institute *Proceedings*, Aug. 1990, 60–62.
19. Don Walsh, "Is It Time for the SSn?" *Sea Power*, Apr. 1989, 137–39.
20. Eric Rosenberg, "Israel to Use $180 Million in FMS Funds Toward Building Subs in West Germany," *Inside the Navy*, 13 Feb. 1989, 1. (This purchase is now in abeyance.)
21. See, for example, Polmar, *Ships and Aircraft of the U.S. Fleet*, 12th ed., 15–16.
22. "Interview with Vice Admiral Cooper," 11.

23. "Navy to scrap plan for new submarine," *London Times*, 26 June 1991, 2.
24. "Interview with R. James Woolsey," *Sea Power*, July 1989, 17.

CHAPTER 11.
Surface Combatants: Quantity Versus Quality

1. Capt. Robert J. Shade, "Marriage of Necessity," U.S. Naval Institute *Proceedings*, Aug. 1990, 31–35.
2. Assistant Chief of Naval Operations, *Surface Warfare Plan 1989* (Washington, D.C.: Department of the Navy, 1989).
3. Comdr. George Galdorise, USN, "LAMP-III: How to Procure a Winner," U.S. Naval Institute *Proceedings*, Jan. 1989, 95.
4. Flannery, "Destroyer, Submarine Under Fire."
5. Robert Holzer, "Navy Scrutinizes Greater Variety of DDG-51 Alternatives," *Defense News*, 28 Oct. 1991, 42.
6. James L. George, "U.S. Destroyers: A New DDG Urgently Needed," *Navy International*, Nov. 1984, 673–78.
7. James L. George, "DDG-51: A Ship for the Twenty-First Century," *Navy International*, Jan. 1985, 26–29.
8. "UK, France to develop new frigate," *London Financial Times*, 3 Dec. 1991, 9.
9. Giovanni de Briganti, "Legal Issues Snarl French Frigate Sale to Taiwan," *Defense News*, 30 Sept. 1991, 16.
10. Joris Janssen Lok, "Koreans complete KDX review," *Jane's Defence Weekly*, 20 Apr. 1991, 632.
11. "Industry Briefing Shows Israeli Sa'ar V Corvette as Spartan, Lightweight Design," *Inside the Navy*, 29 Oct. 1990, 9–11.
12. "Helicopter System Proposed for Early DDG-51s," *Navy News and Undersea Technology*, 13 Aug. 1990, 3.
13. James L. George, "Navy Guns Systems: 'Alive and Well'," *Sea Power*, Oct. 1979, 25–36.
14. "In Dramatic Turnabout, Navy Readies Plan for Upgrading Knox-Class Frigate," *Inside the Navy*, 17 Sept. 1990, 1–7.

CHAPTER 12.
Balance of the Fleet: Maintaining the "Blue"

1. Rear Adm. Worral Reed Carter, *Beans, Bullets, and Black Oil* (Washington, D.C.: Department of the Navy, 1953).
2. Adm. C.A.H. Trost, USN, "A Report on the Posture and Fiscal Year 1991 Budget of the United States Navy," statement before the House Armed Services Committee, 20 Feb. 1990, 15.
3. Peter Grier, "The Short Reach of Soviet Naval Logistics," *Military Forum*, May 1988, 34–38.
4. Duncan S. Ballantine, *U.S. Naval Logistics in the Second World War* (Princeton, N.J.: Princeton University Press, 1949), 11.
5. Ibid.

6. Carter, *Beans, Bullets and Black Oil*, 1.

7. Rear Adm. Henry E. Eccles, *Logistics in the National Defense* (Harrisburg, Pa.: Stackpole Company, 1959), 138.

8. Norman Polmar, *Ships and Aircraft of the U.S. Fleet*, 14th ed. (Annapolis, Md.: Naval Institute Press, 1987), 6–10.

9. Robert Holzer, "Navy Devises Two Ship Classes to Resolve Sealift Gap," *Defense News*, 21 Oct. 1991, 1.

10. Binkin and Record, *Where Does the Marine Corps Go from Here?* 1.

11. U.S. Marine Corps, *Concepts and Issues, 1990* (Washington, D.C.: U.S. Marine Corps, 1990), 5–8.

12. Assistant Chief of Naval Operations, *Surface Warfare Plan, 1989* (Washington, D.C.: Department of the Navy, 1989), 10.

13. Norman Polmar, "Carrying Large Objects," U.S. Naval Institute *Proceedings*, Dec. 1990, 121–22.

14. William Flannery, "Friendly Fire: Army and Marine Corps Fight over Combat Role," *St. Louis Post-Dispatch*, 1 Apr. 1990, B4.

15. Edwin Simmons, "Go Marines! Beat Army," *Washington Post*, 8 Oct. 1989, C1.

16. Bruce Van Voorst, "Who Needs the Marines? From the Halls of Montezuma to the Shores of Redundancy," *Time*, May 1990, 28.

17. U.S. Marine Corps, *Concepts and Issues*, 1-7 to 1-9.

18. Caleb Baker and Robert Holzer, "Marines Pursue Expanded Role on Battlefield," *Defense News*, 25 Nov. 1991, 1.

19. Gregory K. Hartmann with Scott C. Truver, *Weapons That Wait: Mine Warfare in the U.S. Navy* (Annapolis, Md.: Naval Institute Press, 1979; updated edition 1991).

20. Ibid., 239.

21. William L. Greer and Comdr. James Bartholomew, USN, "The Psychology of Mine Warfare," U.S. Naval Institute *Proceedings*, Feb. 1986, 58–62.

22. *Surface Warfare Plan*, 15.

CHAPTER 13.
Lessons of Desert Shield/Desert Storm: Forerunner or Fluke?

1. Department of the Navy, *The United States Navy in "Desert Shield" and "Desert Storm"* (Washington, D.C.: Office of the Chief of Naval Operations, 15 May 1991).

2. Ibid, C2.

3. Gen. Norman Schwarzkopf, USA, "A Tribute to the Navy–Marine Corps Team," address delivered on 29 May 1991 to the graduating class of the Naval Academy, reprinted in U.S. Naval Institute *Proceedings*, Aug. 1991, 44.

CHAPTER 14.
Naval Arms Control: An Unknown Factor

1. For a comprehensive look with a good pro and con discussion on naval arms control, see Fieldhouse, ed., *Security at Sea;* see also Hill, *Arms Control at Sea*.

2. James Lacey, RAND Working Paper on Naval Arms Control, RAND Corporation, 1990.
3. Joshua Handler and William Arkin, *Nuclear Warships and NAVAL Nuclear Weapons, 1990: A Complete Inventory,* Neptune Papers no. 5 (Greenpeace, 1990).
4. Ibid.
5. See, for example, R. Jeffrey Smith, "Design Changes Urged for Nuclear Safety: Scientific Panel, in Report to Congress, Favors Immediate Action on Submarine Missile," *Washington Post,* 19 Dec. 1990, A4.
6. See, for example, Ensign Christopher M. Duquette, "Ban the SLCM," U.S. Naval Institute *Proceedings,* June 1990, 34–38.
7. Department for Disarmament Affairs, *The Naval Arms Race* (New York: United Nations, 1986).
8. For an elaboration of these points, see James L. George, "On Naval Arms Control: Mediums and Messages," *Naval War College Review,* Summer 1990, 32–42.

CHAPTER 15.
Other "New World Paradigms": Do They Really Matter?

1. See, for example, Gregory Flynn, "Problems in Paradigm," *Foreign Policy,* Spring 1989.
2. Halford J. Mackinder, *Democratic Ideals and Reality* (1942; reprint, New York: W. W. Norton and Company, 1962).
3. See, for example, annual *Soviet Military Power* reports from the Department of Defense.
4. George Friedman and Meredith LeBard, *The Coming War with Japan* (New York: St. Martin's Press, 1991).
5. Francis Fukuyama, "The End of History," *National Interest,* Summer 1989.
6. John Wilner, "What's New About the New World Order?" *Fletcher Forum of World Affairs,* Summer 1991, 1.
7. Paul Kennedy, *The Rise and Fall of the Great Powers* (New York: Random House, 1987).

CHAPTER 16.
Conclusions: The Perils of "Less of the Same"

1. "In Dramatic Turnabout, Navy Readies Plan for Upgrading Knox-Class Frigate," 7.
2. "Reduction in DDG-51 Buy Will Have Serious Impact on U.S. Shipyard Industrial Base," *Inside the Navy,* 20 Aug. 1990, 1, 5.
3. Glenn Frankel, "Gulf: A Crisis in Diplomacy," *Washington Post,* 25 Dec. 1990, A38.
4. Ambassador Glaspie has refuted this interpretation, but after congressional hearings, doubts remained.
5. Blechman and Kaplan, *Force Without War,* 1–2.

Select Bibliography

OFFICIAL DOCUMENTS

Cheney, Dick, Secretary of Defense. *Annual Report to the President and the Congress.* Department of Defense, January 1991.

Department of the Navy. *The United States Navy in "Desert Shield" and "Desert Storm".* Office of the Chief of Naval Operations, 15 May 1991.

Garrett, H. Lawrence, III, Secretary of the Navy. *Annual Report on the Posture and Fiscal Year 1992–1993 Budget of the United States Navy and Marine Corps.*

Kelso, Admiral F. B. *The Posture and Fiscal Year 1992–1993 Budget.* Statement before Congress, February 1991.

BOOKS

Albion, Robert Greenhalgh. *Makers of Naval Strategy, 1798–1947.* Annapolis, Md: Naval Institute Press, 1980.

Bartlett, Merrill L., ed. *Assault from the Sea: Essays on the History of Amphibious Warfare.* Annapolis, Md.: Naval Institute Press, 1983.

Beach, Edward L. *The United States Navy: 200 Years.* New York: Henry Holt, 1986.

Binkin, Martin, and Jeffrey Record. *Where Does the Marine Corps Go from Here?* Washington, D.C.: The Brookings Institution, 1976.

Blechman, Barry M., and Stephen S. Kaplan. *Force Without War: U.S. Armed Forces as a Political Instrument.* Washington, D.C.: The Brookings Institution, 1978.

Brodie, Bernard A. *A Guide to Naval Strategy.* 1958. Reprint. Westport, Conn.: Greenwood Press, 1977.

Cable, Sir James, *Gunboat Diplomacy.* 2d ed. London: Macmillan, 1981.

Cagle, Malcolm W., and Frank A. Manson. *Sea War in Korea.* Annapolis, Md.: Naval Institute Press, 1957.

Corbett, Sir Julian. *Some Principles of Maritime Strategy.* 1911. Reprint. 1989.

Fieldhouse, Richard, ed. *Security at Sea: Naval Forces and Arms Control.* New York: Oxford University Press, 1990.

Gansler, Jacques S. *Affording Defense.* Cambridge, Mass.: MIT Press, 1989.

George, James L., ed. *Problems of Sea Power as We Approach the Twenty-First Century.* Washington, D.C.: American Enterprise Institute, 1978.

————. *The Soviet and Other Communist Navies: The View from the Mid-1980s.* Annapolis, Md.: Naval Institute Press, 1986.

————. *The U.S. Navy: The View from the Mid-1980s.* Boulder, Colo.: Westview Press, 1985.

Gorshkov, S. G. *Sea Power of the State.* New York: Pergamon Press, 1979.

Gray, Colin S., and Roger W. Barnett, eds. *Seapower and Strategy.* Annapolis, Md.: Naval Institute Press, 1989.

Grove, Erik. *The Future of Seapower.* Annapolis, Md.: Naval Institute Press, 1990.

Hill, Rear Admiral J. R. *Arms Control at Sea.* Annapolis, Md.: Naval Institute Press, 1989.

————. *Maritime Strategy for Medium Powers.* London: Croom Helm, 1986.

Howarth, Stephen. *To Shining Sea: A History of the United States Navy, 1775–1991.* New York: Random House, 1991.

Mahan, Alfred T. *The Influence of Sea Power upon History.* 1890. 12th ed. Boston: Little, Brown, n.d.

Miller, Steven E., and Stephen Van Evera, eds. *Naval Strategy and National Security.* Princeton, N.J.: Princeton University Press, 1988.

Morison, Samuel E. *The Two-Ocean War.* Boston: Little, Brown, 1963.

Palmer, Michael A. *Origin of the Maritime Strategy: The Development of American Naval Strategy, 1945–1955.* Annapolis, Md.: Naval Institute Press, 1988.

Potter, E. B., and Chester W. Nimitz, eds. *Sea Power: A Naval History.* Englewood Cliffs, N.J.: Prentice-Hall, 1960.

Reynolds, Clark G. *Command of the Sea: The History and Strategy of Maritime Empires.* New York: William Morrow, 1974.

Rosinski, Herbert. *The Development of Naval Thought.* Edited with an introduction by B. Mitchell Simpson III. Newport, R.I.: Naval War College Press, 1977.

Roskill, Stephen. *Naval Policy Between the Wars.* Vol. I. *The Period of Anglo-American Antagonism, 1919–1929.* London, 1968.

————. *Naval Policy Between the Wars.* Vol. II. *The Period of Disarmament.* Annapolis, Md.: Naval Institute Press, 1976.

Ryan, Paul. *First Line of Defense.* Stanford, Calif.: Hoover Institution Press, 1981.

Swanborough, Gordon, and Peter M. Bowers. *United States Navy Aircraft Since 1911.* 3d ed. Annapolis, Md.: Naval Institute Press, 1990.

Till, Geoffrey. *Maritime Strategy and the Nuclear Age.* 2d ed. New York: St. Martin's Press, 1984.

Uhlig, Frank, ed. *Sea War in Vietnam.* Annapolis, Md.: Naval Institute Press, 1987.

Wylie, J. C. *Military Strategy: A General Theory of Power Control.* 1967. Reprint. Annapolis, Md.: Naval Institute Press, 1989.

Index

"Admiral's Revolt," 2, 10, 107
Afghanistan, 35, 207, 212, 217
Aircraft carriers, 17–18, 103–12
    Abraham Lincoln CVN-72, 104
    America CV-65, 106, 109
    Constellation CV-64, 106
    Coral Sea CV-43, 17, 18, 104
    CTOL, 104–6, 108–9
    CVV, 3, 18, 108, 109
    Enterprise CVN-65, 106
    Forrestal CV-59, 106
    Independence CV 62, 104
    John F. Kennedy CV-67, 106, 108, 109
    Lexington AVT-16, 104, 105
    Midway CV-41, 17, 106
    modified mix alternatives for, 108–12
    and NATO, 50, 52
    Nimitz-class, 17, 18, 106, 107, 108, 109, 125, 126
    Ranger CV-61, 106, 109
    reconstitution of, 123–24
    reserve options for, 124–25
    retirement schedule for, 105
    Saratoga CV-60, 106
    Stennis CVN-74, 106, 107
    United States, 10, 106, 107
    VSS, 3, 18, 110
    V/STOL, 3, 17, 18, 52, 106–7, 109–12
Air Independent Propulsion (AIP), xx, 137
Airplanes, 112–23
    A-3, 71, 113
    A-4, 113
    A-5, 113
    A-6, 71, 112, 113, 114
    A-7, 71, 113, 114, 121
    A-12, xix, 112, 114, 116, 119
    ATA (*see* A-12)
    ATS, 112
    AV-8B, 71, 114
    AX, 43, 71, 116, 119, 120, 123
    E-2, 115, 118
    F-4, 114
    F-8, 114
    F-14, 112, 114, 115, 116, 117, 118, 121
    F-16, 114
    F/A-18, 114, 115, 116, 117, 118, 121
    F-20, 122, 124
    F-22, 119, 120
    F-117, 119
    light attack/fighter, 124
    modified mix alternatives for, 118–23

Airplanes *cont.*
  MRF (multi-role fighter), 121
  NATF, 112, 117, 119
  P-3, 112, 115, 117, 124
  P-7 (*see* P-3)
  reconstitution of, 123–24
  S-3, 115, 118
  V-22, 112
Amphibious ready group, 15, 110–11,
  125, 142, 143, 217
Amphibious ships, 166–173
  APD, 143, 155
  LHA, 106, 107, 110, 125
  LHD, 18, 106, 107, 108, 110, 125
  LPH, 106, 107, 108
  LSD, 18, 54
  LST, 54, 56
ANZUS, 76, 101
Arab-Israeli Wars, 14, 184, 188, 211
Argentina, 51, 65, 66, 67, 73, 76, 111,
  127, 211
Armada, Spanish, 8
Army-Navy fight, 83
Arthur, Stanley, 190
Aspin, Les, 44, 83, 221
Assad (Syria), 191
Australia, 68, 111
Auxiliary ships, 159–66

Bacon, Roger F., 128, 129, 141
Barnett, Roger, 7
Baruch, Bernard, 66
Base force, xxii, 19
Battleships, 2, 60, 75, 151, 155, 226
Bennett, Charles, 134
Biological Weapons (BW), 66
Bombers
  B-1, 36–39
  B-2, 33, 38–39, 43, 118, 119
  B-52, 36–39
  long-range, strategic, 32–47 *passim*
Bradley, Omar, 166, 167
Brazil, 6, 65, 67, 111, 208, 211
Britain. *See* United Kingdom
Brock, Bill, 3
Brookings Institution study, 12, 13, 62,
  103, 167, 222, 227, 228
Brown, Harold, 74
Budget, xxii, 5, 19, 20–22

Building and transitional concepts,
  90–95
Burke, Arleigh, 13, 223
Bush, George, 4, 14, 22, 30, 32, 38, 39,
  42, 46, 75
Byrd, Robert, 21

Canada, 49, 50, 51, 58, 137, 138
Carriers. *See* Aircraft carriers
Carter, Jimmy, 18, 34, 35, 104, 109,
  110, 217
Center for Naval Analyses, 6, 62, 90,
  223
Chemical Weapons (CW), 4, 65–66,
  69, 74, 75, 77
Cheney, Dick, 22
Chernenko, Konstantin, 207
Chile, 211
China, 5, 41, 64, 65, 66, 208, 210, 211
Churchill, Winston, 94
CINCLANT/CINCLANTFLT, 55–56
Combat logistics force, 161–62. *See also*
  Auxiliary ships
Concepts, building and transitional,
  90–95
Conference on Disarmament (CD), 65
Conventional Arms Talks (CAT), 194
Conventional Force in Europe (CFE),
  31, 42, 46, 49, 50, 57, 58, 59, 60,
  104, 196, 200, 201, 202, 221
Cooper, Daniel, 135
Corvettes, xx, 153
Crowe, William, 19
Cruise Missile Carrier (CMC), 72
Cruisers, 144–45
  Bainbridge CGN-25, 145
  Belknap CG-26 class, 144
  California CGN-36 class, 144
  gun, 28, 155
  Leahy CG-16 class, 144
  Long Beach CGN-9, 145
  modified mix alternatives for,
    150–51, 155
  retirement schedule of, 145
  Ticonderoga CG-47 class, 17, 144
  Virginia CGN-38 class, 17, 144
Cuba, 199
Cuban Missile Crisis, 14
CVV, 3, 18, 108, 109

David Taylor Research Center, 90, 92, 108–9, 112
Defense, Department of, 9, 96, 99
Delta Force, 75
Deployments
    alternatives, 124–25, 140–41, 157–58, 166, 172–73, 178
    concepts, 100–101
Desert Shield/Desert Storm, 75, 183–93
Destroyers, xxi, 144–46
    Arleigh Burke DDG-51 class, xxi, 18, 146, 147–48, 216, 217, 225
    Charles F. Adams DDG-2 class, 146
    Coontz DDG-37 class, 146
    Farragut DDG-37 class, 145, 149, 150
    Kidd DDG-993 class, 146
    modified mix alternatives for, 151, 154–55, 156
    reconstitution of, 156–57
    reserve options for, 157
    retirement schedule for, 145
    Spruance DD-963 class, 17, 18, 144
Diego Garcia, 68, 104, 185, 186
Dominican Republic, 12, 99

Egypt, 64, 137, 140, 208, 211
Eisenhower, Dwight D., 13, 192
Ellis, Earl H., 2
El Salvador, 75, 212
England. *See* United Kingdom
European Community, 55, 201, 202, 208, 209, 210

Falkland Islands War, 50, 52, 67, 73, 76, 127, 129
Flexible response, 74, 228
France, 41, 48, 49, 50, 51, 52, 54, 55, 57, 59, 138, 208, 209
Frigates, 146–47
    Knox FF-1052 class, 146, 157
    modified mix alternatives, 151–53
    NATO, 53, 60
    Oliver Hazard Perry FFG-7 class, 17, 18, 146–47, 157, 158
    reconstitution of, 156–57
    reserve options for, 157–58
    retirement schedule for, 145

Gallipoli, 2
Garrett, Lawrence H., III, vii, 6, 215, 220
Germany, 5, 42, 48, 52, 53, 57, 60, 206, 207, 208–9, 210, 213, 214
Glaspie, April, 84, 184, 225, 227
Goldwater-Nichols Act, 84, 189, 219
Gorbachev, Mikhail, xxii, 4, 14, 32, 39, 41, 42, 46, 207, 220
Greece, 48, 54, 57
Grenada, 12, 189
Grey, Colin, 7
Guam, 68, 70, 75, 104
Gunboat diplomacy, 79

Haig, Alexander, 56
Hart, Gary, 3, 110
Hayward, Thomas P., 3, 79
"High-Low" mix, 2, 3, 17, 92, 147
Hitler, Adolph, 65, 128, 208
Hoare, Mike, 4
Holloway, James, 3
Hussein, Saddam, xxii, 75, 82, 84, 184, 187, 188, 191, 192, 193, 212, 225, 227

Incident at Sea (IncSea) Agreement, 198, 199
India, 5, 29, 66, 67, 127, 129, 208, 211
Indian Ocean Zone of Peace Talks, 194
Industrial base. *See* Reconstitution
Intercontinental Ballistic Missiles (ICBM), 32–47 *passim*, 69
Intermediate Naval Nuclear Forces (INNF), 58
Intermediate Nuclear Force (INF)
    forces, 32, 41–43
    Treaty, 4, 14, 31, 32, 42, 44, 196, 221
International Atomic Energy Agency (IAEA), 66, 75
Iran, 66
Iraq, xxii, 1, 4, 5, 6, 15, 24, 30, 31, 32, 59, 62, 64, 65, 66, 67, 68, 75, 84, 97, 183, 184, 187, 188, 192, 197, 208, 209, 211, 225
Israel, 64, 67, 137, 140
Italy, 50, 52, 56, 111, 122

Jackson, Henry, 34

Japan, 5, 8, 60, 111–12, 208, 210, 213, 214
Johnson, Louis, 10
Johnson, Roy, 71
Jutland, Battle of, 8

Kennedy, Paul, 214
Kenya, 63
Kenyatta, Jomo, 63
Khomeini, Ayatollah, 191
Khrushchev, Nikita, 207
Kissinger, Henry, 42, 48
Kohl, Helmut, 209
Korea, 66, 68, 69, 76, 100
    war with, 1, 10–11, 12, 15, 20, 22, 71, 102, 114, 166, 212
Kuwait, xxii, 1, 4, 15, 30, 59, 183, 184, 191, 211

Lebanon, 12, 188
Lehman, John, 3, 29, 78, 90, 113
Lenin, 207
Lepanto, Battle of, 8
Liberia, 15, 62, 68
Libya, 66, 67, 70, 71, 73, 74, 189, 199
Lind, Bill, 3
London Naval Conference, 1, 194

McNamara, Robert, 10, 74, 83
McNulty, James, 79
Mahan, Alfred T., 7, 160, 204
Marines, 173–75
Maritime Strategy, 2, 3, 7, 29, 30, 60, 78, 79–80, 85, 228
Massive retaliation, 74, 228
Mauz, Henry, 190
Mayaguez incident, 12
MBFR, 202
Metcalf, Vice Admiral, 73, 219
Midway CV-43. *See* Aircraft carriers
Military Sealift Command (MSC), 164–67. *See also* Auxiliary ships
Mine craft, 175–78
Missile proliferation, 64–65
Missile Technology Control Regime (MTCR), 64, 75, 77
Moffet, William A., 2
Moorer, Thomas P., 223
Multilateral Force (MLF), 13

Multiple or modified mix
    aircraft carriers, 108–12
    airplanes, 118–23
    amphibious ships, 171–72, 179
    auxiliary ships, 165, 179
    concept, 92
    mine craft, 177–78, 179
    submarines, 134–39
    surface combatants, 150–56
Multi-role Fighter (MRF), 121. *See also* Airplanes
Mussolini, Benito, 65

Napoleon, 8
National Defense Fleet Reserve (NDFR), 163
National Oceanic and Atmospheric Administration (NOAA), 178, 179
National Security Strategy of the United States, 29
NATO, 4, 5, 13, 30, 31, 32, 41, 42, 43, 48–61 *passim*, 62, 74, 76, 81–82, 84, 92, 101, 128, 184, 209, 210, 224, 226, 227, 228
Naval arms control, 3, 5, 27, 194–202 *passim*
Naval Institute, U.S., 223
Naval Strategy Think Tank (NSTT), 222, 223
Navy-Air Force fight, 10, 13, 29
NCND (Neither Confirm Nor Deny) policy, 72, 73
Nelson, Horatio, 8
Netherlands, 8, 50, 51, 54
New World paradigms, 3–4, 5
    balance of power, 208–11
    Commonwealth of Independent States, 3–4, 5, 203–8
    condominium worlds, 4, 5
    end of history, 212–13
New Zealand, 76
Nicaragua, 197
Nigeria, 208, 211
Nimitz-class. *See* Aircraft carriers
Nitze, Paul, 30, 212, 222
Nixon Doctrine, 2, 75
Nonproliferation Treaty, 75
Nuclear Proliferation, 4, 66–67
Nunn, Sam, 28–29, 46, 78, 100, 221

Oliver Hazard Perry FFG-7. *See* Frigates
Operation Eastern Exit (Somalia), 111
Operation Just Cause (Panama), 69
Operation Sharp Edge (Liberia), 110

Pakistan, 66, 127, 129
Panama, 68, 69
Peloponnesian Wars, 7, 8, 9
Perle, Richard, 94
Philippines, 68, 76, 77, 100, 104
Pipes, Richard, 205
Polmar, Norman, 18, 133
Portugal, 53

Qaddafi, Muammar, 191
Quick Strike (F-14Q), 116–17, 118. *See also* Airplanes, F-14

Raratonga, Treaty of, 198
Reagan, Ronald, 1, 2, 3, 18, 19, 20, 28, 41, 75, 78, 95, 104
Reconstitution
  of air forces, 123–24
  concept of, 101–2
  of submarines, 139–40, 216
  of surface combatants, 156–57
Research and development, 95–97
Reserves, 97–100
  air forces, 124–25
  amphibious ships, 172–73
  auxiliary ships, 166
  mine craft, 178
  submarines, 140–41
  surface combatants, 157–58
Rickover, Hyman, 2
RIO Pact, 76, 225
Rivero, Horacio, 223
Rogers, Bernard, 56
Royal Navy, 49, 51, 111, 127

Sa'ar (corvette), 153
SACEUR, 13, 42, 49, 55
SACLANT, 4, 49, 55–57, 60
Sacramento AOE class, 163
Salamis, Battle of, 8
SALT I, 4, 33–34, 35, 37, 39, 41
SALT II, 4, 34–35
Samuel B. Roberts FFG-58, 147
Saudi Arabia, 189, 191, 193

Schlesinger, James, 74
Schwarzkopf, Norman, 183, 185, 187, 188, 189, 192
Sea Beds Treaty, 198
Sea Control Ship (SCS), 17, 109, 111, 125. *See also* Aircraft carriers, V/STOL
SEATO, 76
Shevardnadze, Eduard, 212
Sidra, Gulf of, 71
Singapore, 68, 210
Ski-jump, xx, 110–11
Sky-hook, 52, 112, 125
Solzhenitsyn, Alexander, 205
Somalia, 15, 62, 111
South Africa, 6, 66
Spain, 48, 50, 52, 57, 104, 111, 122
Spanish-American War, 8
Stalin, Joseph, 207
STANAVFORs, 56–57, 59, 60, 76–77, 157, 185, 224–25, 226
Stark FFG-31, 147
START, 4, 31, 32, 33, 35–37, 39–41, 43, 44, 46, 47, 221
Stockdale, James, 192
STOVL, xx, 52–53
Strategic Air Command (SAC), 20, 45
Strategic Defense Initiative (SDI), 95
Strategy, 27–31, 74–76
  nuclear, 13, 32–47 *passim*, 74, 81
  "The Way Ahead," 29
Submarines
  and Air Independent Propulsion (AIP), 137, 140, 141
  attack, 129–31
  Ben Franklin SSBN-640 class, 131
  Centurion SSN, 134, 138, 139
  Lafayette SSBN-616, 131
  Los Angeles SSN-688 class, 17, 18, 129, 130, 134, 139
  modified mix alternatives for, 134–39
  Permit SSN-594 class, 129, 130
  reconstitution of, 139–40, 216
  reserve options for, 140–41
  retirement schedule for, 130
  Seawolf SSN-21, 18, 129, 130, 132–33, 134, 135, 139, 216, 225
  SS, 136, 137, 138
  SSGN, 43, 73–74, 77, 129, 130

Submarines *cont.*
  SSn, SSBn, 137, 138
  strategic (SSBN), 13, 32–47 *passim*,
    131
  Sturgeon SSN-637, 129, 130, 134, 136
  Trident SSBNs, 32–47 *passim*, 131
Support ships, 159–66
Syria, 66, 211

Taft, William, 3
Taiwan, 66
Thatcher, Margaret, 70, 201
Theater Nuclear Force (TNF). *See*
  Intermediate Nuclear Force
Thucydides, 7
Tlatelolco, Treaty of, 198
Tocqueville, Alexis de, xix, 206
Tsushima, Battle of, 8
Trost, Carlisle, 15, 29, 159, 217, 223
Truman, Harry, 9, 10
Turkey, 54, 57, 58, 209
Turner, Stansfield, 79

Ukraine, 41
United Kingdom, 8, 9, 41, 48, 50, 51,
  52, 53, 54, 55, 56, 59, 66, 70, 122,
  208, 209, 211

United Nations, 58, 197, 199, 200, 211,
  212

Vietnam, 11, 12, 15, 20, 21, 22, 71,
  102, 104, 113, 181, 197
Vinson-Trammell Act, 102
VSS, 3, 18, 110
V/STOL, xx, 52–53

Warsaw Pact, xxii, 42, 49
Washington Naval Conference, 1, 194
Wasp LHD-1 class. *See* Amphibious
  ships
Watkins, James, 77, 78, 80
Webb, James, 59
Webster, William, 65
Western European Union (WEU), 209,
  210
West Germany. *See* Germany
Woolsey, James, 141

Yeltsin, Boris, xxii, 4, 33, 39, 46, 207,
  212
Yugoslavia, 58, 212

Zumwalt, Elmo, 2, 14, 17, 107, 109,
  147, 220

About the Author

JAMES L. GEORGE is a graduate of the U.S. Naval Academy at Annapolis. During his naval career he served on board destroyers and amphibious ships. He holds an M.A. and Ph.D. in International Relations from the University of Maryland and is a former Public Affairs Fellow at the Hoover Institution on War, Revolution, and Peace. Dr. George has served as a Professional Staff Member for National Security Affairs on both the Senate and House Committees on Government Operations. He is a former Assistant Director for Multilateral Affairs, and for a time was the Acting Director, of the U.S. Arms Control and Disarmament Agency. He was also a Senior Fellow at the Center for Naval Analyses and is currently a Senior Adjunct Fellow at the Hudson Institute.

Dr. George is an internationally known author on both naval affairs and arms control. He is a five-time winner of the U.S. Naval Institute *Proceedings* Arleigh Burke Essay Contest and the author or editor of six books. These books include *The U.S. Navy: The View from the Mid-1980s* (1985), currently on the reading list of the Chief of Naval Operations, and *The New Nuclear Rules: Strategy and Arms Control After INF and Start* (1990).

THE NAVAL INSTITUTE PRESS

THE U.S. NAVY IN THE 1990s
Alternatives for Action

Designed by Karen L. White

Set in Weiss
by BG Composition
Baltimore, Maryland

Printed on 55-lb. Glatfelter antique cream
and bound in Holliston Kingston Natural
by The Maple-Vail Book Manufacturing Group
York, Pennsylvania